DANGEROUS HOOD DREAMS

Saquan Lewis sr
Thank
you
very
much
for
your
Support!

Saquan Lewis

Dangerous Hood Dreams

Second Print Edition:

ISBN: 978-1-7358000-0-4

First, I would like to take the time out to thank God, because without him nothing is possible. I would like to acknowledge the people in my life and during me finding the inspiration to write. I want to thank everyone for pushing me and believing in me. Also, I would like to thank everyone for their support.

Dangerous Hood Dreams

Second Print Edition:

Dangerous Hood Dreams

In the hood where death is an ever-present foe if you sleep you do not eat. Another theory is where it starts, that is where it ends, meaning the life of a hustler never wins. As the older people in the hood would always say, "that boy will be dead or in jail…."

By Saquan Lewis

Table of Contents

Dangerous Hood Dreams iv

Prologue vii

Chapter 1: Man-Child 1

Chapter 2: The growing of a man 5

Chapter 3: Death before dishonor 10

Chapter 4: Family First 14

Chapter 5: Cannot tell me nothing 23

Chapter 6: Seeing me in him 29

Chapter 7: Playing the Phone 40

Chapter 8: Get played 44

Chapter 9: Where Stronger Together 49

Chapter 10: Hard to avoid 55

Chapter 11: Taking chances 59

Chapter 12: Crazy streets 66

Chapter 13: Take what comes with it 73

Chapter 14: The things that happen in the streets 76

Chapter 15: Get'em girls 80

Chapter 16: Remember what his older brother said 96

Chapter 17: Never expected it to turn out like this 106

Chapter 18: Watching What They Both Go Through 115

Chapter 19: Need Some Answers 121

Chapter 20: Hearing me out...130

Chapter 21: It will catch up to you One day 135

Chapter 22: Wish on better days 142

Chapter 23: Thought you were smart..147

Chapter 24: Keep it moving...151

Chapter 25: Missing you for life...154

Chapter 26: Remain focused..160

Chapter 27: Let me school you 163

Chapter 28: Smile just to keep from crying.................................166

Chapter 29: Stick to the script...167

Chapter 30: The funeral 170

Chapter 31: New York City..177

Chapter 32: Feeling the pain..182

Chapter 33: Making moves with family 186

Chapter 34: So much anger and stress 190

Chapter 35: Cannot lie forever..196

Chapter 36: A lot of tension in the air...201

Chapter 37: No stopping just yet 209

Chapter 38: I will hold us down...213

Chapter 39: Time to recruit 219

Chapter 40: Guilt and relief 222

Chapter 41: Making critical decisions 226

Chapter 42: Still not feeling the vibes.........................229

Chapter 43: The drop off.........................232

Chapter 44: When it hurts.........................236

Chapter 45: When a mother hurt.........................241

Chapter 46: Who is being watch.........................246

Chapter 47: Other plans.........................251

Chapter 48: Being blind.........................255

Chapter 49: Reminisce.........................259

Chapter 50: When it is so close.........................263

Chapter 51: Vengeance set in.........................266

Chapter 52: When the time is right.........................269

Prologue

The summer heat was burning, kids running the streets playing games of touch football, the hustlers working their beats and the crack heads walking up and down the streets. This was not just a summer thing in the eyes of a fifteen-year-old boy named Carlos. He turned suspect to the life of crime at fourteen due to his Uncle's flawless lifestyle. Carlos would imagine himself living in a big house with a lot of his favorite cars, with his mother never having to work anymore. This was not only Carlos' dream or imagination either. All his friends and their friends wanted out and wanted a better life for their mother's because most of them had no father in the house, like Carlos. His father left him and his little brother at an early age and never came back. As Carlos sat on his porch mind filled with many ambitious thoughts while he stares down at his little brother who played with his friends with no cares in the world or should I say with no cares in the hood. Carlos was deep in his thoughts; he never saw his Uncle walk up from behind.

Carlos… Carlos! Uncle Larry shouted.

Carlos quickly snapped out his thoughts, looking to his side as he saw his Uncle standing over him.

Hey Unc! Carlos said as he looked at him then glanced away.

Hey…. Hey… that is all I get, boy… I told you… you got an old soul. Uncle Larry said smiling at Carlos.

You caught me in a train of thought Unc, that's all. Carlos said looking back at him.

What's on your mind, nephew? Uncle Larry asked.

When Carlos had the chance to sit and talk with his Uncle, he never held back how he felt; his Uncle was the only male role model he looked up to, he loved the tough love he got when talking with his uncle.

I need some money Unc because this is not working. Carlos said, pointing at his clothes.

Nephew what you need; because I got you, I don't need you caught up in this bullshit out here because this shit out in these streets is a never-ending cycle. Just look around out here, but first look at your little brother because he will follow your lead. While you think, think like you are thinking for both of ya'll. His Uncle Larry said as his hand was swinging back and forward while making his point.

Unc… I feel where you're coming from and I was thinking about Justin at the same time. I just want better, that is all I want…. that is all I want. Carlos repeated as his face frowned up.

You and everybody in the hood, so just appreciate what you have, get your education and enjoy your youth. Here's two hundred, go buy you and your little brother something. Where your mother at? Uncle Larry asked as he handed Carlos the money while walking pass to go in the house.

Doing overtime, as usual. Carlos said, shaking his head.

Carlos knew his Uncle did not want his mother for anything, he only wanted to go either hide something in the house or get something out, Carlos was familiar to where he hid things. One day he walked up on his Uncle Larry while he was hiding it in their closet. Fed up; Carlos knew his Uncle Larry was not giving his mother any money towards the bills. So, Carlos said to himself as he turned to watch his Uncle make his way through the door, I won't be broke for long, with the devilish grin on his face as he was looking back at the money in his hand, caught by surprise as he looked up, Trick and Jay were standing in front of him with big smiles on their faces, eyeing his money.

Damn man, you are holding! Trick said.

Yeah, man, what you about to do with all that money? Jay asked.

Both of ya'll... worried about the wrong thing... but for your information, this is not all mine. Carlos said waving the money in his hand.

Well, you have more than me. Trick said.

Me too! Jay said.

Jay, Trick, Black, Rell, Rock and Lartesha was who Carlos would be around in the neighborhood they were the only ones he felt he could trust around in the neighborhood. Carlos stood up and looked around, something he felt was only normal to do in the neighborhood. He walked close to his friends than pointed towards his door. He gave an eye signal, something like a code that they only knew. Trick and Jay shook their heads then looked back at Carlos with the same devilish grin expressing Carlos had on his face, Jay and Trick would run into Carlos' uncle from time to time. He would not allow them to hang around, Jay and Trick were on the same page Carlos was on. Every time Carlos' Uncle came around, they had this eye signal that they used.

So, what ya'll was about to get into? Carlos asked.

Nothing, we came to see what was up with you. Jay said.

Where everybody else at? Carlos asked.

We saw Lartesha down the street at her grandma's house. Rell, Black and Rock, I haven't seen today. Trick said, shrugging his shoulders.

While they were talking, Carlos' uncle was walking out the door talking on his cell phone; not paying any attention to Carlos or his friends.

Yo, I'm about to take my brother to the store so I can buy him something with this punk ass hundred dollars my uncle gave me for him! Carlos said as he was giving Jay and Trick handshakes.

All right, cool. We'll get up with you! Trick said.

CHAPTER 1

Man-Child

Ring.... Ring.... Ring... Ring...... MOM! THE PHONE! Carlos yelled.

Being that it was the weekend, all Carlos wanted to do was sleep in. When he heard the phone continue to ring, he thought his mother, or his little brother, would get it. To his surprise, no one was home. Carlos mother got called in on her day off, Justin made his way outside to play. So that left Carlos to answer the phone.

Hello... Hello! Carlos answered.

You have a collect call.... from Larry. the operator said.

Carlos took the phone from his ear and looked at it with a sense of disbelief. He wondered to himself, what the hell did my Uncle Larry do. Carlos quickly answered the call, as he was walking around the house to see if his mother was there, he knew for a fact it was her day off.

Hello.... Unc, what's going on? Carlos asked.

Yo Carlos, listen, where is your mother? Uncle Larry asked.

She's not here!! Carlos replied.

Well check this out, tell her I'm locked up and they not giving me no bail. You hear me? I'm not getting out no time soon and she knows what to do! Uncle Larry said.

When Uncle Larry mentioned not getting out Carlos being plotting and did not have any plans on letting his mother know anything; Carlos knew this gave him the chance to make a difference in his house. He was willing to take that risk. He also thought about the advantage he had over his friends. Carlos was sitting on the phone, not paying any attention to what his Uncle Larry was saying. He quickly snapped out his thoughts, so he could end the phone call. Carlos was eager to put his plans into motion.

Unc, I gotcha… When my mother comes home, I will let her know everything you told me. Carlos said.

Thank you, nephew. I gotcha when I come home, hold it down for now, I have to go. Uncle Larry said.

When his uncle said hold it down Carlos smiled to his self because that was what he had intending on doing. With that in mind, Carlos was also thinking how he would do it without being seen. The people that came to mind were Trick and Jay because they would be around the action from time to time when Carlos Uncle Larry was not running them off. They knew who sold and who used. Carlos sat for a minute in his living room, spending some time weighing his options and thinking about the consequences. He knew for young boys their age that people would not take them as serious; he figured he would have to be the muscle if there was any problem. Knowing that; Carlos got up to see what his uncle had hiding in the closet. When he opened the box, his eyes got wide at the sight of the abundance of drugs he was standing in front of, not knowing the value of it. He hurried out of the room grabbed a bag out the kitchen came back; took half of what his Uncle Larry was hiding. The entire time this was taking place, he continued to think of the risk he was taking.

After months of seeing the ins and outs of the game from the sidelines, Carlos continued to not play it close by, not putting himself out in the streets. He watched the backs of his friends, Jay and Trick, who were awfully familiar of who was who and what was what. After Trick and Jay ran through the first half within a few months, they all came together with all their thoughts on how everything should be and who should be in on everything. Rell, Rock, Black and Lartesha made up the rest of the crew. They stayed close to each other in the neighborhood, Trick and Jay were more oriented with the neighborhood than the rest of the crew. So, after counting the money they made from what Carlos' stole from his Uncle Larry, Carlos brought everybody in the picture for his own reason.

As Carlos, Jay and Trick departed from counting their profits, Carlos told them to get in touch with everyone else and meet up at Lartesha's grandparents' house on the porch where they all would hang out.

Slowly approaching his crew, Carlos wanted to make himself clear on where he stood. He had already weighed the consequences of his actions when he stole from his Uncle Larry. Now that he was all in, Carlos could not and would not let his friends cause him to lose everything. Jay and Trick saw the seriousness in Carlos face as he approached them, they had immediately stop with the jokes and got serious while the others never knew or saw what was coming.

What's up, Carlos? said Trick.

You already know, Trick. Carlos said as he looked at everybody before sitting down.

Carlos, what's wrong? Lartesha asked with a concerned look on her face.

Well Tesha this is for everybody ear's… I need ya'll to listen and pay close attention cause I'm talking serious business. Carlos said as he looked at everyone.

Sshhhhh…. Ssshhhhhhhhh! was the noise Lartesha made.

I made a serious decision months ago, keeping it between Jay and Trick. Now that we made it happen. We feel since we are a crew… We feel that we could trust ya'll with our life because that's what this is, our life on the line if this goes the wrong way. Carlos said as he was looking at the ground and back at them.

Carlos, what are you talking about? Come out and say what you are talking about! Lartesha spat.

Okay… okay… give me a chance. Well, when my Uncle Larry went to jail I took everything he was hiding in my mother's house, I did not know what to do with it, but thanks to Jay and Trick in the long run I can patch that back up when it's time to cross that bridge with my Uncle Larry.

No…. No… No! was all Lartesha could say.

No… No… what Lartesha? Carlos asked.

Silence was all you heard.

Yo listen, I need money! If anyone of you don't, that's on ya'll but I do not want to hear any of this going out of this circle. Now if anyone of you wants in, say it. But all I ask is loyalty from everyone. So, for me, Jay and Trick, we each made forty thousand from everything. Carlos said as he stood in front of his crew.

What can I do, I'm not standing on no damn corners? Lartesha said with a serious look on her face.

Chill…. chill. All I want you to do is put the money up. Carlos said.

And for the fella's, Jay and Trick will show ya'll the ropes. My Uncle Larry had a gold mine, he just didn't know it, but we will hold it down just watch, just watch…. Carlos said as he looked around at everyone.

Everyone agreed with Carlos and was ready for whatever.

CHAPTER 2

Three years later

The growing of a man

Carlos was playing a game of cards for money with his boys Rock and Rell. The rest of his crew, Jay, Black and Trick were busy counting the money they made from hustling these last couple of years. The old run-down house belonged to an old head that stayed around the neighborhood; somebody who Carlos developed a relationship with. One day Carlos asked the old head if he could rent out the house. Ever since then they only went there strictly to chill or count their money.

Yo, Carlos, I'm done! I quit, man! This shit keeps going back and forth! Rock said, pushing the cards away.

Shit…...! That's what you think, nigga! Tell Carlos to count his money, ha…. ha… ha…. Rell said laughing.

Awe….! That ain't shit Rell grow up nigga that's why I don't like gambling with you. Rock said.

Yo Rock, I'm done too! I will help these niggas count this money. Carlos said, getting up and heading toward Jay, Black and Trick.

Yo Carlos, did you see that young kid Mack come through the hood yesterday in that six forty-five CI horizon blue with twenty-two-inch rims? Son....! That shit was off the chain. Jay turned around and said as he saw Carlos making his way towards them.

Carlos knew how fascinated Jay was with cars; he would try to get him out of cherishing frivolous things, which was hard. Jay would always spark a conversation up about cars and things of no means. Carlos would give him just what he was asking for every time.

Man, you think I care about some young punk riding around making himself hot. That's nothing to me. I'm on a whole different level than that shit. I'm thinking about spending my money wisely, like where I want to be; I'm about setting goals. I don't sit back and think about what car I will buy with my next couple of thousand. This game is too dangerous for that. And that same kid you saw riding through the hood, I saw the same kid up on the hill in front of the East Coast Market with his car parked right out front... THAT NIGGA WAS still PUSHING THAT PACK... and he got the nerve to be driving the six forty-five CI with chrome. Tell me, Jay, how smart is that? Nigga you may get lucky and be able to buy his car from one of the police auctions in a few weeks. You got to stop looking at them car books so damn much and pick up something that will help you in the long run, like a law book or a business book because it's more than just doing what we do in these streets. The law man does not want to see no black man in the hood make it, he wants to see us behind bars or dead in the hood. Yo, those jails are becoming big business for them and they love niggas who think like you. Carlos said raising his voice giving Jay the annoyed facial expression.

All right... All right...! I understand, just no more, please! It's too damn early in the morning for your long speeches. You need to stop being so serious about everything and enjoy life. Jay said.

I'm enjoying life now so let's finish counting this money because it's already five a.m. and I have to take my brother to get his hair cut. Carlos spat back.

Yo...! Son, I don't know why you got this nigga started this early in the morning, Jay. Because you know he would hit you with that, you need to pick up a book shit like he just got all the damn sense. Man, I'm about to be out! I'm hungrier than a hostage and sleepy as fuck. I'll check Y'all later.

The look that Trick gave as he spoke, Carlos didn't like; he knew Trick was being sarcastic as usual and when dealing with Trick, Carlos didn't have the patience so he immediately stop what he was doing turned in Trick direction. Trick was not the type to back down, and he always wanted the last word.

Trick, what do you mean you don't know why he got me started this morning? Nobody wasn't talking to you... so speak when spoken to nigga!! Another thing, we- not- done- counting- this -money... so when we get finish everybody will leave together. Until then, you are a hostage. Carlos said aggressively as he was walking in Trick's direction.

The look and tone of voice, Carlos responded in; Trick was aware of; it was not the first time that Carlos became aggressive with him. He also knew it would not be the last. He knew Carlos wanted to be in control and could also intimidate people with his serious looks, height and muscle from working out. Carlos knew Trick was not the type to back down to no one. So, Trick came back with the same tone in his voice.

Yo Carlos... I-speak-when-the-fuck- I want to speak nigga! I go when the fuck I want to go... because I'm nobody's hostage and you better watch how you come at me son because you're not my father or boss; so when you have some kids, then that's who you tell what to do. Until then, play your position nigga! Trick said with an aggressive tone in his voice.

That is right where Carlos wanted Trick to go with it, before Trick could get the last words out of his mouth Carlos was all over him just swinging on him. Carlos was so swift that the first blow caught Trick in the temple, sending him down to the ground awfully hard. He started kicking him saying.

Smartass nigga get up! You so hard, get up, bitch ass nigga! Carlos yelled out.

Jay drop the money he was counting, ran over and pulled Carlos back while Rock helped Trick get off the ground. Trick was dizzy from the blows which made him slowly get up off the ground, irritable and frustrated he walked to the bathroom like everything was over, splashing water on his face with his hands. Walking back out of the bathroom, he trudged right up to Carlos without him ever noticing, punching him swiftly in the mouth with a hard blow that almost sent him to the floor. Carlos shook it off, but before he could go back after Trick, Jay was between them both, yelling.

Yo...! WE ARE A CREW! Y'all two need to grow up and stop fighting each other all the time and let's get this money! Jay shouted.

All right... It's over... My bad... my bad; I apologized; my nigga now let's finish this shit because I got to go pick up my little brother. Carlos said, waving his hands in the air in defeat.

Trick looked in Carlos' face when he apologized. He tried to read his facial expression and body language, which was awfully hard, Carlos always had the same serious expression on his face, Trick took it for what it was and never let his guard down around Carlos.

All right. Carlos said.

It's dead, my dude... But never try that shit again... yo like I was saying I'm about to be out. I'll check Y'all later. One! Trick said in a calm tone as he was walking towards the door.

Come on, Y'all...! Let's finish this shit I don't have all morning; it's already six a.m. and I know my girl thinks I'm out here fucking around on her. I am... not trying to hear her mouth this morning either...

when I get in the crib I'm going straight to bed, Yo.... Trick I'll see you in the p.m. be safe. Rell said.

In a minute, I'm out myself. It's done, I'm tired then a motherfucker the count is three hundred and fifty thousand. Black said as he was rubber banding the last stack of the money.

All right then we can all be out together... Yo Rell, you need to take the money and put it up because we can't take no losses right now. I will talk, to Marie about us connecting with her uncle I know with her we might have a chance, so until then I'll get up with Y'all in the p.m. Oh, tell Trick what the outcome was one of Y'all so he don't feel left out. Well, Y'all know who I got to go get bad ass himself all right. Oh, Rell, be careful with that money walking out of here because you know them young boys got McKinley on fire, that's why I don't park my car on this Street, police be riding up and down this street. So, I think Y'all need to park on a different street also start taking shortcuts, especially with the money Y'all be having on Y'all. Just think about it, I'm out! Carlos said as he was walking away.

CHAPTER 3

Death before dishonor

Carlos was leaving out the door, Rell yelled out to him.

LARTESHA! Rell yelled.

YOU ALREADY KNOW WHAT IT IS! Carlos yelled.

Rell was making sure they were on the same page of where the money was going. Lartesha was intelligent and street smart; the fellas called her their ride or die chick; they loved her. She was not the type to let no one get in her business and her favorite words when the fellas would come and drop something off is Death before dishonor, and this was something she lived by. When she wanted to hang with the fella's she always kept her pistol on her; she was serious about her surroundings and could spot a fake person a mile away. That was something else they liked about her. Also, she never bit her tongue for no one, but could say a bit too much. Coming from a young black woman like her a person would not expect it especially men, most men looked at a woman's desirable features that is when she fool them with her five, seven frame that could cause any man on earth's heart to begin immediately pumping all the blood available directly to his manhood. So true in fact those jealous girls used to call her Medusa. Not because she was unattractive but because every young guy in school used to get an immediate erection at the sight of her "C" cup breasts, her incomparably well round ass which she kept stuffed in all the latest designer jeans. She turned boy's dicks into stone at the sight of her. Lartesha's hair was like gentle ripples of a black river. Her silken strands of jet-black hair lay delicately on her shoulder, so naturally wavy that she unquestionably had some Indian ancestor. Her hair frames her cute face, complimenting her beautiful grayish-green eyes that almost seem hypnotic, like that of the siren that lured foolish sailors to their deaths at sea. Her face was so cute that you would not believe that she was a woman of twenty-four with her cute nose in; combination with her baby-like chubby dimpled cheeks gave her the appearance of a younger girl. Her body had more curves than the letter "S". Especially when she walked. She was truly one hundred thirty-eight pounds of pure ecstasy.

I'm coming, Motherfucker...! Lartesha said to herself as she was walking to the phone.

This is Lartesha speaking.... How may I help you, and who may this be? Lartesha asked with a smile being sarcastic.

She already knew who was calling. She never gave her house number out to anyone. The other number she would give out was her cell phone. That was for outsiders.

Stop the games chicken head. I'm on my way over there, you know what it is. I'm on Colvin and Midland, I'm not that far so get ready. I know it's early in the morning and I'm tired then a Motherfucker. Rell shouted through the phone.

All right... All right...! I hope you didn't call to hold a damn conversation, just get your ass over here... I got things to do myself... oh ya, your chicken head is at home waiting for your LAME ASS! Bye Rell...! Lartesha spat back as she slammed the phone down.

Rell took the phone from his ear. Then the light changed; he turned the music back up, pulled off in his 1995 Acura Vigor he brough from the auction one day him and Carlos went. Soon as the first car came pulling in for bidders, he was the first person to bid on it. Rell walked over to the car, looked through the whole car with a big smile. Rell was excited, as if he brought a Mercedes Benz or BMW. They all agreed on not spending over five thousand on a car. The color and interior made the car stand out, that was what he really liked about the car, the metallic grey paint job with the butter soft leather interior, feeling satisfied. He got the car towed to Carlos's shop with all three of the cars Carlos had purchased. The next day he took the car to a shop for window tint and a system installed. He did not want rims because everybody in the crew all agreed on staying under the radar. The whole idea came from Carlos. He did not want any attention on him or his crew, so that's how Rell kept it. After Rell pulled off from the light, he was thinking about all the things he needed to do today being that the weather was looking nice outside everyone was cleaning their cars and going to the mall getting their gear right. But that was not the only thing on Rell's mind. He was also thinking about the sizeable amount of money in his back seat that he was about to drop off. Rell was thinking about the big moves he and his crew were about to make. Rell felt it was right on time. He did not want to take any more risks on the highway, back and forth to New York when they had the connection right under their nose. Rell pulled up in front of Lartesha's apartment, jumped out the car, grabbed the bag of money from the back seat then ran to the door. He was about to hit the doorbell, but she was one step ahead of him, buzzing him in as soon as he got to the door.

What the fuck took you so long? I told you I got things to do! Lartesha Spat as she snatched the bag.

Aw... I bet it's not important, why you got them hot ass pants on, it's hot outside. You ain't been watching the news this morning.

I was listening to the radio on my way here; it said that it's ninety-five degrees today, so all them designer dresses you have would probably be best. Rell spat back as Lartesha snatched the bag.

Nigga mind- your- own-damn- business... I have something important to do. It may not be important to you, but it's important to me. I have a hairdresser and nail appointment! I'll be fine with my tank top and pants. It ain't like I will be outside, anyway. So, when I get back from my appointment, I'll hit Y'all later. Is there anything else nosey motherfucker? Lartesha said with a smile.

Rell smiled back at her.

Listen, heifer, I told you about that smart-ass mouth. It will get you in trouble one of these days. Rell said as he was walking towards the door.

She laughed at his words and pulled her baby nine-millimeter out of her purse and said, I think this would end the trouble for the person who's bringing trouble.

As Rell was walking to the door, he looked back.

Yeah, that would help depend on how fast you are pulling it out. Rell said, then he started laughing as he was going out the door.

Death before Dishonor. Lartesha yelled behind him.

CHAPTER 4

Family First

Carlos was riding through the city streets listening to music in his 2002 Acura MDX SUV headed to go pick his little brother up, so they could get their haircut together. Carlos wanted to fill that void for not having a father in the house, he wanted to step up to be that male figure for Justin. Carlos loved his little brother to death and would give him everything he wanted. Carlos did not want his little brother thinking selling drugs was cool, he wanted him to stay focused on school. Carlos felt he needed to play this position because his mother could not be there. She had to work a lot of hours and never had much time off. Carlos enjoyed the time he spent with Justin, it was all for the love, but it was difficult. Carlos would always tell Justin family first and friends are stepping stool to money, death, or jail. This was how Carlos viewed things. Carlos pulled up in front of his mother's house, blew the horn. Carlos knew his mother was not home, so he didn't see a reason to go in the house. Justin came running out; he jumped in the truck.

What's up… Carlos? What's good… Justin said in a nonchalant voice.

Then he entertained his thoughts with crazy things he wanted to know but did not want to ask his brother because he did not want to hear any long speech this morning. His friend J-love told him about the drug game, how much money he could make, how he's been sneaking getting money at sixteen, only one year older than Justin, Justin was curious and eager to be in the mix of action; he wanted to test the water.

Yo Justin, what's up, Justin.... Justin.... Justin…. What's up, Justin, what's on your damn mind? You were just spacing out for a minute, what's the deal is something going on I should know about, Carlos said with a worried look on his face.

Justin kept quiet for a while, then he told his brother a quick lie because he knew if he would have told his brother about what his friend was filling his head with he would have told him to stay away from J-love, so he kept that to himself.

Oh, what up Carlos? I was just thinking about this bad ass chick I met the other day, that's all. Justin replied.

Man Justin, I told you about them girls! You are too young to be thinking about girls twenty-four seven. How are you doing in school? What are you learning about? I'm telling you Justin, if you don't pass this year, I'm cutting you off from your allowance for an entire year! So, you need to get your act together fast. Oh, that car I said I would get you for your birthday, you can kiss that goodbye! Carlos said.

When Carlos said this, he said it with a serious look with a mean tone in his voice to get his point across, something he did not like doing to his little brother. He felt that he was hurting his feelings. Justin had other things on his mind, when Carlos said no money if he did not pass and no car, that just added to his negative train of thoughts. Justin was thinking about taking J-love on with the proposition of getting money; he knew he was not passing this year. So, he figured, well fuck it! I will just go sneak like J-love and get paid; where at he did not have a clue, but something had to give. I'll just have to repeat my grade next year, was how Justin felt.

Justin… Justin… Justin…! What the fuck is wrong with you? Are you going deaf or what? Should I take your ass to see a psychologist… that has to stop. Carlos said with a worried look on his face.

My bad, I heard what you said, I understand, you made yourself loud and clear. Justin said.

Glad to hear you understand; oh yeah, before I forget… I cannot pick you up to take you to school all next month, I will be out of town. Marie will come and get you, do not… I repeat, do not give her a hard time, do not be jumping in cars with little knuckleheads; when you get out of school, these boys your age have stolen car, guns, and drugs. Stay away from all that little Brody. Carlos said as he was driving.

When Justin heard Carlos say out of town! He heard nothing else; everything else was of no relevance.

They rode in silence with nothing but music playing, Carlos' cell phone started ringing.

Hi Mom, Carlos said as he answered.

Hi Baby! How are you doing? Did you go pick your brother up? Mr. Johnson asked.

Yes Mom, I got this knucklehead right here, how are you doing this morning? Carlos said with a big smile as he tapped Justin on top of the head.

I'm all right baby… just hanging in there and working hard, Baby. Ms. Johnson replied.

Well, don't work too hard, you hear me? Carlos said.

Yes, I hear you… I got bills to pay… I know you understand, listen Carlos before I forget; I called your house, Marie answered. She said to call her; she also said you haven't been home all night; So, call her, it's probably important. Tell Justin I said that I love him and do not be hardheaded, listen to you. Mr. Johnson said with concern in her voice for Marie.

All right, Mom… We love you. Let me call this girl to see what she wants. Carlos said as he was slowing down for a traffic light.

Okay Baby, you and Justin; be safe! Mr. Johnson said, as she was hanging the phone up.

Hanging the phone up Carlos said to his self what could Marie possibly want, she knew where I was all night; she knew what I had to do with the fellas; Carlos let Marie know everything. Holding his phone, Carlos pushed the name WIFY on the screen because that was what he had Marie stored in his phone under, letting the phone ring.

Marie was Carlos first love. Since high school, he never looked back at another girl. She was his one and only. She asked Carlos to move in with her after high school; she already had her own apartment, compliments of her uncle. Her Uncle made sure she had everything she needed. Marie's Uncle brought her and her older brother to the United States from the Dominican Republic, after their mother and father had died. After many years of being in the United States, Marie's older brother fell victim to a drug transaction gone wrong, is what she was told. So, her uncle felt that it was his obligation to protect and get his niece whatever she asked for; Marie was a natural Dominican Woman of beauty had she been born into an ancient civilization; they would praise her as a goddess, a queen whose beauty would have been comparable to Nefertiti herself. Her skin tone was so unique that it was a clear giveaway of her pure Dominican bloodline. It was as if God himself carefully painted every inch of her body with his own personal mixture of colors, reserved especially for her: caramel brown, honey gold, butter-pecan with a hint of cream with hazel brown eyes. Long jet-black hair was past her shoulders and a shape that would make a man drop to his knees in the presence of her five-five frame and all that firm one hundred thirty-six pounds packed in nothing but designer wear. It was not just her appearance; she was also smart in every aspect, with a pleasant sense of humor.

Hello... Hello...! Marie said with a big smile on her face; she knew it was Carlos. She always looked at the caller I. d. before she answered.

What's up, what's going on? I just got off the phone with my mother; she was telling me you had something important to tell me. Carlos asked with a concerned look on his face.

Oh, no... ha... ha... Carlos! You know how your mother is with me. I told her you have not been home all night... boy when I told her I was calling you all night she was like WHATTT!! But I said that because I knew she would ask do you know where he's at, so that's all. But Bobby called from your shop not too long ago. He said something about cars; I think you need to call him. Marie said as she was walking around their apartment.

All right, Marie, I'll get on that after we hang up; are you going somewhere this morning, because we need to talk? It's important. But I have Justin with me, we're headed to go get our haircuts. Maybe we could catch a movie tonight, so pick me something up to wear from the mall, grab some eleven p.m. tickets. We could talk then, all right! Carlos said.

All right, Carlos sounds good to me. See you later and be safe. Marie said as she was hanging the phone up.

Carlos and Marie had nicknames that they would call each other, Carlos loved Marie's accent and the way she pronounced it, she called him Papi and she loved for him to call her Mami, especially when they were having romantic sex. He also loved when she shopped for him, she had impeccable taste; she kept him in the newest Polo, FUBU, Sean John, Rocawear and the rest of similar designer fashions. Carlos hung up the phone and called his shop.

Hello, Automotive Used Car Shop! Bobby said with his deep voice when he answered the phone.

Carlos was talking to bobby while he was pulling over in front of the barbershop, Justin was looking through some CDs trying to find something to listen to.

What's up, Bobby? My girl told me you called saying something about some cars. Did they all come in from the auction today? Carlos asked.

Yeah, they came in; I called to let you know that we need some parts because we're getting low on a lot of things and it's the weekend. So, the order of supplies will not be in until next week. I will need you to go to the auto parts store and pick up a few things. Bobby said.

All right... Make a list out, I'll have somebody come take care of that real soon, is that all right? Carlos replied.

Bobby was Carlos all-around mechanic that could do almost anything to a car. He could make the best hiding places there were. Mostly, that was what Carlos liked about him he was creative and could make things happen. Carlos called Jay to ask him if he could make a run to the parts store for him. So, he called him the faster way, by pushing four digits, then hit a button calling him on his walkie talkie Nextel phone.

Yo, Jay! Carlos yelled through the walkie talkie.

What up? Jay replied with a sleepy voice.

Yo, I need you to run over to the auto parts store to get a few things for Bobby at the shop. Just go to the shop first and get the list. Carlos said.

Yo nigga, I was sleep! Remember, we were up all damn night? Jay spat back.

My nigga, I wouldn't have called you if it weren't important, all right; I've also been up all night and day my damn self, that's part of being a businessman. We will rest after we take care of shit, can you do it? Carlos asked with a frown on his face.

Yeah, I'll do it after I get out the shower. Where you at right now? Jay asked.

Why? Who wants to know? Carlos asked back with a smile on his face, trying to be annoying because he knew Jay did not like that.

Man, fuck you, Jay shouted, with a frown on his face. I'm out. One lifting himself up from where he laid.

One...! Carlos said, ending the conversation.

Justin and Carlos jumped out the truck to walk up in Toni's barbershop; it was the weekend and packed as usual. As Carlos made his way through the door, he saw this one particular person who he had his eyes on and vowed to get when he caught him without his crew, Carlos knew now was not the time because he was with his little brother. So many things were running through his head because Dirty has not seen him yet. So Carlos told Justin to go to the bathroom for a minute, Carlos turned to see if Dirty was looking with a quick glance then he rushed back out to his truck and hit the special compartment to grab the chrome Desert Eagle then he ran back in the barbershop with the Desert Eagle revealed. Dirty was not looking at who was coming through the door his eyes were closed while the barber was cutting his hair, the barber was watching Carlos make his way over towards them. When the barber Tom looked in Carlos face he saw how his eyes were red with a very serious facial expression, then he saw the chrome gun in his hand by that time Carlos was right at the chair tapping Dirty on the chin with the gun. As soon as Dirty opened his eyes, Carlos hit him with the gun right in the mouth. Justin came walking out of the bathroom right in the moment of Carlos hitting Dirty Carlos briefly looked up as he heard Tom.

Please, not in here... Please not in here! Tom yelled.

When he yelled that Dirty was trying to get up, Carlos quickly hit him again, even harder than the first time. Justin was right behind Carlos, watching Dirty's face flow with blood from his mouth and eye. When Carlos turned, he immediately caught eye contact with Justin. Carlos yelled for him to get in the truck Then he turned back around and said to Dirty in his ear.

You're lucky today... thank Tom when you wake up for saving your bitch ass life, Carlos said in a low tone then he walked out got in the truck pulled off in silence.

Carlos adjusted himself in his seat as he looked over at Justin wanting to ensure him, they were still going to get their haircuts.

Little Brody, we still going to get our haircuts. Don't worry about that. Carlos said.

Carlos, why you do that man like that? What did he do to you? Why do you have a gun? Justin asked with a concerned look on his face.

Justin, that dude did something terrible, that's all you need to know. For the gun I have it to protect my business and my family, so don't go thinking it's cool to walk around with guns. You hear me? Carlos said as he was driving.

Yeah, I hear you. So, where are we getting our haircuts at Carlos? Justin asked while he was putting the Clips CD in the deck to play (What Happen to That Boy) then Justin looked in Carlos' direction and started smiling.

Carlos did not smile back he was thinking about the incident that just occur; He was driving in deep thought; he knew he could have handled the situation differently; he knew he couldn't keep giving Dirty a pass every time he caught him off guard for the shit he was getting away with. Coming through the hood robbing dudes, making dudes get naked. He should have caught the first bullet coming out the barrel of the Desert Eagle, Carlos had bigger plans for Dirty. He wanted everybody in on this one. He did not want all the fun for his self. He knew how people wanted to kill Dirty. They have not caught him at the right place and time. Carlos would catch him slipping; but Dirty never noticed.

Yo Carlos, where the hell are you going? Are you going downtown because you just missed the turn to go on Adams Street? Justin said as he sat up in his seat, pointing out the window, making Carlos aware of the turn they missed.

Damn, my bad; I was just zoning out. Yo, we going to go to my homie Boo barbershop on the North side. Carlos said.

Carlos phone rung, before answering it, he looked at the screen it was just the person he wanted it to be.

What's up Rock? What's the deal, my nigga? Carlos asked.

I don't know; you tell me what's popping for the day? Did you have time to holla at your girl yet? Rock asked.

Man, I haven't even been home yet… I spoke with her on the phone. She was kind of busy herself for the day. I will get up with her later man. Do not worry about that shit. Be easy, my nigga. Yo, I got Little Brody with me, we all need to talk… Remember they said the early bird catches the biggest worms. I caught a big slimy one had to put the steel to his face. It was not his time to meet his maker due time… due time; Yo let's meet at Lartesha crib around seven p.m., I'm getting a haircut at Boo shop, then going to the crib, take a shower, lay down for a few. So, I'll holla. All right, my nigga. Carlos said.

I will let everybody know. I'm about to go on the block anyway, so later than my nigga. Rock said.

CHAPTER 5

Cannot tell me nothing

Jay was already in the neighborhood, shooting dice with Young Chris. Young Chris was only sixteen, he liked to do everything from shooting his gun, smoking weed, beating dope fiends up, getting his dick sucked from dope fiends. The boy was a menace to the Neighborhood. Even the other young boys his age did not like to play dice with him. They knew if they won, he would get mad then take his money back with a weapon. Young Chris was much bigger for his age, five eleven stocky, enormous head wore a size eleven in shoes. Jay would always let Young Chris hang around when he came outside; He would try to school him, being that he was six years older than Young Chris. When Jay tried to talk to him that shit went in one ear and out the other. The boy did not have any respect for his mother or father. They were both addicted to drugs, so he never had a role model to look up to the boy stay outside from day to night, getting money, doing crazy things.

YO… YO… bet some more before you roll Jay. Young Chris shouted, putting his feet in the way so Jay could not roll the dice.

Ha… ha… oh you are holding the dice up, yo… ha ... ha… remember when you went in the back with Catman… ha… ha. Jay shouted while he was holding his arm next to his ear, shaking the dice in his hand.

Jay started reminiscing to Young Chris about one hot day everybody was all out in the neighborhood with their barbecue grills out, dice games were going, sidewalks filled with people leaving the basketball tournament in the park, dudes out from different neighborhoods. McKinley was busy with fancy cars riding up and down the street. Jay was on the dice, making bets all around to people who called out for them. Young Chris was making bets right with Jay, talking loud in their faces, laughing loud every time Jay hit his point on the dice. Young Chris was always looking around, watching his surroundings. He looked up and saw this dope fiend name Catman coming down the street. Most of the times Catman had money from taking it from other dope fiends that came to the neighborhood from suburbs areas; or he would try his hand with the young dudes because he knew most of their parents, he even smoked cocaine with Young Chris mom and dad from time to time. Young Chris told Jay to pick his money up when he hit, then he walked off over to where Catman was at. He asked Catman how much he was working with.

What you working with? Young Chris asked.

Let me see it first. How it looks? Catman asked.

All right let's go in the back of the house. Young Chris said.

As they were walking, Young Chris warned Catman.

You better not try nothing stupid. I'm telling you. Young Chris said, emphasizing his words, then he started laughing.

Young Chris had one hand in his pocket with a tight grip on his twenty-five automatic. He knew how Catman like to take advantage, and he refused to be a victim. So, when they stopped Young Chris pulled the cocaine out, then Catman looked at it and snatched the package out of his hand.

I'll hold on to this, just go on little nigga! Catman said with a deep voice, trying to intimidate him.

Young Chris smiled at him, pulled the twenty-five automatic out and shot him once in the stomach, walked up to him, grabbed his packages of cocaine back.

Try holding that stupid. Young Chris said walking away laughing harder than ever.

When he returned to the dice game everybody was looking at him; they heard the gunshot go off. Some dudes ran when they heard it. He did not care about how people felt. He kept betting with Jay because he was still rolling the dice. Suddenly, Catman appeared from the back holding his stomach with blood all over his hands yelling.

HELP! Catman yelled loud.

Young Chris ran over and shouted.

You want some help? Young Chris asked, then kicked him.

Then he ran back to the dice game, laughing. Dudes started picking their money up to leave. Jay was mad; he turned around and yelled.

Son, you got to stop doing that crazy shit...! Jay yelled

Man, I'm not trying to hear that shit! That dope fiend tried to rob me, I bet he won't try nobody else without thinking twice. Young Chris said with a frown.

After telling Young Chris that wild story that he would forever re-member just saved Jay enough time.

Yo Jay, bet the hundred before you roll. Young Chris shouted.

What little nigga… You sure you want to jump out there like that with your little re-up money? Jay said, smiling and laughing as he was shaking the dice in hand.

Nigga this far from re-up over here I got more where that came from. Young Chris said pulling out a stack of twenties with a smirk on his face looking at Jay.

My nigga, you might as well go put that little shit up because if you put that funny money down on this ground, I'm putting it in my pocket. When Jay said this, he had a big smile on his face.

Jay was talking slowly to Young Chris so he could understand that he was not playing, Jay knew how Young Chris was when he lost his money. Jay wanted to make him think twice about jumping out there, so Jay pulled out a stack of hundreds.

Nigga how much you got there? I bet it's not over eight hundred; bet my thousand to that little shit you got in your hand. Jay said, Then Jay peeled off ten crispy hundred-dollar bills from the stack of money, dropping it right on Young Chris' shoes with a smirk on his face.

Nigga, I got over eight hundred on me! Young Chris shouted, then went in his pocket, pulled out another stack of twenty's.

Nigga bet…! I don't know who card you trying to pull… But something must got into your head; Maybe that pussy you ate before you came out here… What she got, lucky charm in that pussy because you are feeling yourself today. Young Chris said with a smile on his face, dropping the eight hundred right next to where Jay dropped his money.

When Young Chris dropped his money, a police car came strolling slow down the street in their direction. Young Chris snatched his money up, ran to the side of abandon house like he had a warrant or drugs in his pocket, Young Chris stayed in trouble. Jay picked his money up put it back in his pocket as he watched the police car ride by slowly, they kept going giving Jay an intimidating stare. Jay was not concern; he knew he did not have any warrants, all he had was a couple thousand in his pocket. Jay started walking towards his car, looking up and down the street, then he heard somebody call out his name. It was Young Chris running back out from the side of the abandon house, laughing, saying something, Jay could not really hear what he was saying; Jay stood by his car waiting for Young Chris to get up closer.

Man, what's so damn funny? You always running when you see police nigga… what did you do now? Jay asked as he was leaning up against his driver side door.

Man, you know the damn police know my face; they fuck with me every mother-fucking time they ride through the hood. I'm dirty, I got a hammer on me and cocaine; plus, I am not doing nothing wrong by running my nigga. I told you; you had lucky charms pussy for breakfast… nigga that money was mine. You better be glad they rode through here. Wait… Yo, is that dope fiend Monica? Son, I'm about to get some head my nigga. Young Chris said, then started running in Monica's direction.

Jay opened the door to his ninety-eight Honda Accord, black with limo tints. Jay knew he couldn't buy nothing fancy, but he sure had plans to go all out one day. His crew had him sticking to the plan they knew Jay had big expectations from looking at car books all the time like a kid with a comic book.

Yo Jay, what's the deal? What the hell are you doing out here by yourself… like you out here hustling. Rock said as he was pulling up on Jay with his head out his car window.

Man, I'm about to shoot to the mall… get a few things. I was out here with Young Chris until that little nigga seen Monica coming down the street. You know that nigga is sick in the head; yo what's up with you my nigga? Jay asked while he was opening his car door.

All ain't shit… bending some corners, Yo, I spoke with Carlos earlier he said he wanted everybody to meet him at Lartesha crib around seven p.m. Yo… Stop parking over on this block… Carlos told you this motherfucker was on fire right now from your little man and the rest of them little niggas? Let it cool off around here or you just watch that Honda going to getting pulled over every damn time the police see it. Rock said.

Yeah, all right Rock, let's go to the mall, you not doing nothing right now. I got to walkie talkie Carlos back anyway to tell him I took care of that stuff at the shop. Jay said.

Son, I'll go to the mall with you, but we will not be bullshitting; you will get what you got to buy then we're bouncing because I know how you do nigga. Rock said with a smile.

All right, my nigga, in and out, just a few things… just a few things! Jay said back with a smile.

CHAPTER 6

Seeing me in him

Carlos and Justin jumped out the truck in front of Boo's barber shop. While Carlos was walking with Justin, he was looking at him taking in his structure and demeanor; remembering when he was his age and how Justin reminded him of himself, with his nonchalant ways. Carlos could see that Justin was developing like a young man. They both had the same facial feature just a little off on the skin tone. Justin was what people would call light skinned, and Carlos was light brown. Justin was growing in height him and Carlos was running close. He was five nine, Carlos was six one in height. Carlos always had hope that one day Justin would play school sports; that was something that Justin was not into. He just wanted the newest clothes, sneakers, and talk to girls. Carlos smiled at the thought of his brother trying to game the girls into dating him; let alone having sex with him, Carlos stop walking wanting to ask Justin a question and wanted to look him in the eyes when he asked him.

Yo Justin... you have sex yet? Carlos asked, tilting his head to the side with an unconvincing facial expression.

Justin stood, caught in suspense at the question his brother had asked him. He did not know whether to tell the truth or lie, Justin stood silent; he took his time not looking Carlos in the eyes, letting his body sway; Justin asked Carlos a question back with a straight face.

Why Carlos, what does it matter to you if I'm having sex? What, I'm not supposed to have sex? Justin asked.

Carlos immediately saw Justin's reaction and the face he made to the questions. Carlos knew that he caught Justin off guard with the question. Carlos also knew when Justin would lie because he would ask you the same question back. The same thing happened to Carlos when he was Justin's age; Carlos had remembered when he was playing like he had all the girls to his Uncle Larry, his uncle caught him in a quick lie, Uncle Larry asked Carlos what color was it, was it wet, how it felt when he put it in... And the number one question that broke his back was where the hole at.

Now, little Brody, I didn't want you to take it like that. I was just asking because I know how you got all the girls. Carlos said walking up towards the barbershop door.

When Carlos said this, he gave Justin a smile and started walking. Justin caught up with him.

Carlos, I had some the other day. Justin quickly replied as he was walking behind Carlos while they were both making their way towards the door.

Carlos knew Justin was lying, which left Carlos no choice but to ask him the question his uncle asked him, Carlos stopped walking, turned around and faced Justin with a smile.

All right... that's what I'm talking about! So, how was it? Carlos asked.

Justin stood confused and surprised at his brother's question, also at the reaction he gave.

Man, that shit was wet, you know I don't mess with ugly chicks either Carlos. Justin said, feeling confident and excited at the same time.

Carlos was setting Justin up, he wanted to see how far Justin would go with it, so Carlos asked Justin another question.

Yo… was that shit hairy and brown? Carlos asked, then started laughing.

Man, I wasn't looking at all, I just put it in, did what I had to do. What's so damn funny, Carlos? Justin asked with a frown and the shrugging of his shoulder.

So, you just put it in… you didn't even look or feel? How you know if you in the right hole, little Brody? Carlos asked, then started laughing again.

Carlos was laughing, Justin was not laughing; he knew his brother was on to his lies.

All right… all right Carlos, I didn't have none yet; can we go get our haircuts? Justin spat, feeling annoyed.

Carlos stopped laughing and gave his brother a serious look. He put one arm around his shoulder and told him he did not have to lie. Then they walked in the barbershop. When Carlos walked through the door Boo started making jokes about him; Carlos knew he would crack jokes as soon as he walked in the door, Boo had a sense of humor, Carlos knew that whenever he went to Boo's shop, it was all good vibes.

Damn, look at this science project coming through the door, What's up with you, Carlos… What brought you on this side of town, my nigga? Don't tell me Tom fucked you up again? Boo asked, then started laughing.

I know this spidery monkey ain't talking! Nigga, you should be glad I'm coming to visit you with those binoculars on your face… you probably don't get that many customers with your ugly ass. Carlos said, then started laughing.

But no… Boo what's going on. I thought since I was around your way, I would stop in to get my haircut! Carlos said as he was standing in front of Boo's chair as he spoke.

Boo's shop had a crowed; he had one guy in the chair, Carlos was sitting waiting, then his phone rung.

Yo Boo, take care of my brother after you're done. Carlos said as he got up to make his way outside to answer his phone.

All right, you funny looking nigga. Boo shouted.

Carlos wanted to step outside to take his phone call; he did not know the person in Boo's chair. Carlos did not want to have an important business conversation in front of a stranger. Looking at his caller I. D. he knew who was calling.

What's up Jay, what's popping my nigga, did you do that for me? Carlos asked as he made his way out the door.

Yeah, I took care of that my nigga, that's why I called you. Jay said.

Yo, did you see Rock or talk to him? Carlos asked.

Yeah, me and Rock are leaving the hood right now… about to go to the Mall. Jay said.

Yo, ask Rock did he talk to Black, Rell, Trick or Lartesha yet if not then he should get on that shit. Carlos said. Jay started laughing; he knew Carlos always tried to demand somebody to do something like he was their father, Jay was telling Rock everything Carlos was saying at the same time he was laughing try to instigate the situation. Rock found nothing funny; he grabbed the phone.

Yo nigga… who the fuck you think you talking to… you better stop acting like you somebody father… telling me what I should do… you got me fucked up, that's why you and Trick got into it this morning… you need to stop that shit Carlos, we grown ass men, not your kids my nigga. Rock said then he hung up.

Carlos went back into the barbershop just smiling to himself and saying to his self.

I know this bitch ass nigga…didn't just hang up the damn phone on me, because of Jays stupid childish ass, now I got to straighten Jays ass out for this shit. Carlos said.

As soon as Carlos walked back into the barbershop, his phone rang again, this time it was Rell calling. Carlos and Rell had a closer relationship amongst the crew. They held better conversation; Carlos turned back around and took the call.

Yo Rell, what's up? I just got off the phone with Jay and Rock, I bet they didn't even call you yet? Carlos asked

Nah, I just got up my nigga… my girl just left the crib to go somewhere… she yelled through the house what time it was before she slammed the door harder than a motherfucker, I guess she has an attitude, but oh well. Rell said.

Hey… she'll get over that shit… yo, check this out though, I need you to be over Lartesha's crib around seven pm because I need to holla at everybody about something; Jay and Rock made me mad as fuck… Jay blew some shit up, getting Rock upset causing him to scream in my ear then hang up the phone on some bitch shit. I just wanted to reach through the phone and choke the shit out of Jay's childish ass for that shit, I'll see him later though. Carlos said.

Man leave that nigga alone Carlos, don't even sweat that shit, you know how Jay is, Rock didn't probably mean nothing behind that shit, it probably annoyed him. Rell said.

Yeah all right, if you say so, but that nigga Jay got to learn to stop blowing shit up amongst us before somebody gets hurt. I'm too damn old for games, you nah mean Rell. Carlos spat back.

Yeah, I feel you my nigga… I will talk to him my nigga, just chill all right, son. Rell said.

All right my nigga, but yo, I'm about to go get this cut out the way so see you at seven pm. Carlos said.

All right… I'm about to get up, take a shower… shoot to the Mall; hit up the bookstore for some reading material, see you later my dude. Rell said.

Carlos hung up the phone and went back into the barbershop. As soon as he came through the door Justin was getting out the chair Boo was still joking.

Nigga… you ain't that important… why you keep going outside every time that damn phone rings… you better get in this chair… I'm closing early today… you funny looking nigga. Boo said.

Damn… Man you did my brothers' hair real quick… that shit better be sharp or we going to jump your ass in here… nobody here to save your ass, after we knock your ass out, I will have Justin cut your hair off. Carlos said jokingly, then started laughing.

Yeah… then where ya'll going to live after. Boo asked as he was laughing.

Yo Justin… watch this funny looking nigga… if he moves wrong… hit him in the mouth as hard as you can. Carlos said and started smiling at Justin, but he did not catch the joke.

Justin was not looking in their direction, he was looking at the T.V., deep in his thoughts; re-playing all the things that happened since he's been with Carlos. He was also thinking about all the things his friend J-Love been telling him. Justin remembered J-Love told him about the time he was in the hood; how Jay and Young Chris were out on McKinley and Elk getting their hustle on, he also saw Trick, Black and Rell coming out of Slow-Cooker house with a big duffle bag; he heard that Slow-Cookers house was the spot all the big drug dealers would go for her to cook their drugs up; Slow-Cooker had skills for cooking cocaine. She knew all the tricks. J-Love said one day he would rob who ever came out the house with another big bag. Justin was anxious and could not wait until he got home, he loved being around Carlos, there were things he did not understand; Justin knew there were things Carlos was not being honest about.

Yo Justin you ready, let's be out Little Brody, Boo, I'll holla at you in a minute. Carlos shouted.

All right, my nigga... be safe out there; peace Justin. Boo spat back.

Peace Boo! Justin replied as he was walking out the door.

As Carlos was getting back in the truck, his phone rung.

Yo Carlos, that phone stay ringing, cut it off. Justin said with a frown.

Nah... Justin, that's part of business; Hello, what's up Black, what's popping my nigga? Carlos said as he was answering the phone.

What's up, Carlos? Black asked.

Same shit different day, I'm just leaving Boo's shop with Justin, I'm on my way to drop him off, what's up with you, have you spoken to Jay or Rock yet? Carlos asked.

Nah... I rode through the hood... but the only person I saw was Toya as usual. She ran up to my car, banged on my window; I cracked the window to see what she wanted. She said that Slow- Cooker went to jail last night for stabbing a white guy who was acting crazy in her house. Toya said she brought the white guy there for some sexual pleasures with him. When they got in the room, he started telling her to do crazy things; she said he asked her to lick his ass... ha... ha... suck his balls... ha... ha... She told him that ain't what he paid for plus; she does not do that. She said he got mad, punched her in the face. She ran out the room with his money screaming; that's when Slow-Cooker came to see what all the commotion was about. Toya ran right past Slow-Cooker screaming with a bloody mouth; Slow-Cooker went in the room to tell the white guy he had to leave; he grabs Slow-Cooker

35

swung her on the floor saying he paid his money. Toya said she came running back in the room to help Slow-Cooker, she pushed the white guy off Slow-Cooker, so they both could get away instead of Slow-Cooker running; she got up, grabbed her knife, then started stabbing the white guy. she stabbed him twenty times; the police came, took her to jail, they took the white guy to the hospital in critical condition. Black said as he was laughing in between telling Carlos the story.

Word, yo, what are the charges they hit her with? Carlos asked.

Man... Toya said they hit her with possession of a weapon, attempted murder, and they got her for possession of drugs. Black said.

Damn! That's fucked up, but she'll beat that shit if they hit dude with the rape charges, I hope Toya told them that the dude was trying to rape both of them. Carlos said.

Yeah, Toya said that the police took her downtown for questioning and she told them everything. She also said the dude had just got done beating his wife badly, before he saw Toya, so I think she would beat the charges. Black said.

Black... since you haven't spoken with anyone yet; I need everybody to meet me over Lartesha's crib around seven o'clock. I'm on my way to drop Justin off. Then I'm headed to the crib to take a shower. We will talk more about this tonight, all right, son. Carlos said as he was pulling over in front of his mother's house.

All right... I'll be there, I'm about to head up to the college campus. This one chick is having a cookout, and she invited me; I washed the whip up this morning before I went home... yo the weather is nice out here playboy. Black said as he was driving through the city street.

Black was one of them dude who kept his clothes and car clean, he bought the two thousand three GS four thirty from the auction along with everyone, tinted his windows had a system installed that sounded like a club built in the trunk Black did not have to sell drugs or be in the street because his family already had money. Black wanted street respect, which he got from every hood. He knew how to network and communicate with people; that was what his crew loved about him, especially Carlos. Black did not get the name Black because of his skin tone. Black was his middle name which everybody made a joke of it then eventually it stuck with him; he wanted everybody to call him that. Black was brown skin, 5'9, with a bodybuilder physique from working out, something he and Carlos would do often. While Black was driving down South Salina, talking on the phone, on his way to the cook-out with the black GS shinning sunroof open. Hanging up the phone he turned his music up then started bobbing his head with the beat playing Fabulous (Keep it Gangster).

All right, Black... see you in a minute... yo be safe you know how them Syracuse football and basketball players be acting about them girls up there... Just look what happened to them midland dudes in that bar a few years ago. Yo... them niggas had to cut them big ass niggas... they went to jail for that shit. Carlos said warning Black before hanging up.

Yo Carlos, they know me, ain't nobody going to try me... they know how I get down... you hear the song I'm playing nigga, see you at seven, one. Black spat back.

Justin was sitting listening to Carlos' entire conversation that he had with Black. He blocked the music out. He turned it down a little, acting as if he were doing it for Carlos. Which in turns he was doing it for his own benefits? Justin knew what Black did in the streets thanks to his boy, J-Love. Justin was now more curious about what Carlos had to talk to Black about. He was only hearing bits and pieces, not the entire conversation. The last part Justin had already known about; everyone was talking about it. Justin heard some teachers in his school talking about the fight. What the hell; that had to do with Black, Justin said to himself, Carlos hung the phone up, then Justin quickly turns the music back up; they were pulling up to his house.

Yo Justin, remember what I said; don't give Marie a hard time. She will pick you up for school and come get you; be where she drops you off; all right… do not forget what I said about you passing your grades in school, oh yeah,… how much money you got on you? Carlos repeated his self again to make sure Justin understood where he stood.

All right Carlos, I won't give her a hard time… I only got fifty dollars on me… Carlos why are you gone so long? Justin asked.

Justin… I have business to attend to… that's why I will be away long… here; take this money, I will see you when I get back… don't be around them damn hoodlums; and tell Mom I will call her later. Carlos said.

All right, Carlos. Justin said.

Justin was happy when Carlos told him he was going out of town; he was more excited when Carlos gave him six hundred dollars. Justin got out the car with one thing on his mind; that was to call J-Love soon as he got in the house. Carlos pulled off thinking and debating with his self on how they would handle Dirty. Carlos didn't want no sloppy jobs. He knew the word was out about what he did; he did not want to make any more mistakes. Dirty had a reputation in the streets, Carlos knew if something were to go wrong with his plan, they would point the finger in his direction. Carlos had plans for Dirty; and he would not get his hands dirty; all he had to do was watch everything go down. He knew Dirty loved to be in the crowds, especially where all the girls were at; Carlos been watching his moves; One night Dirty pushed up on one of Lartesha's home girls in The Groove. Carlos wanted to get the scoop on that from Lartesha, Carlos needed to know if she took his number. That's what he was looking for. He knew Lartesha was down with what the crew was down with. Carlos pulled up in front of Marie's apartment building and sat in his truck for a minute; just playing the situation out. Then a voice came over his Nextel walkie-talkie.

CHAPTER 7

Playing the Phone

Carlos...! Carlos...! I know you're there, this Lartesha... pick up.
Lartesha shouted.

What's up, baby girl? Call me on my phone, I don't enjoy conversing
on this walkie talkie's plus I need to holla at you.

All right... all right! Lartesha spat back.

Lartesha started dialing Carlos's number while she was leaving out
the door of her hairdresser. Lartesha headed toward her 2003 Navy
blue X5 BMW; which her Dominican friend Jordan brought as a gift;
in Lartesha mind she would say it was for her bomb sex she gave; But
in reality, Jordan was on to something bigger. Money or sex was not
in the picture. Lartesha other friend Vince who bought her the twenty-
two inches with a system to go with her SUV did not get the same
treatment as Jordan; he still gave her things. Vince was another one
she did not know much about; Lartesha never wanted to get serious
with none of the men she was seeing. She kept her relationships to
herself, Lartesha knew Carlos would not agree with some guys she
was seeing. Carlos looked at his self, more like a big brother to her.
Today Lartesha was feeling good, after getting her hair, nails, and car
cleaned; she headed home to put on something more relaxing. She
wanted to show her sexy honey brown legs off with her new platinum

ankle bracelet that her friend Jordan purchased. When he was out of town on business, he wrote a note with the bracelet. Lartesha had the right outfit in mind, Lartesha was no slouch; She was feeling like some thong sandals today; she wanted to show off her beautiful feet with her Laperle top and her Gucci skirt. Lartesha was driving down South avenue, talking to Carlos on the phone.

Carlos, what's going on... why didn't you want to talk on the walkie-talkie... is something wrong? Lartesha asked.

Nah, ain't nothing wrong. I just didn't want to hold a conversation on that shit. So how are you today, baby girl? Carlos asked.

So far, I can't complain, I got everything out of the way now I'm headed back home. Oh, yeah... Rell's funny looking ass came by this morning. Lartesha said.

So, I suppose nobody hasn't called you since, then right? Carlos asked.

Nah, why somebody supposed to tell me something? Did something happen? If so, just come out and tell me... stop beating around the bush with me. Lartesha said

Nah... Nah... stop jumping the gun. I told Jay and Rock to call everybody... Jay is probably high; that nigga Rock... he thinks niggas be trying to boss him around; Those niggas have serious issues. Anyway, yeah, I had a brief run in this morning; I wanted to talk about it with everyone... I know it's probably already in the streets. Carlos said

I'll be at the crib... I just have to pick up around the house then change my clothes... should I get something from the store for Y'all to eat while I'm out? Lartesha asked.

Nah... I'm not staying... I told Marie to get some movie tickets for tonight... So, I'll be taking my lady to the movie... I will be over your crib before we go... I told everyone seven o'clock all right. Carlos said.

All right, then. Carlos please do not get bent out of shape about Jay and Rock. Tell Marie I said hi and to call me. Lartesha said.

Oh yeah, before I forget what's up with that girl Veronica… One night I seen her and that nigga Dirty talking, he brought her a drink. Is he fucking her or what? Carlos asked.

Now hold the fuck up! Why the hell are you inquiring about her? You have a faithful lady, Carlos! Lartesha yelled through the phone.

When Carlos asked about Veronica, Lartesha was not trying to hear nothing. She had the up most respect for Marie; she liked her so she would not cross her. So, before Carlos could explain, Lartesha cut him off, waving her finger in the air as if he could see her. Lartesha was shaking her head back and forth like she was making her point through the phone.

Now wait a minute, Lartesha, let me. Carlos said in his defense.

No… you wait one-minute nigga… You better get that mother-fucking thought out of your head; trying to cheat on Marie. She has been nothing but good to you all these years. Now you want to fuck with a girl I associate with… Come on Carlos, don't be like the rest of these niggas out here.

All right… all right… Lartesha, would you stop running your damn mouth for one minute… calm the fuck down; listen… I don't want that bitch for the record; I just need you to find out if she got the nigga number that night, find out if she hooked up with him yet. I'll talk with you later about everything else, oh yeah, another thing… you trying to counsel me with the bent out of shape attitude shit; you need to start with yourself. Carlos said.

Lartesha could not say a thing, she knew Carlos was right; she jumped the gun as usual as Lartesha tried to play it off.

All right Carlos, I jumped out there bad; I like Marie and you know how I feel about most of these chicks out here, my bad. I'll get on that. See you at seven. Lartesha said.

All right, baby girl. Carlos said with a smile.

CHAPTER 8

Get played

Carlos jumped out the truck to walk in his apartment building then his cell phone rung; looking at the phone screen made Carlos shake his head with a smile on his face.

What's up Marie... what are you doing on this adventurous day? Carlos asked as he answered.

I'm still in the mall... I was thinking since I'm in here I might as well pick you up one of those new books that just came out. It's called THICK FACE, BLACK HEART; I looked through some pages... I think it's something you may like... Do you want it? Marie asked.

Sure Marie, get it. When are you coming home? I'm about to jump in the shower, I'll be laying down until you get home. I got to go meet the fellas at Lartesha's crib around seven o'clock. Oh, yeah... before I forget Lartesha wanted you to call her. Carlos said.

All right... I'm about to buy this book, then I'm on my way; I'll be there soon, Carlos... I love you. Marie said.

I love you too, Mami, bye. Carlos replied as he was walking through his apartment build hallway.

Being it was the weekend, the Carousel Mall had a crowed; Marie knew she would run into someone she knew; Marie approached the entrance of the store, she could see Rell in the bookstore with a few books in his hand. He also had the novel in hand that she mentioned to Carlos; when Rell saw Marie, he smiled, and she waved at him, then went to the cash register with her book. Marie did not have time to talk, she wanted to get home to Carlos, Marie daydreamed as she waited in line, her body was yarning to be next to Carlos. The thought of him getting in the shower made Marie tighten her legs as her panties got slightly moist as she stood waiting to cash out. Marie really tried hard to think about other things. When she did, she remembered the movie tickets she had to get. So, she quickly paid for the book than rushed out the store. Marie did not want to miss her man getting out the shower. While rushing out to the store, Rell was getting in line, he saw that Marie was rushing; he thought something was wrong. He shouted out to her, apparently; she did not hear him, so Rell did not pursue her. He waited in line, thinking about his boy Trick. Rell said to his self, why hasn't Trick called me all damn day? That was strange, Rell was thinking, so he hit the walkie-talkie.

Yo Trick… beep… I know you hear me nigga. Rell yelled through the walkie talkie.

It took Trick a minute before he answered Rell back. When he did, Rell knew by the sound of his voice what was up.

Man, what up Rell… not now, I'm a little busy. Trick shouted

Playboy hit me in a few, all right. Rell replied.

Trick took the walkie-talkie away from his ear. In the process he kept his hand on the button, holding the phone close to the side of his leg, while she was performing oral sex. Rell could hear the girl's lips smacking real clear through the walkie talkie receiver, Trick continued to hold the button to the walkie talkie. Then he let go of the button, smiling to his self. Trick had a few girls to creep with, no one he would call his own; they were always someone else's. Trick was enjoying pleasures the young lady was giving until she stopped; when he was on the verge of ejaculation, she held his penis in one hand as she wiped the saliva from her face with her other hand; she looked up at Trick in a arousing and seductive way.

Fuck me in the ass daddy. The Young lady said as she turns around slowly.

Trick looked at her like she was crazy. He never had a woman tell him that before. He put a condom on, then started stroking her from behind. She was making freaky moaning sounds, Trick ejaculated then pulled out with an expression of disgust on his face, like he could not believe what he just done. Then his walkie-talkie broke his train of thought.

Yo Trick, who's bitch you fucking? Rell said; he knew that would make Trick mad.

Trick picked up the phone, smiling. He knew Rell was trying to be annoying; Trick knew just what to say to get back at him.

Aye yo Rell...! I didn't tell you. Trick said, smiling hard.

When Trick said that; Rell knew something smart was coming with it, so he got quiet. He just was not expecting what was about to come out Trick's mouth.

Nah, you didn't tell me... Yo, don't be a smart ass. Rell said

Oh, yeah... well since you want to know so damn bad; I was fucking the brake off your girl... nosey ass nigga; she had some fire ass throat to go with it. Trick shouted through the phone.

After Trick fell out laughing. He knew Rell was mad. What he did not know was Rell's location. Rell did not respond, Trick waited a few minutes then hit him back again; Trick started laughing in the walkie-talkie, while laughing he was telling Rell he was joking. Rell was ignoring Trick while he paid for the books he had. Rell tried to get out the bookstore as fast as he could. He refused to let Trick play with him like that. Rell felt embarrassed standing in line to cash out, so he let Trick call his name repeatedly as he continues laughing; but it was not a question if he was mad it showed through his the facial expression he made as he rushed to his car.

Yo Rell...! Rell...! Oh, now you mad at me because you were being nosey, man I was just playing nigga, stop being so sensitive. Trick shouted.

Trick continued laughing through the walkie talkie; he knew Rell was mad. Trick knew how his boy felt about Kelly, even though they have tried plenty of times telling him she was no good; he insisted on being with her. Rell mother made him leave her house at seventeen. He went to apply for section eight. He moved into an apartment in the Pioneer Home Projects when he met Kelly; she was living with a friend in the same projects. She fucked and sucked his dick so good; he moved her in. They would fall out from time to time; Rell knew his boys did not like Kelly, he refused to let them disrespect her. One day Black, Trick, Jay, Rock and Carlos were all together at the mall. They saw Kelly with three of her friends talking to some guys. They called her name just to let her know they saw her, Kelly look at them, smirked and rolled her eyes. She continued with her conversation; they told Rell about what happened; he got mad, went to confront Kelly about it; she denied it; told him a quick lie and everything was back to normal with them. When his crew came back over his house; it made Carlos and Jay's blood boil to see her still there; they did not know what Rell saw in her; they felt their friend could find better. Carlos would try to school him; Jay would come out in say how he felt about Kelly and her friends to Rell's face. One day as Jay was smoking marijuana while they were riding through the city streets with his seat reclined. He looked at Rell, then shook his head. Jay said in between puffs.

Yo Rell... what the hell do you see in that trifling ass bitch; She must suck some good dick; she must have a mean fuck game... Because ain't no bitch going to be eating, sleeping and shitting in my crib not paying bills… going around fucking the next nigga for free… You know what homie… just face it… you are a sucker for love ass nigga. After Jay said that, he started laughing and choking off the marijuana smoke.

Rell quickly pulled over; throw the car in park, turned his body with a wild swing, hitting Jay off guard with a blow so hard that sent his head hitting the window with his marijuana flying to the floor. Rell jumped out with a lot of hostility running through him he ran around the car to the passenger side meeting Jay as he was getting out with his lip bleeding face twisted from the pain as he touched his lip looking at Rell charge towards him they started fighting until they both got tired. After fighting, they both got back in the car rode to the neighborhood in silence not wanting to speak to each other for a few days. Eventually they got over it; Jay knew Rell would continue loving Kelly's dirty draws. Walking out the mall, Rell's blood was now boiling when he got to his car door. He yanked the car door handle, snatched the phone off his waist, pushed the walkie-talkie button real aggressively.

Trick…! I already told Y'all niggas about playing with me like that if I were in your presence; I would have broken your jaw… But you got that one; for future references, whatever ugly ass girl you got over your crib right now… you need to ejaculate… Have an ugly ass baby that looks just like her… then you could have somebody to play with… I will not tell Y'all again… I was just hitting you up to let you know that everybody is meeting at Lartesha's crib around seven o'clock, stupid ass nigga, I'll see you then… one. Rell yelled through the walkie talkie.

Trick did not respond, he heard what Rell said about meeting at Lartesha house. Trick was sitting on the edge of the bed trying to figure out in his head what the meeting was about, while he was thinking the Young Lady that was laying across the bed naked had, being falling asleep, he turned around and slapped her on the booty then he told her to get dressed.

CHAPTER 9

Where Stronger Together

Carlos… I'm home… are you still in the shower? Marie asked as she yelled through the apartment.

Marie yelled out as she made her way through the door with bags in hand, dropping her bags at the door Marie rushed straight to the bathroom where she thought Carlos would be; She could not hear the shower running, saying to herself; well maybe he was drying off with that thought of him drying off made her change direction. Marie turned and headed straight to the bedroom, when Marie walked through the room door, she took all her clothes off. Then she stood in the middle of the room as her natural skin glowed with her red Victoria's Secret matching thong set; she wore. Marie was hornier than ever, waiting for Carlos to walk through the bedroom door. She heard the door shut to the bathroom... which made a big smile come to her face, Marie was excited imagining how Carlos always appeared when he got out the shower, with a towel wrapped around his waist revealing all his muscles on his body, especially his eight pack which she loved rubbing, Marie had the picture in her head. Carlos stood in the doorway with his towel wrapped around his waist with a big grin on his face from the sight of his lady's perfect skin tone and perfect features. Carlos's manhood arose from under the towel pointing in Marie's direction. Carlos began laughing, then Marie started laughing even harder as she walked towards him. When she got in his arms,

Marie gave Carlos a seductive look, then she started taking her bra off. Carlos let his towel fall as he took Marie closer in his arms, picking her up and walking her over to the bed placing her down on the soft Versace Barocco cotton sheets passionately; Carlos started kissing Marie all over her body sending chills through her spin, he slowly guided his hands and tongue down her body; massaging Marie's legs as he slowly spread them open, Carlos began gently caressing Marie's clitoris with his tongue; when he saw that Marie was loving it, he started performing other tricks with his tongue. Carlos would gently pull Marie's clitoris in his mouth then momentarily releasing it; Carlos kept repeating it, sending Marie's body through many sensations as she climaxed; Marie placed both hands on the side of Carlos cheeks pulling his face up to her face whispering in his ear.

Put it in Carlos, I want you in me now! Marie said seductively in Carlos' ear.

Carlos was gently kissing Marie as he slowly guided his manhood inside her; she insisted him to go faster. They went on for twenty minutes as Marie came to another climax, Carlos began ejaculating in Marie as he stroked her loving all the sensations that traveled through his body. Carlos and Marie were both drained as they laid in silence, smiling to themselves.

Carlos… I love you… I never want to let you go… The thought of you; makes my panties wet. Marie said as she had a big smile on her face.

Marie… I feel the same way about you… I never want to lose you. Carlos said looking over at Marie.

So, Carlos… what is it you wanted to talk about? And don't you have to meet somebody at seven o'clock? Marie asked.

Yeah, I have a favor to ask you… Remember what I asked you before; about me connecting with your uncle Victor? Well, I need you to talk to him for me; see if he will deal with me just this one time. I really need this Marie. Carlos said.

Carlos, I don't have any problems asking my uncle for a favor for you. But you understand that my uncle is very stubborn; also, he's serious about his business. Marie said.

When Marie was explaining this to Carlos; she spoke in her soft Dominican accent. She was looking him in the face, expressing how serious her uncle was about his drug business. Marie did not want Carlos disappointed if her uncle did not want to move forward.

Marie... I understand... I really hate to be asking you for this favor... I need this one big move... if he says no; I won't be mad; I'll just have to keep going the way I've been going. All I'm saying, Marie, that it's worth a try. Carlos said.

All right, Carlos... your right, it is worth a try; for your benefits not for mine... I want you to be happy Carlos... but I want you to stop what you are doing... I do not understand why you won't just run your car shop; I do not want to lose you like I lost my brother. I don't know what I'll do without you, Carlos. Marie said as the emotions set in, tears started coming down her cheeks.

Watching the tears rolling down Marie's cheeks, made Carlos grabbed Marie tight in his arms to console her. Carlos looked Marie in her brown eyes; he told her how much he cared for her; Carlos also expressed how he felt about the drug game. Carlos explained to Marie how far they came together. He assured Marie that now was not the time for her to be breaking down, while he was wiping her tears away.

Marie... please be strong for me this time, I need you the most. I cannot have you thinking bad things right now. All I need is this one run... I got it laid out; we will be straight for a long time. Carlos said.

Carlos, you do not understand me; I do not care about money. What I am trying to say is that you are out there selling drugs... who knows what else… A lot of things come behind that lifestyle Carlos… When people live that life, they end up dead or in jail… I am not trying to lose you to none of that... Then you run around here saying how you want to keep your little brother away from the street shit… But here you are doing wrong yourself, Carlos… I will do this one favor for you… I love you and I know if something were to go wrong, I cannot blame nobody but myself. But Carlos do not get your hopes up because I told you he was stubborn. Oh, and I do not feel like going anywhere tonight; so just go have fun with the fellas, I will just stay in so I can read. Marie said.

After Marie was finish expressing how she felt, she got up from where she laid and headed towards the bathroom. Marie did not look back; she knew Carlos would get up and follow behind her, entering the bathroom Marie got in the shower letting the water run over her face; to mix in with the tears that came down her cheeks. She was thinking about her family as Carlos was getting in the shower. Marie had her back turned with the water running over the front of her body; with most of her head under the water. Carlos eased up close to her and let his hands rest on her shoulders, then he slid them down to her waist as he started kissing on her neck; between every soft kiss, he would explain to her why; he was taking the risk he was taking.

Marie… I need you to hear me out… I am not trying to make a career out of selling drugs… I just need two hundred thousand to get the shop where it needs to be... Right now, it's not bringing in that much money… I buy cars from the auction… I need you to understand that my uncle left me that shop and I've been trying my hardest to keep it running… Look at me when I say this Marie; I need you to stand your ground like you have been doing; with no doubts about your man, okay. Carlos said.

After Carlos was finish explaining to Marie; he knew he had to get going because he had some unfinished business to attend to. That was a side Marie never saw or never perceived him as being the type to kill; which he left in the street, in the presence of his queen; he played his role of a king. Carlos stepped out of the shower, grabbed his towel and began drying off; Marie stepped out behind Carlos reaching to grab her towel to dry her body off, Carlos walked over to her grabbing the towel from her hand let his eyes roam her body as his hands guided their way all over her body with the towel. Marie saw the look in Carlos's eyes. She also felt the arousal in his manhood, making her blush at him. Carlos smiled back at Marie. He knew she felt it. She shook her head at him, gesturing no. Marie kissed Carlos on the cheek, then told him to go get the bags at the front door. Marie attempted to walk by Carlos, when she got by the door with her seductive sway of her hips; he was grabbing her in his arms, putting his tongue down her throat. After he pulled back, smiled at Marie and told her how much he loved her. Then they both walked in different directions. She went to put on her pink matching Victoria's secret thongs and bra set. Carlos put his polo cologne on with his polo robe then he walked towards the front door where the bags were. When Carlos looked in the bags, he had a smile on his face; he knew his lady would pick him out something nice. He took the bags in the room only to find Marie was lying on the bed smiling at him. She knew he would like the blue Sean John denim jeans with the white Sean John t-shirt, white Sean John zip up hooded jacket with white Air force ones. Carlos was a man of perfection, especially when it was time to get dressed; Marie loved to watch when that time came. She would help; just to get her a few good feels in. but the way Carlos made love to her. She felt exhausted. All Marie wanted to do was lay across the bed and watch Carlos get dressed.

Marie, I need you to pick Justin up and take him to school... I also need you to pick him up from school... Would you be able to do that for me Marie? Carlos asked.

Yeah, I don't see a problem with that Carlos. I love your little brother, he's a little cutie. Marie said with a smile.

Oh yeah, I think you better get that out of your little brain because he's only sixteen… I'm not sharing you with anyone. Carlos said, looking at Marie, smiling.

Carlos, you need to stop with that… you know all this is yours… You just make sure that thing in your pants doesn't come out… Marie said, with a smile and slight laugher. Marie said.

Carlos started laughing when Marie mentioned his manhood. She would remind him every time they made passionate love. Marie was serious as her expression on her face showed. Marie had a sense of humor and could be funny. Carlos got dressed; then he leaned over Marie, placing both his hands on each side of Marie's beautiful, dimpled cheeks, then he put his tongue in Marie's mouth in a way that made her hot all over. Then Carlos pulled away with a big grin.

Marie… I have to go… but I'll be back later on tonight. Oh yeah, I will take your truck. Carlos said

All right Carlos, the keys are on the glass end table… I'll call my uncle tonight… if he agrees to talk with you, I will call you in hang up. That will mean he agreed… if he does not agree I will wait for you to come home then we will talk about what he said. Marie said.

All right, Marie… that sounds good to me, oh when you go pick Justin up do not… I repeat do not tell him where I am; I told him I was going out of town; He gets a little too nosey. Carlos said.

Okay, Carlos… don't worry... I know how to handle your little brother; I'll see you later. I love you and be safe. Marie said standing in the doorway with her pink matching Victoria's secret set on.

I love you too Marie and don't worry, I'll be safe out here. Carlos replied as he was walking out the door.

CHAPTER 10

Hard to avoid

It was a nice Saturday weekend; Carlos walked outside with his mind entangled with things he had laid out for his crew. The temperature was cooling down, everyone was outside enjoying the weather. Carlos walked to his truck to open the door and grabbed his chrome desert eagle out of a special compartment Bobby installed for him, Carlos leaned over and checked the clip of his gun, wanting to see if it was full with hollow points. Carlos tucked the gun in his waistline, closed the door; then headed towards Marie's zenith blue 2002 ML320 Benz SUV her uncle bought her. Carlos loved driving it to hide behind the tint, jumping in the truck he was hoping Lartesha had the chance to contact her friend Veronica; Carlos felt she was the topping to their cake. Carlos had the sunroof open cruising down E. Fayette St. He usually took the scenic route, tonight he felt like riding through the inner city he wanted to see everyone in their nice cars and the lady's walking around in their tight jeans, leggings or shorts.

Riding pass Rolling Greens projects, the eastside of town impoverished neighborhood with high crime, he stopped at a light; on the opposite side of the street, standing in front of the corner store, was a group of young boys. Carlos was watching their every move, the young boys were not aware of Carlos looking at first, then one of the young boys noticed Carlos staring through the tinted window which made the young boy throw his hands up and yell.

WHAT THE FUCK ARE YOU LOOKING AT? Young Boy yelled, throwing his hands up.

Carlos continued watching when the young boy yell, putting the desert eagle on his lap Carlos smiled and said to himself I wish you would little nigga. Carlos saw Mack leaning against the store with his BMW 645 Ci parked out front. Carlos shook his head in disbelief. Then the light turned green. Before he could pull off a bottle flew pass his windshield. Carlos tapped on the gas before his windows got broken, turned the corner, threw the truck in park. Carlos jumped out the truck threw his hoodie on enraged, jogging to the side of the store; he put his back up against the wall, then started easing his self slowly to the corner of the store. When he got close to the corner, he cocked the desert eagle back real slow. As soon as he was about to turn the corner to shoot, the young boy who shot the bottle was coming around the corner to see where the truck had gone. But little did he know he was in for a surprise, soon as he turned the corner Carlos grabbed him, threw him up against the wall of the store stuffed the gun barrel in his mouth knocking two bottom teeth out. The boy could not scream. One of his friends came running to the corner; when he saw what was going down. He tried pulling his gun out. The Young Boy was not fast enough. Carlos let go of the Young Boy he held on the wall; he began shooting at the Young Boy, who was attempting to pull his gun. Carlos moved quick with his first shot, catching the young boy in the shoulder. The impact of the desert eagle with hollow points knocked him clean off his feet. The Young Boy was on the ground rolling around in pain, screaming at the top of his lungs, while the other Young Boy was trying to run around the corner holding his mouth. Carlos caught him in the back with a hollow point. Then Carlos turned around to run back to the truck; is when a few more Young Boys came running around the corner shoot loud shots at him. He knew he could not win; he threw the truck in drive, stepped on the gas. When Carlos was pulling off Mack ran to the corner to see who his Young Boys were shooting at. Unfortunately, when he got to the corner, he saw his little cousin on the ground holding his shoulder. That is when Mack looked up with nothing but rage in his eyes. All he could see was the taillights of the ML Benz turning the corner. Then young Slim ran up to Mack and said that he saw the truck he did not see the face. Mack stood there for a minute in a state of shock, seeing his cousin bleeding with his man lying on his stomach with blood coming out of his back. Young Slim tapped Mack's arm, telling him the police were coming, they had to go; Mack refused to leave his cousin in pain, he picked him up put him in the car not caring about his other man on the ground. Mack took his cousin to Upstate Hospital with tears and the look of revenge in his eyes. Carlos was speeding in and out of lanes of night traffic, when he jumped on the highway on Teal Ave. Carlos could not imagine how old those Young Boys were out there trying to make a name for themselves. Carlos knew Rolling Greens projects were rough; so, he knew what to expect when coming through there at night in a car that was not familiar. Carlos had a few good dudes that he did business with in Rolling Greens projects, he said to himself, was Mack one of them niggas shooting at me Carlos was on his way to get off the highway at the Brighton exit, when his phone rung he glanced at the screen then answered.

Lartesha I'm on my way… I had to handle something… I'll talk about it when I get there; Is everybody there yet? Carlos asked.

Yeah… Everybody is here; that is why you need to hurry because this nigga is working my nerves. I think he had too much for tonight. Lartesha said with the rolling of her eyes.

All right… all right… I'll be there; did you talk to your girl Veronica yet? Carlos asked.

I called her house right after we got off the phone earlier today, but she did not answer… I left a message on her answering machine. I will call her again right now… what do you want me to say to her? Lartesha asked

I don't feel like explaining it right now… tell her to get dressed. We are celebrating tonight.

Okay, I'm about to call her Bye Carlos. Lartesha said.

Carlos hung up the phone, then started thinking about how his day was going. He knew it was not good; he figured it would all play outright, when it was all said; and done.

CHAPTER 11

Taking chances

Meanwhile, Justin was home changing his clothes; he could not wait until his mother walks through the door. Justin had plans. He wanted to see for himself what the street life was all about. He picked the phone up; to call J-Love.

J-Love… what's up? I'm glad I caught your ass at the crib. Man, I'm trying to hit the block with you tonight. I'm ready, I got my all black army fatigue a couple hundred… see what's up with your man for me. Justin said excitedly.

Damn Justin, you right on time… I bought this new car… what time you want me to scoop you up? Don't worry about that package… I got that handled. J-Love said.

Yo I'm waiting on mom dukes to get home... Yo I will tell her… I'm staying the night at your crib, then I will call you I needed you to be on the same page as me all right. So, what kind of whip did you buy? Justin asked.

Oh, it ain't nothing fancy, it's a Pontiac 6000. I copped it from that used car shop named Dirty Dave's on Salina Street. I only paid $700 for it. I put some tints and a system in it, so we can get money… you nah mean? J-Love said.

Yeah, I feel you… When you come pick me up; I got to holla at you about something all right; So, watch your phone. Justin said as he was hanging the phone up.

All right, Justin… don't be all damn night. J-Love spat back.

Mom… Mom… Can I go stay the night at Jason's house tonight? I did all my homework from yesterday. Justin said, lying and hoping she did not ask to see his homework at the same time.

Boy, calm your ass down… What the hell has gotten into you? Let me get in the damn house; why are you so damn hyper? Why do you have all that black on like some damn hoodlum Justin; Does his mother know you're staying the night over at her house? Mr. Johnson asked.

Yeah, she knows! Jason already asked her, that's why I came to you. Justin said.

All right, I guess it's okay Justin. Mr. Johnson replied.

When Mr. Johnson said yes, Justin went straight to the phone called J-Love.

Oh yeah, Mom… Carlos said, he would call you… he has to go out of town. Justin said.

Mr. Johnson knew what Carlos got himself into in the streets. That was her oldest son. She loved him no matter what.

J-Love was outside blowing the horn, waiting on Justin. J-Love had his music level up high, the weed circulating throughout the car. When Justin jumped in the car J-Love was just puffing away bobbing to the music.

What's good, Justin? I see you ready for the field. J-Love said, after he let the smoke out his nostril.

What's up nigga? I'm glad you know how to pass that weed… Yo you can pull the fuck off from in front of my house now; before my Moms come out on the porch and get a whiff of this sticky green. Justin said, as he was taking the weed from J-Love.

All right... nigga do not start that scary shit! J-Love said.

Whatever, nigga, I ain't never scared. Turn this music down for a minute; we need to talk. Justin said, as he was puffing the marijuana.

All right nigga, what's on your mind... it had better be good. Oh, one more thing, don't ask about this. J-Love said as he threw a sandwich bag on Justin's lap.

Okay... That's what's up... how much is this... Justin asked, picking up the sandwich bag.

Just give me one hundred and fifty dollars, it's about forty to forty-nine dime bags... shit they could go for twenties. J-Love said.

All right, no problem... that's not what I'm trying to talk about. Justin said as he was counting his money.

Well, what's on your mind, I ain't no damn psychic nigga. J-Love spat back.

All right, remember when you were telling me about them niggas Black, Jay, Rock, Trick and Young Chris? Well, I was with Carlos today... mostly all of them niggas were calling his phone. I did not get to hear all the conversations... they were talking about meeting up at Lartesha's crib around seven o'clock tonight...

Yo... Son we went to Tom's barbershop this dude named Dirty was up in there, Carlos went crazy on him... He was just slapping the dude around with his gun... Man my brother was out of his mind today. Justin said.

When Justin was explaining what he heard J-Love had a conniving look on his face like he was up to no good. He already knew about Carlos and the rest of his crew from the word on the street. He did not believe it was true; Carlos never was on the block, J-Love knew Carlos had a car shop. Now everything was starting to all come together with the information Justin had. J-Love knew all about Dirty, he wanted to put a few bullet holes in Dirty his self, J-Love was grinning at Justin when he mentioned Dirty's name.

Yo Justin… I know you're probably not going to believe me, but your brother is the man around the hood… That's what I'm hearing and them niggas is down with him… But for that nigga Dirty… I wanted to put a few bullet holes in his ass myself… that nigga be coming through the hood making niggas get butt-naked robbing niggas. Word… Son, he did that shit to my nigga L.A. one day, so that's good for his ass. J-Love said.

J-Love was still smoking the roach while he was driving. He burned his lip; causing him to toss the roach in the ashtray. Then he asked Justin to roll another cigar while he was riding down W. Bellevue St. He saw a few dudes he knew. As he rode by, he blew the horn at them. They did not know his car, and he was smiling to himself, enjoying the fact that nobody knew what he drove.

When J-Love told Justin that his brother was the man, Justin did not believe him. Justin was thinking to himself. My brother never had on anything expensive, except for Jewelry.

Yo… Justin, I heard that crack- head Slow Cooker went to jail… Remember I was telling you about her… But they said; she got out from stabbing a white dude twenty-nine times for trying to rape her and Toya… Man if I see a nigga coming out of her crib tonight with anything that look like a come up, I will put this.38 to his head. J-Love said as he was pulling a gun from under his seat.

Man… I came out here to make some money… I'm not robbing anybody nigga… Yo, I'm not trying to be like Dirty. Justin said, then he started laughing.

Awe… Now you want to get scary nigga… Trust me if a nigga sees you out here and if he caught you slipping; you are good as got son…

that's how it is out in these streets. Yo Justin; ain't no love in these streets... there are a lot of cutthroats, and you entered this dangerous life... so take this, give me a hundred. J-Love said, handing Justin a fully loaded 38 revolver.

Yo J-Love... I- am- not -going to- tell -you again... I ain't got no type of bitch in my blood so you can stop saying that scary shit to me. Justin said with a serious look on his face, snatching the gun out of J-Love's hand.

After Justin snatched the gun out of J-Love's hand, J-Love made a quick turn on Elk St causing him to step on the brakes as they both stared at the yellow tape with ambulance trucks and police directing cars. There were people standing around watching what happened. J-Love saw what was going on; he put the car in reverse and backed up real fast. Then he went to park on McKinley St; he wanted to see who was being put in the ambulance in a body bag.

Yo J-Love... why in the fuck did you park on the next street over? You know we got drugs and guns on us, what the hell you about to do? Go back over to be nosey? like all the other people whose standing around! Justin said with his hands up and a frown on his face. Giving J-Love the expression of this makes little sense.

Here we go again with the scary shit... Nigga it's not called being nosey... I'm just trying to see what went down in the hood... I saw L.A.'s Mother and Sister hugging each other crying... so I'm trying to see what's up. If you want to stay in the car, then I'll be right back because I'm about to run through these shortcuts real fast... You can put the gun and drugs under the seat and bring your ass on nigga. J-Love said, in a firm tone of voice.

Yo... do you kid I'll chill right here... Oh and another thing nigga... I'm done telling you about that scary shit, that's it; next time we will take it there, and that's that. I feel you are trying to call me a bitch on the low nigga. Justin spat.

Man, whatever nigga… if that's how you feel. J-Love said as he was getting out the car.

Justin changed his mind, got out the car right behind J-Love, then followed him between two houses. When they got on Elk Street, it was the same scene with more faces the first person to see Justin was Toya; She ran over to J-Love because she did not know Justin; to be asking him for any drugs. She knew that Justin was Carlos' little brother from seeing them together many of times.

J-Love… J-Love, you wouldn't believe what just happened! Toya said all hyped up as she ran up on him.

First calm the fuck down… before you bring all the attention over here on us. J-Love said putting his hands-on Toya's shoulder bringing her more in between the houses.

All right… all right… let me tell you because I was out here to see it all… L.A. came out here; he had some drugs; I ran him a few sales, so he gave me a quick hit. After that, Sky and Ty came walking up, and they had drugs to… I ran a sale for Sky, and he gave me a hit. After I smoked what they both gave me I tried to get another hit from Sky. He said that he was out… somebody stole his shit the other day… he said what he gave me was all he had… I said, all right I'll get some from L. A. since it all tastes the same… he said what with a mean tone in his voice, walked over to L.A... they started arguing about something I didn't hear what it was about… I saw Sky hitting L. A, then they started swinging hitting each other. That's when TY ran somewhere and came back quick, shot him twice in the head… So, since I just told that long ass story J-Love, can I get a hit… My high went down; let me get a hit please… Why you got Carlos's little brother out here… I know he ain't trying to hustle when his brother got all that money… Toya said, smiling at Justin.

Man, mind your business Toya… did the police arrest Ty and Sky, did anybody else see what happened beside you? J-Love asked.

No, they didn't arrest them yet because they ran after it happened... yeah, a few people saw it. The police had one crackhead I doubt he knew Ty and Sky names... shit I ain't saying a damn thing to no police so you ain't got to worry about me... so now can I get a damn hit or do I have to sit here and get interrogated by you some damn more? Toya asked.

All right... but if I give you this hit, you better not tell anyone you saw Carlos' little brother out here with me tonight. J-Love said as he was handing Toya some dope.

J-Love and Justin started walking back towards the car, J-Love knew that they could not hustle on the block tonight. With the police all over, no telling what the crackhead said to the police.

Yo Justin, if I see those niggas Sky and Ty before the police catch them niggas... They better get ready to wear a group picture on a t-shirt... not just one saying, R. I. P. L.A. either... I fucked with that young nigga... they got to get it for that shit nah mean? J-Love said before they got in the car.

I'm with you, my nigga... it's whatever with me. Justin replied as he was getting in the car.

Yo Justin... I got some bitches crib we could go over... you could probably come up on some pussy tonight... What's up with it we could come back out here later on when shit dies down... We could ride to that bar called The Groove... people be out there and I'm not just talking about grown up's either... I'm talking about some bitches we could come up on nah mean... we might catch a nigga slipping. J-Love said.

Yeah... I'm all for it my nigga... let's hit the weed spot again before we go to them bitches' crib. Justin said.

All right, son. J-Love said as he was pulling off.

CHAPTER 12

Crazy streets

Pulling in front of Lartesha's apartment building; Carlos jumped out the truck rushed to the door, before he could touch it Lartesha was buzzing him in when he reached it, entering the apartment everybody was sitting around on Lartesha's butter soft leather sofa; Watching college football on the 62 inch plasma flat screen. Carlos made sure he got everybody's attention quick as he walked in the living room. Everybody could see by the look on his face that something was wrong. Rell was the first one to speak up.

Carlos, what's up with you? Rell said, with a concerned expression on his face.

What's up.... I'll tell you what's up... I just had to put some damn bullet holes in two of them young niggas up on the eastside; right in front of that store on E. Fayette St... I don't know what got into them young niggas, but they fucked with the right one tonight. I saw that nigga Mack standing out there with them young niggas, but I don't know if he was shooting too. Because I was running to the truck after I shot two of them little niggas. Man... They couldn't be no older than 15 years old. Carlos said with a high pitch in his voice as his adrenaline ran high walking back and forth.

Trick jumped up to say something, but Lartesha cut him off quick.

Ya'll got to hold the damn noise down. This is an apartment building; not only could I hear ya'll, but the neighbors could too. So, lower the tone of ya'll voice please and excuse me Trick for cutting you off, but I had to get some order in my crib. Lartesha said, waving her hands in the air.

All right, Lartesha... calm your ass down... YO, Carlos, let's go back up there later tonight and let a couple more of them niggas have it. Or we could just step to that nigga Mack. Trick said

Nah... Those dudes are not a factor to us right now... I got some unfinished business to handle... ya'll going to like this; Remember that nigga Dirty who niggas say be coming to the hood doing all that foul shit... Well today, I saw his ass at Toni's barbershop; I slapped his ass all around with the desert eagle; I know I should have put one in him but I had my little brother with me... I wanted to put an end to his clown ass... I know it's probably already on the streets, So I came up with a good idea... listen this is not the first time I've caught him slipping... It's been many times. Today I let him have it... Yo so check this right, I saw him and Lartesha's friend talking in The Groove one night. So, I was thinking maybe we could use her nah mean. Carlos said as he was pacing back and forth.

OKAY CARLOS... YOU WAIT ONE MINUTE!!!! So that's why you wanted Veronica, well I will tell you this right now; she can't hold water... So, if you're trying to get her involved in a murder; then I think you better go back to reading your law books because you will need them after that shit goes down... But she called me back; she was with the going out shit... So, what you want me to call her back to tell her get in touch with that nigga. Lartesha said

Yo Lartesha, don't even worry about her. Carlos said and gave Jay a head nod.

We will make sure she won't say shit. Just get back in touch with her, tell her to call or text him to meet her at The Groove tonight. Then you go pick her up, take her to The Groove with you. Get her drunk then tell her you have to use the bathroom then leave her there... I'll be in the truck outside; then we will handle it from there, that's all you got to do. Carlos said, Lartesha just nodded her head then went to call Veronica back.

Jay for you... I want you to call that young crazy nigga; Young Chris tell him that were coming to get him so be on the block when we come through... Jay, also I want you to ride with Trick... Lartesha, after you get off that phone go get them things for me... Rell, Black and Rock going to ride with me. Carlos said

Yo Trick and Jay ya'll can handle this right? Because we can't afford to make no mistakes! Carlos said.

What Mistakes... Nigga you got us fucked up... Yo, I want to push this chump's cabbage back. Jay said jumping up real hype referring to killing Dirty.

Nah Jay, calm down, he's just talking about the mistakes like he made, right Carlos? Trick asked, with a grin being sarcastic.

Whatever smart-ass nigga... just don't fuck up! Carlos spat back, looking directly at Trick with a serious look.

Yo Carlos, how do you know that clown ass nigga will fall for that shit? Rock asked.

Man, just let me handle this... everything will go just right. Carlos answered. When Lartesha got off the phone, she went straight to grab the two beautiful 9mm's with silencers on them. As she made her way back to the living room, she stopped to close her window blinds. Before doing so she looked out and saw somebody sitting in an all-black tinted out Porsche Cayenne; with the interior lights on moving around. Lartesha thought nothing of it as she continued on her way after closing her blinds.

Here you go Carlos... I already made sure the clips fully loaded so don't worry about that. Oh yeah, that stupid bitch said; that she ain't fucking that nigga Dirty; so that's out the question. Lartesha said; then started laughing.

Man, she ain't got to worry about fucking him because they both going to be slump... now how that sound? Trick said, with a serious look in his eyes.

That stopped Lartesha right in her tracks all around as she headed into her kitchen. She got back to herself fast when Trick mentioned them both. Lartesha did not believe that they would take it as far as killing Veronica. She just thought they would just scare her up. Lartesha was thinking in her mind that she needed to convince Trick into letting Veronica live. she knew that it would be hard.

Wait... wait; hold up Trick, why in the fuck did you just say both? You do not have to kill her... All ya'll need to do is just scare her up a little... I think ya'll taking this shit too far... Carlos, that girl does not have to die. Lartesha said, with a sign of sympathy in her voice.

Lartesha don't start getting all soft on us... You, the one who said, she couldn't hold no water, so I decided maybe we should just plug that hole up instead of taking chances going off emotions like you're doing right now. I'm being safe than sorry so stop the games now, Let's go. Carlos said, then walked off.

When Carlos walked off, Lartesha was right behind him trying to get him to change his mind.

Come on Carlos, ya'll are doing this all wrong. That girl has nothing to do with this nigga... here we are setting her up with him just to get her killed... I could understand if she did something to one of ya'll... but ya'll don't even know her... She probably got kids... ya'll don't know; ya'll sure didn't ask. Lartesha said pointing and shaking her head right with every word she said.

Lartesha, you just said a mouth full right there, we don't know because we didn't ask. What that tells you, we don't care... Now can we go... We got business to take care of. Jay said smiling at Lartesha.

You listen here you smart mouth motherfucker... I'm about five minutes from putting this damn meat cutter in you... I think you need to shut the fuck up for tonight... Your high anyway this might just sober your ass up. Lartesha said, walking towards Jay standing all up in his face.

Carlos quickly walked between them both to break it up. He took the knife from Lartesha; turned and told Jay to leave it alone. Jay walked off mad at Lartesha for pulling the knife on him like that.

Lartesha listen... Please, I need this chick and you know this right... okay if they can let that nigga have it without her in the way then she can live but other than that, shit happens. You already know this, so stop getting all bent out of shape and act like the woman of the crew baby girl. Carlos said, with his hands on Lartesha's shoulders, staring in her eyes as he was talking to her.

All right Carlos, I will go get my purse... But you need to tell the hot-headed itchy finger ass nigga what to do because him and his little protégé just might take it in their own hands and kill her, anyway. Lartesha said, then walked off.

Carlos told Jay and Trick to follow him to the hood then he yelled back at Lartesha as they were walking out the door, then his phone rung. He looked at the phone screen and smiled as he picked up; it was the call he waited for from Marie. Carlos picked up, then hung up. In his mind he wanted to tell his crew they got the connection. But he told his self to wait, he did not really know if it was official. Carlos kept it to himself. When they all got in Carlos's truck, they never notice the person sitting in an all-black Porsche Cayenne. They were so busy cracking jokes on Jay about how fast he got quiet when Lartesha pulled that big ass knife out on him. While Lartesha was still in the apartment getting herself together. She strapped her snub nose.38 under her Gucci skirt, then she headed towards the door. Lartesha cell phone rung, causing her to stop at the door to look at the caller I.D.

Hi Vince, how are you doing? Lartesha ask when she picked up.

I'm doing fine. What about you, is everything all right with you? Vince asked.

Yeah, I can't complain. I was just about to head out for a few, so maybe I could call you later all right? Lartesha replied.

I see you don't waste no time with the conversation, you just take complete control before I could make any arrangements to see you tonight. Vince said with a slight laugh.

No... No... No, it's not even like that Vince... I'm not trying to brush you off or nothing like that... It's just that I promised my girl that I would take her out tonight, Like I said I'll try to call you later okay? Lartesha said as she was shutting her apartment door.

Okay Lartesha, just don't forget to call me because I'll be around. I was thinking of going out myself. Vince said, as he was smiling to himself.

Vince put a listing device under Lartesha's sofa months ago when he first started the investigation on Carlos and his crew. He got all the papers signed by the judge, then he went from there without getting approval from higher up his captain. Vince had a thing for Lartesha. He was feeling sorry for her on how deep she was in this, as he sat listing to the crew plans; tonight he had her on accessory to murder, not to mention all the other things he was hearing over the device. Vince enjoyed getting pleased at the same time. So, when he hung the phone up with Lartesha, he sat in his all Black Porsche Cayenne writing everything down.

When she stepped out the door, he wanted to break his cover at the sight of her, Vince continued writing. Lartesha was too busy thinking about what she was about to do to her friend Veronica that she did not even look in Vince's direction. Vince stopped writing and began staring; he was loving every bit of her in his sight. Lartesha jumped in her truck, pulled off, not looking in her rear-view mirror.

CHAPTER 13

Take what comes with it

J-Love and Justin were just leaving the weed spot; as they were getting in the car, J-Love's cousin Pooky ran up to him grinning. J-Love knew he was up to something, he could not catch it right off hand.

J-Love... J-Love, what's up nigga where you been? Pooky asked.

Yo, what up Pooky... What's the deal...? I was just chilling. J-Love said. So, where you headed J-Love... You want to match a few sacks? Pooky asked, showing his weed bags.

Nah, not right now Pooky... I'm about to head over to these girls' crib. But if you be out here later tonight, when I come back through, then we could do something. J-Love said, as he was opening the car door.

All right nigga, I'll see you later than. Pooky said, walking away.

When J-Love got in the car, Justin was rolling weed up; between licking the cigar leaf Justin started asking J-Love questions.

Yo J-Love, who in the hell was that funny looking nigga? Justin asked; looking back and forth at J-Love as he licked the cigar leaf, making sure he did not mess it up.

Man, that funny looking nigga is my cousin. Why... Who the fuck wants to know? J-Love asked sarcastically.

Yo son, who the fuck you think you talking to like that? Nigga you better get some act right in you and get out cha' body playboy. Justin spat back as he was drying the cigar leaf off with his lighter.

Oh... I'm not in my body nigga, don't take it like that, I was just letting you know that's my family, and ain't nothing funny about him. That so call funny looking nigga bust his gun, and he is a money getter. Yeah, so what you got to say about that? J-Love asked.

Yo I didn't ask you all about that nigga, and yeah that's how I will take it. Because that's the way you put it out there, now I'm done with that nigga so take this and shut up, you need to be calling them chicks before we get over there; to make sure they're at the crib. Justin said passing J-Love the cigar.

J-Love took the cigar as he was laughing at Justin's smart remark; then he took a couple pulls and passed it back. J-Love then picked his cell phone up to call the girls he had in mind. J-Love dialed the number and got an answer on the first rang.

Hello.... Carmen answered in a soft tone of voice.

What's up... What are you, doing? J-Love asked.

Nothing... just sitting here with jazzy watching TV. Carmen said.

Well, I'm on my way over there... it's not to be watching T. V either... tell jazzy my homie is trying to see her. J-Love said.

Yo J-Love... Is that police coming up behind us? Justin asked, looking through his side rear-view mirror then turning the music all the way down.

Hold up Carmen... Yo Justin stop being so damn paranoid I got this my nigga, back to you Carmen. J-Love said as he was putting the phone back to his ear as he was coming to a stop sign on Brighton and Cannon Street, with the police on his bumper.

Okay, I'll be here waiting… but for your friend; I hope he's not ugly because my girl doesn't bite her tongue, she'll let him know. Carmen said with a slight giggle.

Well, all right, we will be there in a few minutes, that's if we don't get pulled over. J-Love said as he was pulling off from the stop sign slow.

J-Love had some insecurities about his self. He did not want to show it. He looked over at Justin then sat the phone down, turned the music back up slowly, looking through his rear-view mirror. When J-Love saw that the police car turned off, he pressed the volume button all the way until the music was blasting. J-Love turned, looked at Justin with a smile before snatching the cigar out of Justin's hand.

CHAPTER 14

The things that happen in the streets

Carlos pulled up on McKinley avenue, with Rell, Black and Rock in his truck. Behind them, Jay and Trick were following; in Tricks green 2002 Q45 Infiniti. Jay jumped out the car, called for Young Chris to come where they were standing. Young Chris was on the corner with a group of young boys talking about the incident that happen with Sky and Ty killing L.A. That had Young Chris mad when he found out how it all went down Young Chris wanted to do something to Toya for what happened. Young Chris made his way towards where Jay was standing, as he approached Jay could tell by the looks that something was wrong.

Young Chris... what's up nigga... Why are you looking like that? Jay asked.

Man, you wouldn't believe what happened, Jay. Young Chris said, balling his fist up with the rage in his eyes.

Yo that stupid ass dope fiend Toya ran her mouth to Sky and Ty crazy asses, they shot L. A; over some petty ass shit... If she would have just kept her damn mouth shut, then that shit wouldn't have happened. Young Chris explained.

Oh, yeah... Jay said in surprise.

Yo my nigga… do not sweat that shit… We'll see her for that shit, but right now we got some real shit to handle. Jay said, putting his arm around Young Chris' shoulder and walking him over to where Carlos was standing.

Yo, what's up young nigga? Carlos asked when Young Chris walked up.

Yo, I got a minor job for you and I know you will like it. Carlos said, grinning at Young Chris as he pulled out the 9mm's with the silencers on them, handing one to young Chris and the other one to Jay.

Young Chris just stood there in silence, looking back and forth at Jay and Carlos. Then it was like Jay said the magic words that broke Young Chris silence; when he mentioned the person name Young Chris got hype and ready to make moves.

Yo… we are about to let that clown ass nigga Dirty have it. Jay said, moving his head from side to side with every word.

So, what's up are you rolling or what? Carlos asked.

What… Am I rolling… Nigga all you got to do is show me where he's at, then just sit and watch… This the moment I've been waiting for… Just to catch that so-called gangster ass nigga slipping. Young Chris said, as he was tucking the gun in his waistline while he was talking with excitement in his voice.

All right… Shit, let's go then. Carlos said, turning, walking toward his truck.

Jay and Young Chris started walking towards Tricks car, when a car with loud music started riding up the street. They could not tell what kind of car it was, so they both pulled out their guns. As the car got closer Jay recognized whose car it was that's when he told Young Chris. Young Chris was eager to shoot the car up, Jay had to get in the front of him to talk him out of it.

Son... That's that nigga Dole from over there on Bellevue Ave... Man fuck that nigga. Jay said, standing in front of Young Chris, tucking his gun back in his waistline.

Shit, that's more the better nigga... That lame ass nigga be riding around here looking like all tough... I said to myself if this punk motherfucker come back through here, I'm going to Swiss cheese that nigga Benz up... So, fuck that. Young, Chris said, as he was lifting the 9mm up.

No.... Jay shouted as he grabbed Young Chris' arm when the car rode by.

As Dole was riding by, he was bobbing hard to his music looking toward Young Chris and Jay. When he saw the gun coming up in Young Chris' hand, he stepped on the accelerator. Dole did not look back; he turned the corner, tires screeching from speed. After Jay and Young Chris saw how fast Dole turned the corner, they started laughing as they were walking towards Trick's car. Young Chris started tucking the gun back away. Carlos was sitting in the truck with Rell, Black, and Rock watching Jay and Young Chris.

Yo ya'll niggas need to put a little pep in ya'll step and stop bullshitting! Carlos said, as he rolled his window down.

Man shut up nigga... stop whining Jay said putting his arm around Young Chris shoulder laughing.

Ya'll niggas crazy. Young Chris said, in between laughs.

Man fuck you... Nigga just hurry your ass up! Carlos yelled out.

Jay got in the car, ignoring Carlos' harsh words. Trick was shaking his head at them both. Then they all started laughing. Jay turned and threw Young Chris a bag of hydro weed.

Son... you were not about to shoot that car up. Trick said while he was laughing.

Hell yeah… I don't like that nigga, anyway. Young Chris said as he was looking at the bag of weed, trying to see what kind it was.

Damn… Nigga you got to examine the weed; man roll that shit up. Jay said, turning his head around.

Oh nigga… You can smoke this to the face, I got some purple haze right here in their fat bags… You know we don't smoke that bunk around here. Young Chris said, tossing the bag on Jay's lap; he started dangling his bags in the air.

Y'all not about to smoke my car out like that, so after that first one, do not light another one… you both know I don't smoke. Trick said, looking back at Young Chris, then over at Jay with a serious look.

Here we go again. Young Chris said.

Pulling off, turning on S. Salina street, it was busy tonight as usual. The scenery was beautiful, everybody was standing on the corners with their crew or riding up and down the streets with their nice cars. Carlos turned off McKinley, headed toward Colvin Street; wanting to check the fish market out, he figured it would have a crowd. As Carlos drove up Colvin Street; he made a quick left on South Ave. When he rode pass the fish market, there were a few people hanging around. Moet's had a little crowd, Carlos kept driving pass, then he turned down Brighton Ave, heading towards The Groove.

Yo Carlos why you didn't stop up in Moet's, that shit had a nice little crowd? Rell asked as he reclined in the passenger seat with his fitted hat down low, looking out the window.

Nigga because I'm driving and I'm not trying to see nobody up in Moet's… Now any more questions? Carlos asked, smiling at Rell.

Man, whatever nigga… Rell said, looking back at Carlos with a smirk.

CHAPTER 15

Get'em girls

Lartesha pulled up across the street from The Groove; When she got out her truck, it was like everything came to a standstill for her. The scenery was jumping; dudes were standing around their cars with their doors open as the music played loud coming through the speakers, you had dudes in dice game with large amounts of money on the ground enjoying the warm night's atmosphere as the headlights of cars filled the dark streets and music, marijuana smoke and hot young lady's played there game trying to get the older guys with a name.

The spotlight immediately turned on Lartesha the way she walked across the street; It was like she was walking down a runway with every step she took; it deserved a snapshot. It was nothing but confidence in her walk. A lot of dudes noticed, that's why they did not come at her with any stupidity. Lartesha did not have a problem shooting a dude down quick with their fake sophisticated approach. Veronica was right behind following suit, dressed to kill in her black leather tight Dolce and Gabbana outfit with every curve showing as she walked, Veronica had a 5'6 frame and blessed with a flawless shape with her beautiful dark-skin with dark brown eyes to complement her complexion. As they made their way through the crowd, a few dudes tried to holla and lots of girls were cutting their eyes. Lartesha and Veronica returned the same looks never missing a beat in their step towards the entrance, it was this one dude who caught Veronica's attention; his name was ringing bells throughout the town the girls were all over him, leaning against the hood of his silver 2003 Navigator with 24-inch rims with all four TV's playing in the headrest. Veronica tapped on Lartesha's shoulder, trying to tell her who she just saw, but Lartesha was ignoring her. Lartesha was mad that she had to do what she was about to do to Veronica. She was not in the mood for a friendly conversation with Veronica; She wanted to get into the bar, have a few drinks to herself. When they got to the door Veronica grabbed Lartesha's wrist and tugged on it.

Excuse me... Miss thing, but I was talking to you... What has gotten into you...? You asked me to go out with you... here you are giving me the silent treatment... Is something wrong, girl. Veronica asked, looking in Lartesha's face with a frown.

No... There is nothing wrong; I just don't want to hear about that damn Terry right now... I'm trying to have me a few drinks, anyway he's a damn hoe; you see all the girls who would run up to him, so don't even waste your time girl... Now come on let's go have fun. Lartesha said, pulling Veronica through the doors.

Walking through the doors, they received a few more distasteful looks; that did not bother them. They made their way towards the counter where the bartender was serving drinks. As they were approaching Jade already had in mind what the girls wanted to drink. Jade was awfully familiar with the girls. Lartesha's mind was elsewhere; she never thought to look behind her.

Vince was coming through the door looking around observing the crowd, he spotted Lartesha quick, Vince played it off like he was not following Lartesha. So, he went in a different direction. Lartesha and Veronica were holding a conversation with Jade. Veronica turned around to fill the place out, spotting Dirty over in the corner with a few other dudes. She turned her nose up at the sight of him tapping Lartesha on the arm.

Girl… I see that ugly ass nigga Dirty over in the corner with some other niggas. Girl… do not turn around so damn fast; I don't want him to spot us… I need me a few drinks to be in the presence of his ugly ass. Veronica said.

Lartesha took a slight turn to see what Veronica was tripping about. When she saw Dirty's appearance, she turned back around with the same look Veronica had.

Excuse me… Jade but we will need two hypnotics a piece, just the sight of that ugly ass nigga gives me the chills girl… Why you didn't tell me he was so damn ugly. Lartesha said, rolling her eyes with her words and with a frown on her face.

Shit, I thought you knew, that's why I said he ain't getting none… I wouldn't let him fuck me from the back girl… how ugly his ass is. Veronica replied with a slight smirk.

Shit for that money I'll bet you'll turn those lights off and give that nigga some… I heard he was sitting on some dough girl. Lartesha said, with her gold-digging ways.

Here are your hypnotics girls, I don't mean to be all in on your conversation but that guy ya'll talking about is a big spender in here… it looks like he's heading this way. Jade said, handing them their drinks.

Veronica tried not to turn around but could not hold back, soon as she turned around Dirty was up on her. Grinning, loving every bit of what stood in front of him. Dirty looked Veronica up and down, then took a quick glimpse at Lartesha's booty.

Well… Well… Well… Look what we have here… Is she with you? Dirty asked, with his deep husky voice with his eyes roaming back over Lartesha's body trying to catch the same view.

Lartesha turned around in time to catch him looking her over. Lartesha gave him a smile; then she sipped on her drink as she introduced herself.

Hi... My name is Lartesha, what's yours? Lartesha asked with her fake puzzled look, as if she didn't know his name.

Call me Dirty! Dirty said taking her hand, getting another look of her body like he intended.

Veronica saw the lust in his eyes as he was looking Lartesha up and down. She could not believe how Lartesha was playing it off, when she saw Lartesha give Dirty a seductive look is when veronica knew her girl was up to something. Veronica cut in quick.

Excuse me... Lartesha could I have a few words with you... Walk with me to the bathroom please. Veronica asked, giving Lartesha a strange look and pulling her by the wrist.

From the signs Lartesha was giving Dirty felt he was a lucky man tonight, when Lartesha gave him those seductive looks as they were walking off Dirty was watching with a big grin on his face trying to hold his composure. Lartesha was not making the situation any better for him as they walked off. She felt him looking at her, which made her put a little extra sway in her hips. That drove him wild until Dirty turned around and told Jade to give him another drink, making it six straight shots of Hennessey. Meanwhile, Vince was over in the bar's corner watching Veronica and Lartesha's every move. He could not believe what his eyes were seeing. Vince wanted to interrupt the conversation that Dirty and Lartesha were having because he saw how Dirty was looking her up and down was something he did not like. Vince conscience was telling him to stay where he was; at that very moment Veronica and Lartesha were walking off. As they were walking off Vince saw how Lartesha was moving her hips for Dirty as he watched.

He started thinking how could Lartesha even flirt with a funny-looking dude like that. Vince started putting things together in his head; he figured maybe this was the guy they were trying to kill. Then he said to himself well why Veronica was not doing the flirting, why Lartesha was not leaving her like they told her too. Vince smiled to his self he felt that something would happen soon, and he would stay out of the way to find out. Veronica and Lartesha made their way towards the faint bathroom sign that read lady's room, walking through the door there was no one in sight; to make sure Lartesha checked all the stalls taking extreme precaution, she knew Veronica was about to go off on her for how she was acting with Dirty. Lartesha had to make sure it was clear before she did any talking; Lartesha wanted to break it down to Veronica as much as possible. Lartesha did not want Veronica to die tonight if she could help it.

Lartesha... What in the hell has gotten into you girl... you're out there making that nigga think he's getting some pussy... I saw how you were flirting with that nigga, what's on your mind please let me know. Veronica said, snapping her head around with a frown on her face.

After Lartesha was finish checking the stall, she quickly turns and rush over to Veronica.

Girl... Would you calm the fuck down... it's not even what you think. Lartesha replied walking close to Veronica.

Shit, if it's not... Veronica spat back, snapping her neck and rolling her eyes.

I can't say names, just listen, they saw when Dirty gave you his number, so that's why I called and had you to tell him to meet you here... Now all I'm trying to do is make it where's you leave with me and not with him, because if you leave with him there's no telling what will happen to you... Now are you hearing me out? Lartesha asked with a concerned look on her face.

So, who is this person? Veronica asked with a worried look.

Lartesha how could you put me in such a position then, act like you're so damn concerned whether I live or die... If that were so... you wouldn't have never put me in such a predicament because friends don't do friends like this... You said that he robbed some important people... God only knows how many people he killed; this isn't a game Lartesha. Veronica said, pointing her finger at Lartesha and rolling her neck as she spoke out of anger.

Veronica ... Veronica... just calm the fuck down... go along with me this one time. Lartesha replied, coming closer to Veronica.

What... Go along with you, that's why I'm here now in this situation I'm in. Veronica said throwing her palm in the air telling Lartesha to save it.

I know... I know... just trust me and nothing's going to happen all right... Now get yourself together and just play along with what I'm doing, okay? Lartesha asked, as if she was pleading.

Lartesha, if something happens to me, I promise you will regret it for the rest of your life. Veronica said, pointing in Lartesha's face as she walked by, headed for the door.

I know... I know... Veronica, please do not go out here with an attitude... I understand that you're mad, but just play it off and follow me. Lartesha said as they were leaving out of the bathroom door.

Carlos pulled up outside The Groove with his crew. They were all scoping the scenery; Carlos was looking to see if he could spot Lartesha's truck. Trick was checking out all the young lady's not looking for Lartesha truck or Dirty's car. Trick saw his friend Tenisha ride by in her whip he started smiling to himself; Jay caught the smile and asked him was he having sex with her, Trick shook his head yeah. Carlos interrupted the conversation when he spotted Lartesha's truck over in the parking lot.

Okay... okay... I see Lartesha truck right there. Carlos said as he spotted and pointed at Lartesha truck.

Then he started looking around to see if he could spot Dirty's car, when he saw the car Carlos pulled out his desert eagle and cocked it and set it on his lap.

Rell looked over at Carlos and started smiling.

Yo, I thought you said that you would let Jay and Young Chris handle it. Rell said, referring to killing Dirty.

They are... I'm just trying to stay on point, it's a lot of other niggas out here... I'm sure them niggas from the East side is out here, and probably know this truck, so I'm not trying to take any chances. Carlos replied looking at Rell, then back out the window.

Aye yo Carlos... Look, there's your man. Black said, looking out the window and laughing hard.

Oh... You got jokes Black, now that's my man... I heard you were planning on starring in his next video. Carlos said, laughing even harder referring to a gay porn movie.

Yo ya'll need to stop with the gay jokes; especially you Carlos because you already know how you got a short temper nigga. Rock said.

All right, let's leave that shit alone, ya'll. Carlos said. Looking out the window, trying to pay close attention to the door of The Groove.

Damn... What's taking Lartesha so damn long in there, I thought you told her to leave that bitch. Rell said with a frown on his face, looking at Carlos.

Man, I don't know what's going on, I just hope she didn't get up in there and start running her mouth with no nigga. Carlos said as he continued to look out the window.

Lartesha and Veronica came walking out the bathroom Veronica was trying to relax herself; she did not know what Lartesha plans were; she kept saying to herself, just follow along.

Lartesha approached Dirty. When she got up close, she could see a bruise on the side of his face; Something she did not notice before she went to the bathroom. She played it off like she did not see it and went back to flirting with him.

So Dirty… How about if we just leave this place and have our own little fun somewhere else? Lartesha said; slow while sticking her tongue out and licking her lips.

Dirty was tipsy. When Lartesha told him, she wanted to go have her own little fun somewhere else; he straightened up quick, with a big smile on his face, that's when Lartesha knew she had him.

Yeah, this place is dead, so we could go back to my crib. My whip is right outside. Dirty said; with a drunk slur referring to his car.

Are you sure you could drive? Veronica asked with her nose turned up with a frown on her face from the way Dirty smelled like alcohol.

Yeah, girl, now is ya'll ready to go? Dirty asked.

Well, we will follow you… I'm not trying to leave my truck around here. Lartesha said.

Shit, that's cool with me, let's be out then. Dirty said; taking another swallow of his drink while throwing a tip on the counter, then he headed towards the door.

Vince was sipping on soda, watching Lartesha and Veronica's every move. He kept contemplating on going over and making Lartesha aware that he was there. When he saw how close Lartesha got up on Dirty, that is when he got mad, he kept his cool. Then he saw how Lartesha and Veronica were following behind Dirty, whispering to each other. That is when he knew something was about to go down. So, he followed behind. He kept his distance between them. When they walked out the door, he waited for five minutes, then he walked out behind them. He rushed over to his truck in an incognito way, then sat there waiting until they pulled off.

Aye yo Carlos… There Dirty go right there coming out the door and look… Lartesha is right behind him with another girl… Is that the girl Veronica…? Because if so, she's bad as fuck. Rell asked, leaning over the armrest, pointing toward the front entrance.

Nigga calm the fuck down Rell, you got a girl anyway… I'm trying to figure out why in the hell is Lartesha with this chick and they look like they're going in the same direction, towards her truck, and Dirty looks like he's going to his car… Could ya'll please tell me what the fuck is going on with this picture? Carlos asked, throwing his hands up in the air.

Yo, it looks like to me; Lartesha got her own plan. Maybe you should hit her on her cell phone before she goes any further with this. Black said, looking out the window toward Lartesha in her truck.

Carlos was dialing Lartesha's number, but before he could push the send button Trick was buzzing in on his walkie talkie.

Yo Carlos… Yo Carlos… What the fuck is Lartesha doing? Trick asked with anger in his voice.

Yo Trick calm down my nigga… I was thinking the same thing… I'm about to call her right now… to see what's up. Carlos said, in a calm tone of voice.

Lartesha and Veronica jumped in the truck, Veronica was still dwelling on the situation that Lartesha put her in. She could not believe that Lartesha would do something so trifling to her like that. Veronica started thinking maybe she did not know Lartesha like she thought she did. Lartesha was looking out the window, watching Dirty as he was pulling around to where she parked. Lartesha quickly planned before Dirty pulled in the parking lot. As he was pulling up Lartesha's phone began ringing. Lartesha rolled her window down before answering her phone she wanted to tell Dirty wait a minute, when Lartesha answered her phone she rolled the window back up.

Hello... What's up, Carlos. Lartesha said low enough so Veronica could not hear his name.

What's up... What's up... Come on Lartesha, you tell me what's up? Carlos asked with anger in his voice.

I got this Carlos... just tell them to follow behind his car and don't worry, it's all good. Lartesha said as she answered referring to Trick, Jay and Young Chris.

Don't worry... I never told you that... All you had to do was drop her off and get her drunk then leave her ass, but no, you wanted to play a man's role, so now you got it and you better not fuck it up. Carlos yelled through the phone.

Dirty started blowing the horn and getting impatient. Lartesha hung the phone up with Carlos and then she got out her truck, Veronica was looking at Lartesha with a strange look wondering why she was getting out; Veronica was also wondering who in the hell was Lartesha on the phone with and why was she whispering like she was. Veronica wanted to know why was Lartesha holding information back from her like she was; Lartesha was approaching Dirty's car, Trick pulled around by the parking lot so he could get a better look. Young Chris was in the backseat hyped, ready to jump out and let Dirty have all the bullets in his gun and he didn't care who saw it. Trick phone rung. He quickly glanced at the caller I.D. and picked up.

Yo, what's up...? Carlos? Trick asked.

I just got off the phone with Lartesha; she said to follow that nigga car when they pull off. Carlos said.

All right but yo check this, I just pulled around here where they both are park and I see Lartesha getting out of her truck going over to where this nigga is park... Yo that nigga can't go forward he got to back up to get out this parking lot... man this young nigga is hype ready to let him have it so what's up? Trick asked, referring to how badly Young Chris wanted to go shoot Dirty.

Shit, if you get the drop then let that nigga have it, but if not then don't fuck it up. Carlos said.

Carlos gave Trick the okay that is when he turned then gave Young Chris and Jay a head nod, with no hesitation they both jumped out the car ducking behind all different cars getting closer and closer to where Dirty was. Lartesha asked Dirty to roll his window down so she could tell him something.

Hey Dirty... Something just came up with my girl Veronica, I have to take her home. Lartesha said as she was leaning in the window of Dirty's car trying to distract him by showing a little cleavage.

Okay, so what's that got to do with you? Dirty asked smiling and looking down Lartesha shirt at her breast.

Lartesha moved her hand swiftly underneath her dress, gripping her snub nose.38; Dirty never noticed because of the lust in his eyes. Lartesha made him more horny when she started licking her lips, she looked down and saw that his manhood was about to bust out his pants, Lartesha looked back up at Dirty as he smiled hard, she leaned in the car and started reaching for his manhood, at the same time she was coming up with her gun in the other hand; grabbing Dirty's manhood, she brought the gun to his temple. Lartesha had so much finesse the way she moved; it was as if she did it before.

Well, I don't think there's anything stopping me on my behalf, Mr. Dirty, or should I call you Mr. Tony? Lartesha said with his manhood in her hand with a tight grip with the gun to his temple.

How do you know my actual name? Who sent you, stop that hurts...? Ah... please... please.... let go... Why are you Ah? Dirty yelled as he was in so much pain from Lartesha squeezing and pulling his penis.

Lartesha... What in the hell is going on...? Why are you leaning in that car window like that, and why is he screaming like that? Veronica asked as she was walking up behind Lartesha.

GO... get back in the truck... Veronica right now... Lartesha yelled, turning her head to see how close Veronica was.

That was a big mistake for Lartesha, Dirty took full advantage of the situation when she turned her head. He leaned away from the gun, swinging with a wild blow that caught Lartesha in the chin, sending her stumbling backwards out the window. When Lartesha hit the ground, her gun fell out of her hand, she was in a daze from the blow; Veronica was standing from a far screaming and crying. Dirty was getting out the car with his .357 revolver in hand, Jay and Young Chris popped up from behind a car nearby which Dirty never noticed. He was so focused on Lartesha as she was trying to get up off the ground. While Lartesha was attempting to get up, she spotted her gun on the ground; she tried going for it. That is when Dirty caught her with an even harder blow to the jaw. When Jay saw how Lartesha hit the ground from the blow, he had tears of rage in his eyes. Young Chris stopped a few feet away, then positioned his self for a good aim.

Aye Dirty... pop... pop... pop... pop... pop... Jay shouted to get Dirty attention before he started shooting hitting Dirty in the chest.

Dirty fell on the ground a few feet away from where Lartesha lay; Dirty was still alive, moaning from the pain. That is when Young Chris ran up to him, put the gun to his head.

Yo Dirty... you hear me... well too bad you won't never hit another woman or rob another nigga where you're going pop... pop... Young Chris said to Dirty with a big smile and then he fired two shots to Dirty head killing him.

Lartesha was on the ground knocked out, Veronica was in complete shock from all that has happened in front of her eyes, she could not move; Jay was yelling at Young Chris, telling him to help him pick Lartesha up. That is when Veronica found the strength to move when she heard Jay say help Lartesha, but as soon as she moved Young Chris was pointing the gun to her head. Veronica was nervous in complete shock that she never felt the urine coming down her leg as she begged Young Chris not to kill her. Young Chris had his hand on the trigger of the gun about to pull it, Jay yelled for Young Chris at the right time than they heard the police siren; Jay urged Young Chris they had to leave.

Aye yo Jay this girl is a damn witness, she got to die. Young Chris said, pointing his gun at Veronica's head.

NOOO... NOO... NOOO...!!! Now let's go before the damn police get here... Aye yo Veronica... help Lartesha get to her truck. Jay said, as he was picking Lartesha's gun up and putting it in his pocket, then pulling on Young Chris to run.

Veronica baffled Jay spoke her name; she was trying to figure out in her mind how he knows her name, that maybe he was a good friend of Lartesha's. Veronica leaned over and tried to wake Lartesha up. It was hard at first. But when Lartesha opened her eyes, she tried to smile but Veronica stopped her real quick then helped her slowly off the ground. That is when police pulled up from everywhere.

V-e-r-o-n-I-c-a... Who called the police? Lartesha asked, with the sign of pain in her voice as they were walking to her truck.

I don't know... I did not see anyone come around here except the guys that put the gun to my head and did that. Veronica said pointing at Dirty's body all covered in blood.

Oh... I didn't do that... well where is my gun... I can't leave my gun. Lartesha asked as she started looking around.

We have to leave; police will ask a lot of questions and one of those guys said my name. I'm already scared, I don't have any patients for the police. Oh, I saw the guy who said; my name, pick your gun up. So, get in Veronica said; opening the door to the truck for Lartesha to get in on the passenger side.

Vince was watching everything from his Porsche Cayenne turbo with his dispatcher in hand, talking on the radio, giving a description of Jay and Young Chris. Vince stayed where he was; not wanting to blow his cover. When he saw how hard Dirty hit Lartesha, he wanted to jump out the truck and get into police mode; but he knew he could not jeopardize breaking his cover. As Vince continue watching he was feeling sorry for Lartesha and asking himself why she would want to live this life. He wanted to give her a better life before he found out what she was into; that is when he had to look at her differently. It was still hard for him to do when Vince saw Jay and Young Chris run off. He made sure they would not get away. He started describing everything that they had on; what kind of car they were in; he then warned them they are armed and dangerous. The dispatcher then asked him for his name and police number repeatedly, which he refused to give it to her. Vince did not want his name written as a witness, he knew it would mess his investigation up badly, he also knew it was too early for that.

Jay and Young Chris jumped in Trick's car, out of breath with sweat dripping down their foreheads.

Man go .... go, Jay yelled, when he jumped in the car; he started jumping up and down in the seat, pounding on the dashboard.

Yo, what the fuck just happened out there. Who called the police? Because I didn't hear shit... I had my window down. Trick was shouting as he sped off real fast.

Yo, I think somebody set us up. Young Chris yelled from the back seat with anger in his voice.

Aye, Yo! Did Carlos call you yet? Jay asked with a frown on his face.

Nah... why was he supposed to call... Ah shit, police are all over us man; they're coming up behind us. Trick shouted as he was looking in his rear-view mirror.

Don't pull over! Don't pull over! Young Chris was yelling from the back seat, bouncing up and down.

Yo shut the fuck up... and let me drive and stop bouncing around in my damn backseat. Trick said with a real serious look on his face and keeping his eyes on the road.

Man, somebody set us up! Somebody set us the fuck up! Jay said as he was punching the dashboard.

Yo, Y'all two nigga's just need to calm the fuck down up in my car especially you Jay, you keeping fucking punching my dashboard nigga. Trick said, as he kept looking in his rearview mirror.

When Carlos saw the police chasing Trick's car, he knew in his mind that somebody had fucked up. Carlos picked his phone up immediately to Call Jay on the walkie talkie, but Jay was one step ahead of him.

Aye, Yo Carlos! Jay yelled.

Yo, what up… Who the fuck called the police? Because we sure didn't hear no shots go off. Carlos asked.

Man, fuck that… Just have my damn bail money and my lawyer ready nigga! Jay screamed back through the walkie talkie.

Yo Jay, tell Trick to just pull the car over and stop panicking. Y'all know where to put the guns at! Carlos yelled back telling Jay to put the guns in Tricks special compartment.

Trick was in his own world trying to cut corners at 65 M.P.H. in a school zone where the speed limit is 35 M.P.H. Trick made a sharp turn on W. Newell Street, making the car almost flip.

Yo... Trick, we might as well give up. They will not find nothing. Jay said looking at Trick.

Man, fuck that! I'm not trying to get charged for no accessory to murder; they'll never put that on me. Trick shouted as he continued to keep his eyes on the road.

Yeah Trick, don't stop this shit! Young Chris yelled from the back seat.

Trick made another sharp turn on Midland Avenue, this time flipping the car over three times before crashing into a house porch. Carlos was following the police siren but did not want to get close on the police cars. When Carlos turned the corner, a sharp pain went to his stomach from the sight on how bad Trick's car was.

CHAPTER 16

Remember what his older brother said

J-Love and Justin were jumping out the car heading into Carmen's apartment. Justin had butterfly's in his stomach from the thought of having sex, also the question his brother Carlos was asking him earlier in the day. Justin did not want to be embarrassed when put in the position of having sex. When they approached the door, J-Love turned around to glanced at Justin catching him with a worried look on his face.

Yo, Justin, if you don't stop that shit acting like this your first time around a girl, nigga these girls ain't shit, so just be yourself, okay. J-Love said to Justin.

All right... all right. Justin said, shaking his head.

Oh Yeah! Another thing we ain't staying over here long. So just spit your game and if she gives you some pussy, cool. If not, don't worry, just get her number, her name is Jazzy. J-Love said, as he was knocking on the door.

When Justin stepped into Carmen's apartment, he admired what he saw about it, being that she was only 18 years old and had her own apartment laid out. Carmen quickly smiled at Justin when he walked through the door. J-Love caught the smile and grabbed her by the wrist;

putting her in a bear hug then he started putting his tongue down her throat like he was a pro at his age. Justin stood watching and waiting for one of them to give him the directions to the living room.

Damn nigga, you just going to stand there and watch us or are you going to go kick it with Jazzy in the other room? J-Love asked, giving Justin a what you are looking at stare.

Justin, that's what they call you right… Never mind him come with me, I'll show you the way to the living room and I'll introduce you to my friend. Carmen said, as she was breaking away from J-Love, rolling her eyes at him with a frown.

Damn… Carmen, let him find his own way and introduce his own self. We got our own business to handle. J-Love shouted, giving Justin an evil look.

Justin loved the hospitality, especially from a good-looking girl like Carmen. He knew J-Love was getting jealous because he was getting more attention than him. Justin was thriving off J-Love's jealousy because he felt the funny vibe. But Justin remembered what his brother Carlos told him about friends. He would always say that they were nothing but envious people in life and if you were ever doing wrong, you could never trust them. When Justin thought about that, Carmen tapped him on his shoulder and brought him out of his thoughts.

Oh… Excuse me, Carmen; I was just thinking about something. Justin said, turning his head, giving J-Love a mean look.

What's up, Jazzy? My name is Justin… well, that's what I prefer people to call me, by my actual name. Justin said, giving J-Love a glare.

All right, they met… He's straight, now come on Carmen because we don't have all night. J-Love said, looking at Justin, emphasizing his last few words.

Well, ain't that too damn bad. Carmen replied by pointing her finger in J-Love's face.

Justin was not paying J-Love any attention. He started holding small talk with Jazzy. J-Love and Carmen went about their own way. Justin gave Jazzy his cell number; when it came time for him to receive her number, she had a skeptical look on her face about giving him her house number. So, instead, she gave him her cell phone number. The time was flying by as Justin got to know Jazzy, and feeling out her personality, he came to see something different about her. It was nothing like how J-Love was portraying Jazzy and Carmen to be from his perspective. Justin was very humble about the situation. He did not see a need into rushing a good thing, even though he never experienced the love making and passionate side of a woman. He felt Jazzy was very mature for her age and sophisticated from just the conversation she would spark up. It was not like talking to an ordinary teenager; she was on a higher level for her age. He really could not relate to some things that she would talk about. He was still young; still getting a lot of his grown-up ways from his brother Carlos; who he really looked up to. Justin wanted to test the waters with someone three years older than him. He was thinking about what his brother told him about finding the right one. Carlos would always tell him if he ever got a girlfriend, feel her out with small talk and never rush things. Let her do the rushing. That is how you'll see what they're about and where their mind was at. Justin always paid close attention to most of his brother's speeches, but not all of them.

So, Justin, I'm happy we can be on first name bases. I don't see any need for any nicknames; especially if we're trying to get to know each other. Jazzy said, in her soft preppy tone of voice.

Well, since it's you, I don't mind at all. Justin replied smoothly.

That's the attitude I like. Jazzy said with a big smile.

So, Justin, what do you want out of life or should I ask what you are looking for in a woman. Jazzy asked, raising her eyebrow with the question.

It's funny that you asked that question because everything I've been looking for is right in front of me right now. Justin said, smiling at her.

How could you say something like that? And we just met. You do not know me to say that I am the one for you; I think you should try to get to know me better before you just jump into something Justin, I'm feeling you, for your age, you're very mature. Jazzy said.

Jazzy, it's not like I'm trying to jump into a relationship with you. You asked me what I was looking for in a woman and I said, you. Just from our little talk we been having, I've enjoyed mostly, and I have never come across a young lady so articulate as you are. Also, the quality I have been seeking in a young lady you brought forth. Just to sum it all up Jazzy, you have a hell of a personality. Justin said, looking into her eyes.

Thank you for the compliments, Justin. I really appreciate them, but I really prefer going slow with anything I do. So, no disrespect, but I am not ready to get into any relationships right now. But I sure would not mind if we could be friends. There is my cell phone number. So, you know how to get in touch with me. Jazzy said; with her soft voice, looking into Justin's eyes.

All right... all right. I understand Jazzy. But one more thing I never give up, so just remember that. Justin said, giving her a wink of an eye.

Well, I hope not Justin. Jazzy spat back with a wink of her eye.

J-Love walked into the living room, pulling his black hoodie over his head and fastening his belt buckle with a big grin on his face. Jazzy looked at him and rolled her eyes in a sign of disapproval. J-Love caught all the eye signs she did and just smiled it off. Justin turned his head and caught J-Love smiling after he saw Jazzy roll her eyes, so when he looked at J-Love; he gave him a curious frown.

Justin, what's popping… Let's be out my nigga! J-Love yelled out. Go ahead, I'll be out there, Justin spat back.

All right, nigga, don't let that bitch get your ass left! J-Love said as he was walking off.

Fuck you! I got your bitch nigga! Jazzy yelled back.

Jazzy... Jazzy! Calm down; don't even feed into that childish shit. Yo, I got the number so be expecting my call. Justin said, looking into her eyes.

All right, all right, just make sure you call. Jazzy said.

Justin got up to catch up with J-Love so he could get a few things off his chest. Justin was not feeling J-Love tonight. He felt that J-Love was getting besides himself. He wanted to straighten him out. So, when Justin got into the car, he put all jokes aside and gave J-Love a serious mean mug as J-Love was about to light another Dutch.

YO SON... I don't know what's up with you tonight; but you need to get yourself straight real fast. I do not know if this car is getting to your head. But you better not come at me sideways no more son. Justin gave J-Love a serious mean mug as he emphasizes his last words.

Damn, I know you're not getting in your body over me calling her a bitch my nigga, like I told you before we came over here, these chicks wasn't shit, but here you are trying to make that hoe your wifey... Niggas done ran through her ass, ya... ya... ya. I know she looks good but she ain't nothing believe me. J-Love spat back at Justin.

J-Love pulled off with his left hand on the steering wheel while he pulled on the marijuana smoke. Justin was mad. He wanted to say a few more words. He kept looking out the window and back over at J-Love with a frown.

Nigga don't put her in this, I'm talking about this whole damn night. You were coming at me sideways starting from the scary shit all the way until we went up in Carmen's apartment nigga, don't play dumb with me nigga. Justin yelled out.

Nigga you need to calm your ass down... because ain't nobody coming at you sideways. That scary shit; I was just messing with you, so you really need to stop getting in your body over nothing, here nigga hit this. J-Love said, passing the marijuana cigar to Justin.

All right, whatever nigga I will leave it alone for now. Justin said, as he started reclining his seat and puffing on the marijuana cigar.

J-Love was driving towards The Groove to check out the scenery. He knew they could not get in; he also knew that mostly everybody would be outside. When he got close; he saw that something was not right from the looks of the scenery. There were no cars anywhere. He did not see one person on the sidewalk. When he got close enough, that is when he really saw why nobody was out. The Groove parking lot was all yellow tape. That is when he knew what was up, that is why he kept driving.

Man, that's the second time tonight; J-Love that we saw yellow tape word. Justin said, looking out his window as they passed the bar.

Yo this ain't nothing new Justin, nigga's getting killed every day that's what I've been trying to tell you. J-Love spat back, looking over at Justin as he stared out the window. These niggas don't give a fuck who you are, especially if he's starving. You feel me. J-Love said.

Justin shook his head in response to what J-Love said. Then they rode down Midland Avenue. When they saw the tow truck putting a car up on the flatbed, J-Love slowed his car down to get a good look. When he saw who car it was, he was in shock from seeing how badly they damaged the car, that made him step on the brakes.

Damn... I wonder if that nigga made it through that disaster right there. J-Love said, pointing to Trick's car.

You know who car that is? Justin asked.

Do I know who car that is... hell ya, I know, shit you should know too because the nigga be with your brother. J-Love responded.

WHAT... he be with my brother? What's his name? Justin asked with a sad face.

Man, this isn't the time to be getting all emotional. You don't even know if your brother was in that car and the dude name is Trick. J-Love said.

Nah, I can't picture his face with his name, but I'm hoping like hell my brother wasn't in there. How shit is looking, a nigga needs a miracle to still be alive after that word up. Justin said, shaking his head.

Yo my nigga we going to go back to the block because it's probably some money out there right now. J-Love said, looking at Justin.

All right, my nigga. Justin said still looking at the car thinking about his brother.

They drove in silence all the way until they got to the block and, as usual, Toya was running back and forth to different cars in competition with the other crack heads who wanted to sell their body's for drugs. Another dope fiend name Dollar was flagging the cars down for her. Dollar thought he had all the games. One night; J-Love was in the cuts between the houses, pumping his crack real heavy. It was like nobody did not have any crack on the whole Southside the way he was moving his package that day. So, Dollar kept coming and spending; but he was not spending his own money; he would stop a few people and then tell them he could get them a better deal. Then when he came back with their crack, he would already skim something from off the top. So evidently, he would end up burning his bridge, so that is when he felt he needed to try his hand. Dollar walked up to J-Love; trying to play it off good like he was still running sells to him. Then he put a folded-up dollar in the palm of his hand, then tried to throw J-Love off, like somebody was watching him by looking all around, then he told J-Love to give him 3 for 20. When J-Love threw the bags in his hand, he disappeared in the blink of an eye. J-Love did not like how that went down, so he looked at the money before he put it in his pocket. It was a one-dollar bill and ever since then, J-Love has not seen Dollar until this day. Not knowing who car he was trying to flag; Dollar was in for a surprise. J-Love stepped on the gas, trying to run Dollar over. When Dollar saw that the car would not stop, he jumped out of the way falling to the ground cursing the person who was driving the car which he did not know who it was. So, he got up, picked a stick up then shot it at the car just missing it by inches. J-Love backed up trying to hit him again, this time Dollar was not moving, J-Love hit him with a soft tap. When J-Love saw that Dollar would not move, that just made him hyper; Justin was laughing hard. Dollar was mad and refuse to jump out the way this time. when Justin turned and saw the look on J-Love face. Then he immediately stops laughing.

I know you're not about to hit this man? Justin asked with a frown on his face.

Just watch me. J-Love spat back, stepping on the gas.

You don't even know him or do you? Justin spat back.

Do I...? He's lucky I don't get out and shoot him over that stunt he pulled on me. J-Love said, then all you heard was Boom!

Damn you hit that man hard J-Love you just lost your mind somebody going to call the police. Justin yelled out.

Who cares, I bet he won't try to pull that shit on nobody else around here, I will let him see my face. J-Love said cocky.

J-Love got out the car, as Dollar was rolling around on the ground screaming that his hip hurt, then he yelled for someone to call the ambulance. But as soon as he saw J-Love's face, he looked like he saw a ghost. J-Love was not smiling at all, he just stood over Dollar in silence, then Justin got out the car right behind J-Love.

Well... Well... Well, what up Dollar? What you thought you would never see me again or something? I hope you didn't think you could hide that good. J-Love said, with both of his hands behind his back making Dollar think he had something.

Wait.... wait, don't shoot me over that... I'm sorry I was just geeking that day terrible; here I got your money right here, please... please. Dollar begged for J-Love to just take the money.

What in the hell is going on over here? Dollar, why are you on the ground like that? Toya asked as she was running up behind; J-Love and Justin with her crack stem in her hand.

Yo Toya, for once in your damn life you need to just mind your business before you find yourself caught up in the same boat. J-Love yelled at Toya, pointing in her face.

Nigga please...! Toya said, throwing her hand up as she was walking away, giving J-Love a back hand like she was saying whatever.

Man, J-Love, just take the money, he ain't even worth it. Justin said, walking up close to J-Love.

What nigga... If I let him get away with what he did then everybody else would try to do it. Fuck that...! J-Love said as he snatched the money out of Dollar's hand, then kicked him in the face.

Ah... Ah... Ahh......... Ah! Dollar was screaming, holding his face with both hands.

Damn nigga you ain't have to do that, at least he was trying to pay your ass. Toya said, standing her distance at the same time.

Fuck you, crack head...! J- Love yelled out.

Yeah, your daddy likes this. Toya yelled back.

Toya, don't make me fuck you up... Just go ahead because I'll knock your ass out quick. J-Love said to her.

Ya... get your ass cut trying. Toya spat back, pulling out a rusty ass box razor.

Ha... Ha. Ha... You better put that shit up before it be another homicide out here, stupid. J-Love said, pulling his.38 out laughing at Toya.

Nigga put that shit up... She ain't going to do nothing. Justin said, putting his hand on J-Love's shoulder.

Shit, you can't underestimate nobody, especially no crack head... You saw what this one did. J-Love said, kicking Dollar again.

Man put that shit up... Yo Toya, let me holla at you for a minute. Justin said, walking towards Toya.

Somebody better talk some sense in her head because I ain't going to play with her. J-Love yelled out as he was tucking his gun back in his waist.

Hold up, Toya. We came out here to make some money, especially me, so let's work something out like every three or four sells. Justin said like he wasn't new to the hustling game.

All right, for you; but just keep that nigga away from me. Toya said, pointing her box razor at J-Love.

I don't need your ass anyway... Dollar get your ass up nigga; you going to run me some licks for that shit you pulled on me. J-Love said flinching at Dollar like he would kick him again.

CHAPTER 17

Never expected it to turn out like this

Carlos was in the hospital waiting room pacing back and forth, hoping and praying his friends would make it. When he saw how the fire department had to come and cut his friends out of the car, Carlos knew it was serious. Then he kept saying to himself. Why... why they ain't listen, I told them to just pull over. Rell, Rock and Black were mad and trying to stay calm at the same time. Rell wanted to tell Carlos to sit down and chill, but he knew how Carlos was, so they all just let him walk off the anger. Jay's mother rushed in the hospital's waiting room first; she was thin, young looking for her age; her eyes were very puffy from crying on her way to the hospital. When Carlos called her and Trick's mother, he did not express to them how bad the accident was. All he stated was that their sons were in a car accident and they needed to get to the hospital immediately. Then he hung up; Carlos never gave them the chance to ask how badly. When Jay's mother walked up to Carlos, eyes filled with tears, Carlos grabbed her in a bear hug then told her it would be all right. Carlos and his crew all knew each other since they were the age of six, they have all been close ever since. When Trick's mother walked in, she saw how Jay's mother was hugging and crying on Carlos. Then she fell to her knees at the entrance of the door. Rell hurried over to get her back to her feet, then over to a chair. She kept asking Rell the same thing repeatedly. Looking in her face, Rell could not hold back the tears. Trick's mother was a heavy-set woman with a young appearance for her age; also, she knew all the crew very well. Rell was hugging her real tight as he let his tears flow. When the doctor walked in the waiting room everybody got silent, except for the mothers they were crying out loud. The doctor asked out loud who the parents were for Mr. Robinson. Everybody looked at each other because no one knew Young Chris's actual name except for Carlos. So, he stepped up and said that he was there on Mr. Robinson's behalf.

Well sir, I'm here to tell you he's alive. But he also suffered some very severe injuries... I also have to let you know that we will release him in the custody of the Syracuse Police Department, sir. The Doctor said, keeping direct eye contact.

Excuse me, doc, may I see him, please? Carlos asked.

Sir, immediate family only, are you? The doctor asked, looking in Carlos' eyes.

No, but I'm an awfully close friend and about the only one who cares. I think that should be good enough under the circumstances doc. Carlos said, in a very hostile way.

Sir, just calm down. Let me check with the officer at the door. Do you have your I.D. because he might need to see it? The doctor asked, very respectable.

Excuse me, doctor... Excuse me... how is my boy... Is he all right, huh... huh? Jay's mother asked, running up behind the doctor.

Ma'am, I have a lot of patients right now. If you could, please bear with us. The doctor said.

Excuse me, doctor! What about my son? Trick's mother yelled out.

Ma'am please relax... I will assure you that every doctor and nurse in this hospital is doing their best? So please relax. The doctor said, then walked out.

Well, try your best to come right back. Rock yelled out.

Baby calm down... just calm down, everything will be alright. It's in the lord's hands. Trick's mother said, putting her hand on Rock's hand.

Carlos was taking Jay's mother back over to sit down when a different doctor and nurse popped up in the doorway with some unpleasant looks on their faces.

May I speak with the parents of Mr. William, please? The doctor yelled out.

Over here, sir. Jay's mother said as she was crying harder.

When Jay's mother got up, she could hardly walk, Carlos had to help her and from the looks on the doctor and nurse faces, there was not any good news. So, when they got up close to the doctor and the nurse, they told Jay's mother that she needed to come with them. Carlos refuses to let her go by herself until; she assured Carlos that she would be all right. That is when tears being fallen from Carlos' eyes; he knew from the looks that his boy did not make it. He whispered in her ear; that he was here for her then kissed her on the cheek then turned around; and sat down in pain. As soon as Carlos sat down, the doctor for Young Chris's was walking back through the door waiting for Carlos to come with him. Carlos got up fast, then went with him. The doctor took him straight to Young Chris' room where a police officer asked him for his I.D. Carlos gave it to him, then he patted Carlos down and open the door. When Carlos saw how badly Young Chris was, he did not know what to say. He just walked up to the bed side, stood there for a while speechless, starring, then Young Chris eyes opened.

Don't talk.... Don't talk, just listen. I gotcha lawyer so don't worry and I will get you a bail. So don't worry. I know you can hear me, but don't talk, okay? Listen to me, move your hand a little, just a little for yes, all right, and don't move them for no. Now did Y'all put the guns in the special compartment? Carlos whispered close to his ear because he did not want the police to hear him.

Young Chris moved his hand. Carlos did not want him to talk because he saw how badly his jaw was; also, he knew they had Young Chris on many pain drugs.

All right, then that's good, don't give these people a hard time and get better. I'll be back to see you real soon. Carlos said, as he was walking out the door.

When Carlos was walking down the hall to get back to the waiting room, he was in his thoughts just thinking about his crew. He did not intend on this to end like this, especially with him and Trick. He knew he never had the chance to hold a sociable conversation with him since their last fight. That was eating at his conscious. When Carlos walked in the waiting room, Rell ran right up to him.

Carlos... They said that Trick suffered some severe head injuries, and he's in a coma, but they're doing their best. Rell said; with tears running down his cheeks.

How is his mother holding up? Carlos asked, nodding towards Trick's mother.

Well, she's doing all right so far; she's trying to handle the pressure behind all of this. But Jay's mother, we just got the news about her. They got her on some medicine. Because when they told her that Jay didn't make it, she almost had a heart attack until one nurse saved her. Rell said as tears were coming down harder from mentioning Jay's name.

Aye, yo, Rock... Black... Come here for a minute! Carlos yelled.

Carlos wanted his homie to have the best burial there was, and he wanted to give Jay's mother the other half of his money in the stash. But he also wanted to make his crew aware of the plan.

Yo, here's what we'll do. We will pay for all the funeral arrangements then give his mother his half of the stash, for Trick we will do the same, if he does not make it. But for right now it is our job to make sure we come to see him once or twice a day, also see how his mother is keeping up from time to time. I did not want to tell Y'all because I did not want to be jumping the gun, but fuck it, it is better to let you know now, tomorrow not promised. Remember when I told Y'all about Maria's uncle, well he will talk with me, so keep the faith all the way around the board. Oh yeah, Young Chris will make it. I told him I will get him a lawyer, so Y'all don't worry about that, I will handle that. Is Y'all with me? Carlos asked.

Everybody nodded their heads in agreement with everything Carlos said. When he spoke about the connection part, they gave him a strange look. When he said, he did not want to tell them about the plans but as they listened; they understood.

Yo Carlos, you think when Trick comes out of the coma; they going to charge him too? Rock asked.

Yeah, more than likely they will because he was the driver. Carlos replied.

Man, let us not worry about that part right now. Let's pray that he makes it out of the coma strong all right. Black said and walked back over towards where Trick's mother was sleep.

Rell's phone rung. He looked at the caller I.D. then answered.

Hello, what's up, Kelly? Rell asked.

What's up.... what's up...? Nigga you tell me what's up? Kelly yelled through the phone.

Man, listen, I'll be home in a minute. Rell said in a calm tone of voice.

Shit, you ain't got to leave that bitch, stay right where you're at. Because I will not be here when you get here nigga. Kelly said, hanging up the phone on him.

When Rell got off the phone, he looked at Carlos. Carlos looked right back at him, shaking his head because he heard Kelly yelling through the phone.

Man, I told you about that girl. She is not good for you. You need to move on... word. Carlos said, then he walked off to go sit down.

I know... I know... I know. Rell said, walking right behind Carlos, shaking his head.

When Carlos went to sit down, he started thinking about Lartesha, Carlos was wondering if she made it home safe.

Ring, ring, ring.

Hello... Hello! Lartesha answered.

What up, Lartesha? Carlos asked with a sad voice.

Carlos, why you sound so down and out? Did something happen? Lartesha asked.

Hell ya, something happened. Every damn thing went wrong tonight, but I don't feel like talking about it just now. Jay is dead, Trick is in a coma, and Young Chris injured badly now the police are taking Young Chris into custody when he gets better. Carlos spat with anger.

No... No... Please Carlos say it ain't so... Please say it ain't so... Jay and Trick, what happened. Lartesha yelled as tears started flowing down her cheeks.

Lartesha... Lartesha... We are coming over after we leave here. First, we got to make sure the mothers are all right. I will need you to call Marie and let her know where I'm at, tell her to come over and stay with you until I get there. Carlos said.

All right, Carlos, all right, I'm about to call her right now. Lartesha replied.

See you soon. Carlos said, hanging the phone up.

As soon as Carlos hung the phone up with Lartesha. He saw the doctor that was handling Jay's mother walk by; so, he got up quickly and rush to the door.

Excuse me... Excuse me...! Carlos yelled.

Yes, how may I help you, sir? The doctor turned around and asked.

I'm inquiring about the mother you took for the accident victim that didn't make it. Carlos asked, looking in the doctor's eyes.

Okay, okay, ya. I remember she is right down the hall. It was hard on her. We have her on some medicine, but you could see her if you like. That's if she's not asleep. The doctor said, as he was turning to show Carlos the way to Jay's mother room.

Yo, Rock, come here! Carlos shouted.

What's up, Carlos? Rock asked as he was walking up to him.

Yo, I'm about to go check on Jay's mother quick. See if Trick's mother will stay the night here or would she like for one of us to take her home and bring her back in the morning. When I come back out, we will shoot over to Lartesha's crib to see what went down all right. Carlos said turning around and walking out the door.

Cool, no problem, I'll get on that right now. Rock said, turning around and walking towards Trick's mother.

As Rock and Carlos were talking Black and Rell was giving them suspicious looks, hoping that nothing went wrong with Trick. When they saw Rock turn around, they tried hard to read his facial expression as they watched him make his way towards Trick's mother; both of their heads went to their laps just praying it was not bad news on their man.

Excuse me, Ms. Walker, would you like for me to take you home, and bring you back in the morning, because you need your rest. Rock asked in a soft tone of voice.

Oh, that's all right honey, I will stay by my baby's side. I will just fall to sleep by his bedside; Y'all get some sleep. I'll be fine. Trick's mother said.

Okay then Ms. Walker, we'll be back in the morning. Rock said as he stood up and walked off.

Yo, Rock, what was that all about? Rell stood up and asked.

Oh nothing, Carlos wanted me to ask her if she was staying, that's all. Rock, responded.

So what did she say? Black asked.

She said... she was all right and she will stay, Man why Y'all asking all these damn questions. Rock asked.

Nah.... nah, just out of concern, that's my nigga. Black said.

Carlos stepped in the room where Jay's mother was at without even knocking. When he approached the bedside, the sight made him even mad seeing her with I.V. in her arm. He started debating with himself whether to stay or leave her bedside because she was asleep; he did not want to wake her. When he made his mind up to leave, her eyes popped open.

Ms. William, I was just coming to check on you; it worried me and the fellas; we heard about the heart attack. Just get your rest; we will handle all the arrangements, so do not worry about that part. I'm sorry this happened, Ms. Williams. Carlos whispered in a soft tone of voice, holding her hand.

Thank you, baby... Thank you. But do not worry about me, I will stay strong, it will take a lot; but I'll make it. Jay's mother said, with the little of strength she had left.

Ms. William, I have to go but I promise that if I cannot make it back tomorrow morning; I assure you we would be here checking on you. Here is my house number and cell number also, if you need anything, just call me Carlos said; before he left.

CHAPTER 18

Watching What They Both Go Through

Justin did not have a lot of drugs left from what J-Love had sold to him. Toya was not about any games; she was bringing Justin sales from everywhere. He was loving the game just from seeing how fast he could double his money. J-Love was between some houses, watching Justin get his money. He was mad at himself for letting Dollar get away; he knew Dollar would not come back when he had the chance to get away, J-Love did not make that many sales.

Yo, J-Love, I'm almost ready to re-up my nigga. Justin yelled out.

All right, my nigga, yo, I'm about to run around the corner to Deb's to get some more cigar's, you want something? J-Love asked.

Nah, I'm straight. Justin yelled back.

Yo, when I get back, we going to hit a few dutches and call it quits, all right? J-Love said.

That's cool with me; yo don't be all day around there because the next sell I get, I'm done. All right... All right. Justin said, running off.

J-Love was at the store holding conversation as he waited in line. Dollar ran up to him from out of nowhere talking about he had a big sell for him around the corner. He told J-Love to hurry before the man left, J-Love tried to give him the drugs, but he would not take it.

J-Love, he told me, he will not take nothing from me or give me his money. He wanted to buy directly from the man. Dollar said, looking all around like he just smoked something.

All right, here I come, let me go give this to Justin and grab my package. I'll be right there, matter of fact, let him know to pull around here. J-Love said.

Justin was talking to his cousin Murder Black when J-Love walked up. Murder Black was 17 years old with a 1999 CLK 320 Benz with 20-inch rims. Murder Black got his name when he caught an attempted murder case and beat it. So people started calling him Murder Black. He used to hang around the neighborhood getting money until he started making the drug addicts page him with sales from everywhere.

Aye, yo Justin... what the hell are you doing out here... I know you ain't trying to hustle nigga. Murder Black said.

What nigga, I'm trying to push something like this; nah mean. Justin said.

Does Carlos know your ass is out here hustling little nigga? Murder Black asked.

Hell nah... shit, don't go running your mouth either. Justin said.

Yo Justin, hold this, I will be right back. I'm about to catch this big lick. J-Love said, as he was walking up.

Man, I know you ain't with this lame ass nigga yo. If you want to make some actual money, hit me on my cell. I'm about to be out. Murder Black said to Justin as he was looking real mean at J-Love.

J-Love gave him the same look back and then ran off to where the sell was waiting for him. Then he jumped in the car, then handed the dude the drugs. As soon as he opened the door to get out, that is when the police pulled in from everywhere. J-Love jumped out and tried to run, but an officer was all over him, tackling him down to the ground when Murder Black saw all that was going down. He told Justin to get in the car. J-Love knew Dollar set him up, and he wanted to kill Dollar for it.

Yo Justin, this block shit is dangerous, you can't sell to anybody, you can't let these stupid ass crack heads bring you sales either. Murder Black said.

Well, shit...! How you know who the fuck to sell to and who not to sell to? Justin asked.

That's what I'm saying, it's a dangerous game, little nigga, a dangerous game. Murder Black said, emphasizing his last words.

Aye, yo, what were you about to get into? Justin asked.

Shit, I'm just chilling, riding around catching my licks on my pager. Why you ready to go home... Your man just brought himself a jail ticket. He will not be getting out soon, especially if he got caught with a lot. Murder Black said, with a slight smile.

Nah, I'm chilling, I told my mother that I was staying the night over J-Love's house. Justin said.

So, you lied to my aunt? Now what if that were you out there instead of your man, that shit would have fucked your mother up because you lied to her. Murder Black said.

Well, how else was I going to get out the crib; by telling her.... well mom, I will hustle on the block tonight. Justin asked.

Nah, I'm not saying come straight out and tell her, but I'm saying you should not have lied to her. That is all I'm saying, you shouldn't be out here hustling anyway, because I'm sure Carlos gives you plenty of shit where you don't need for nothing. Murder Black said.

All right.... all right, I'm not trying to hear that shit nigga. You shouldn't be out here hustling. But look what you have from getting money on your own. Justin said.

Ya, and it's no fun having to watch my back every five minutes just to make sure nobody don't rob my ass or watch who I serve so I don't be like your man there with the jack ass look. Murder Black said, with a little laughter.

Yo, what Y'all don't like each other? Did he say something about me? Justin asked.

Well, your man is the one who has the problems, because I'm smashing that bitch Carmen. She tells me shit; that he says about me. Murder Black said.

I know the nigga ain't going out like that. Yo come to think about it though, that nigga had an attitude tonight. She wanted to show me where the living room was; she was smiling at me, J-Love got mad. Justin said.

Aye yo... you just need to watch who you are around, especially that clown ass nigga. He ain't nothing but a small-time kid to me, anyway. That nigga is working for somebody else, anyway. Don't let him fake you out. Murder Black said.

I know he's working for somebody and since we're on that subject, you might as well let me get money with you. Justin asked.

Nigga... Carlos ain't about to fuck me up. Murder Black said.

Come on fam, how will he find out, plus you just told me if I wanted to get some money, holla at you. So here I am getting at you for some love; so, what's up? Justin asked.

I'll think about it... what's up with them cigars? You got something to go with them. Murder Black replied.

Hell, yeah what you think, I just got them for show nigga. Justin said.

I did not know you smoked weed, shit your car sure does not smell like you smoke. Man, you must have some good ass air fresheners or a hell of a cleaning game, because this shit be clean every time I see it. Justin said, as he was splitting the cigar, referring to how clean his cousin's car was.

Hold up! Murder Black yelled.

Huh, put that shit in this bag right here, try not to waste anything. Man, a nigga that ain't use to having his own will cherish it when he gets it, believe me fam. I will keep my shit up, like it's straight off the car lot! word.... ha... ha. Murder Black said with a laugh.

Justin was recline back enjoying the night out he was having with his cousin, as he was rolling the cigar Justin was in his thoughts thinking about the drug game. He figured that if people did not want to play fair, then he would not play fair. That thought brought a slight smile to his face. Justin looked over to his cousin wanting to ask him why he feared his brother, but he just left it alone, grabbed the lighter to fire the marijuana up. Murder Black was taking the back streets trying to enjoy the night without getting pulled over by police, being that they had drugs on them. So, he figured he will play it safe.

Yo fam, have you seen my brother at all today? Justin asked as he was smoking on the marijuana.

Justin was just trying to get more information about his brother out of his cousin.

Nah, I haven't seen Carlos today. Why? What's up? Murder Black asked.

Do you know this dude name Trick? Justin asked.

Do I....! He is making moves with your brother, why did something happen Justin... Because you sure are asking a lot of questions. Murder Black asked.

119

Yeah, something happened tonight, I was just trying to make sure my brother wasn't in the car, because he told me he was going out of town. Justin said. Nigga, then what happened? Murder Black yelled.

Man, calm down. Ain't no sense in getting all loud and hyped. Justin said.

Shit, if it ain't… I hate secrets so say what's on your mind. Murder Black said.

All right… tonight when me and J-Love left Carmen's apartment, we rode down by The Groove. Everything was close, for what reasons, I don't know. Then we rode down Midland Avenue J-Love stopped the car to see a car that was getting put up on a flat bed. It was all crushed up; he said the dude's name was Trick. That's why I'm asking so many questions. Justin said.

Hell ya…. I know him stupid; man, he is part of your brother's crew. They all be getting money together. Sometimes I buy my cocaine from them, shit the operation shut down, stop acting dumb like you didn't know your brother was doing his thing around the hood. Murder Black said.

For real, for real, I didn't know until tonight when I did my thing, but you like the third person to say that tonight word. So now I know. Justin said.

CHAPTER 19

Need Some Answers

As Carlos was walking out of the room, his cell phone rung, he knew it was only Marie, so he did not bother to even look at the caller I.D., he just pushed the button.

What's up? Carlos asked.

Carlos, I'm over here at Lartesha's house. How long are you going to be? Marie asked.

Excuse me... sir... you need to cut that phone off in the hospital, please. A doctor said, as he was walking by Carlos.

Marie, I have to get off the phone, but I'm on my way right now. Carlos said.

As Carlos got off the phone and walked in the waiting room over to Trick's mother and gave her a big hug.

Ms. Walker, he will make it through this, he's strong. I know he is... I know he is. We just got to keep the faith. Carlos said, as he was hugging Trick's Mother.

I know, baby.... I know. Trick's mother whispered.

Ms. Walker, is there anything you need before we go? Carlos asked.

No, baby, I'm fine. Ms. Walker said.

Well, here are my phone numbers if you need anything, I mean anything just call. One of us will be back tomorrow morning to check up on you. Oh, Ms. William is down the hall in room 1306 okay. So, if you get the time, then pay her a visit, we love you very much Ms. Walker. Carlos said kissing her on the cheek, then standing to leave.

What's up, Y'all ready? Carlos asked.

They all got up and walked over to Trick's mother and gave her a hug and kissed her on the cheek, then walked out behind Carlos.

Carlos, Rell, Black and Rock got in the truck without saying a word. Everybody was in their own thoughts about how everything went down.

Somebody got to answer for this. Carlos said out loud, breaking the silence in the truck as he was driving.

Carlos, who you think might have called the police? Did Lartesha say anything about who might of did it? Rell asked.

Nah... Nah..., but we're about to find out as soon as we get there. And if the story does not sound right, that bird ass bitch Veronica is dead. She is lucky that Young Chris cannot talk, but when he's able somebody will get it, if the story doesn't match. So, they better be praying that he doesn't get well because when he does; that's what I'm waiting for. Carlos said, with rage in his eyes.

Yo, Carlos, about the money you said; we would give Jay's mother; his half, now why won't we just flip it first then give her the money. I mean, we are paying for the funeral, because if we do that, we are not looking at that much. Rock said.

Urrrrr...... Carlos stepped on the brakes so fast, causing the tires to make a loud noise as he pulled over.

Nigga...! My man is dead, and that's what you're thinking about, some money... How could you even say something about some money? We got our man dead up in that hospital, and his mother had a damn heart attack, and you're speaking about money nigga. Carlos yelled as he was about to reach over the seat to hit Rock.

NO! Carlos. Rell said, grabbing Carlos' hand.

Rock did not know what to do when he saw Carlos step on the brakes with extreme anger. He started explaining how he felt the same way everyone else felt. He thought he was giving some friendly advice.

Man, I didn't mean nothing by that Carlos, trust me... I was just thinking, that is all. I feel the same as everyone, but after we get through mourning for a few days, it is back to business. Nigga I loved Jay too, so do not come at me like that Carlos, you need to calm the fuck down. Rock said, expressing his self with the waving of his hand as if he was pleading his case.

Nigga, you need to watch the words you use up in here at a time like this... THAT'S MY WORD. Carlos said as he shouted his last words, then he turned around in his seat, adjusted his self and sped off from the side of the road.

Vince was outside of Lartesha's apartment, tired and ready to call it a night because the coffee he stopped to get at the gas station was not doing him any good; he was getting sleepy. As soon as he saw Carlos truck pull up, then Marie jumped out of it then run up to Lartesha's apartment building door, woke Vince right up. Inquiring to himself on who Marie was because he knew the truck, but he just never saw Marie before. Vince thought to himself, damn; another beautiful woman caught up in this madness! Vince sat and watched, hoping to hear some conversation over the hiding listing device in Lartesha's apartment. Lartesha was in the bathroom putting on some makeup, trying to cover up the black and blue bruise on her face. But the pain was too much to bear; the way her jaw felt. She thought he broke it at first until her friend Veronica checked on their way home. She told her it wasn't broke. Lartesha did not want Marie to see her bruised up so badly, but under the circumstances, she needed her there. Lartesha knew the questions would come at her as soon as Marie or Carlos walked through the door. After she got herself together, she walked through her apartment dimming the lights. While she did that, her doorbell rang. When she went to answer the door, she made sure that she stood behind it. While Marie was slowly entering Lartesha was hoping she would walk right into the living room; without saying a word. But it was the opposite. As soon as she walked in, she stopped directly in front of Lartesha.

Hi Marie, come on in. Don't just stand there staring at me. Lartesha said as she was trying to turn her face away.

NO... Now what happened to your face Lartesha, and why do you have all that make-up on trying to hide it... Hold up, turn some of these lights on, let me see that bruise. Marie said, stepping closer and putting her hands on Lartesha's face.

I'm all right, I'm all right! It's no big deal, Marie. Jay is dead, that's what's on my mind, Veronica said he saved my life, do you hear me? He saved my life, Marie. He shouldn't be dead, it's my fault... it's my fault. Lartesha said repeatedly as tears started running down her beautiful, bruised face.

Come on Lartesha, let us go sit down, then we could talk about it. Marie said as she put her arms around Lartesha and gave her a big hug.

NO... NO... I do not want to talk about it. I should not have done it. I shouldn't have done it. Lartesha said as she was crying and hugging Marie back.

You shouldn't have done what... Lartesha, why are you hiding shit from me... Just calm down, I'm here for you, so you don't have to hold nothing back from me... Now let us go have a seat. Marie said, as she pulled away and headed for the living room.

Lartesha locked her door then followed Marie into the living room As Marie was walking, she was thinking how and why this happened to Jay, Trick, Lartesha and Young Chris. This was starting not to make any sense to her. She wanted some answers. As they sat down, Marie moved closer to Lartesha with the look of sympathy written all over her face, right when Lartesha said something; she heard some doors slamming outside of her apartment. She jumped up and ran towards her window to peek out to see who it was, taking a quick peek she quickly rushed towards her door buzzer to press it, so they could get in the downstairs door. Carlos pulled up outside Lartesha's apartment building, throwing the truck in park aggressively, then he jumped out as if he would run to the door. Rell, Black, and. Rock hurried up and jumped out, also following right behind. Carlos did not notice that he pulled up right behind Vince's truck. When Vince saw the truck pulling up, he sunk real low in his seat hoping to not be notice. While he was adjusting his rear-view mirror so he could see who it was pulling up behind him. When he saw who it was, Vince started writing notes down. Carlos was walking fast, Rell, Rock and Black gave up trying to keep up with him. Carlos yanked the door so hard that it hit the building wall, making a loud thunder sound. Then he met the steps as if he were in some race the way he flew up the stairs not even looking back. His boys were trying to keep up right behind him. Lartesha heard the loud sound of footsteps coming up the stairs. She knew in her mind who the sound belonged to; just from how violent it was sounding. When she opened her apartment door, Carlos was staring her right in the face; with eyes redder than the devil himself. Lartesha could not stand anymore of the pressure, so she hurried and got out their way as Carlos and the rest of the fellas walked right by giving her a look of disapproval. When Marie saw all the men faces, she could feel all the tension floating in the air. As she approached Carlos, she could see the redness in his eyes. Something she never saw in all the years of being with him. She was speechless, not knowing what to say or how to say it; without making him turn his anger on her. she just stood there with a blank look on her face.

Marie... why are you just standing there staring at me... You could leave now. Carlos said, trying to hide his anger.

What... I'm not going anywhere... You had me drive all the way over here to be with Lartesha; and now since Y'all came here mad at who knows what. Not even stopping to see how she is doing for God sakes... I mean she has been through a lot just like everyone else has, so I really think Y'all should show her some concern. She has feelings also! Marie spat back, stepping up in Carlos' face.

Marie, I'm really not in the mood, so please... GO... stay out of this. I will be home real soon. This does not concern you. We'll talk about it when I get home, all right? Carlos said, putting his hands on her shoulders.

Marie just go please; I'll be all right... I'll call you later, or tomorrow I promise you, okay. Lartesha said, walking up behind her.

Marie jerked her body away from Carlos' hands and turned around to look Lartesha in the face to read her expression, something she was good at doing. She really did not want to go, but she agreed anyway.

Lartesha, you make sure you call me, especially if he gets out of hand. Marie said, walking off, rolling her eyes at Carlos.

As Marie was walking out the door, she heard Rell shout first So; she slammed the door and stood outside of it trying to hear what was going on, but she only could make out bits and pieces of the conversation, Marie went home holding on to the anger felt towards Carlos.

Lartesha, why in the hell didn't you do what Carlos told you to do? Rell yelled out.

I'm so sorry... I'm so sorry. I thought I had it under control. Lartesha said as she started crying and stuttering as she spoke.

Hold up... Hold up... wait one-minute Y'all before it even gets out of hand. Let us just skip the small talk; because my patience is running low and I'm ready to hurt someone. Lartesha, I want to know what made you think you had the drop on him… What the hell was Veronica doing, because this shit does not look right to me? Carlos asked.

Carlos, what do you mean this does not look right…? When I was about to put some holes in that nigga; Dirty! Veronica walked up behind me and threw me off; that is how it got out of hand. Now what happened after that, I do not know that nigga caught me off guard and knocked me out. When I woke up the police were coming, so I asked Veronica who called the police, she said; she did not know. For me acting on my own, I truly apologize. Lartesha said, as tears were coming down her cheeks.

Well…. the question is if she didn't call the police, then who in the fuck did. That's what I'm trying to find out because whoever called; that's who's responsible for Jay's death. Trick's coma, and Young Chris injuries… I'm letting everybody know, right now… As long as I live… and I stress; as long as I live, I will not let this rest. I am determined to find out who put my man's and them in the hospital. And in the casket! Carlos said, as tears rolled down his cheeks as he spoke the anger showed.

After Carlos said what he had to say, nobody never said a word because they understood where he was coming from; they felt the same way. But Lartesha was feeling so bad. She walked up to Carlos, then gave him a hug. Whispered in his ear as she was trying to control herself from the crying. She said death before dishonor. Kissed him on the cheek, then walked over and sat down.

Lartesha, I want you to watch Veronica, just to be on the safe side. Also, I need you to get the funeral arrangements taken care of for me. I will tell Marie to help you out on that. I will take care of Young Chris' lawyer and in the meantime, everybody keep your eyes open and ears to the streets. I'm about to be out. Carlos said.

Lartesha followed everyone to the door. She had enough for one night and wanted to be alone for the rest of the night. Locking her door, Lartesha headed towards her bedroom, then her cell phone started ringing. In her mind, she knew it was Jordan or Vince calling this late, hoping to come over for some sex. When Vince's name popped in her mind, she remembered assuring him she would call later. When Lartesha looked at her caller I. D, she let out a deep breath knowing she had to tell a quick lie.

Hi Vince, I'm sorry I didn't have time to call you back when I got in the house. Lartesha said as she walked through her apartment holding in the pain, hoping Vince did not catch on.

Oh... that's okay Lartesha.... I was out and about... I was on my way home myself; I could not get your sexy ass out of my mind. I was hoping you wouldn't mind if I stopped by to keep you company for tonight. Vince asked; with a big grin on his face sitting outside of her building watching Carlos and everybody else leave.

Oh No... I will pass on having company for tonight baby I'm not feeling too good, I'm about to go to sleep, anyway. Lartesha said, rolling her eyes to the back of her head.

Lartesha peeped the game Vince tried to run on her real quick. She knew he wanted to come over and have his way with her, but she did not fall for it. She made the conversation real short; as possible.

Oh, so you're not feeling good, then shit, that's more the better baby girl. I will come and wait on your hand and feet. I will be your personal doctor. Vince said as he smiled to himself.

How sweet... But I will pass for tonight, baby. I am not in the mood for company tonight; it has been a rough night and I just need to be alone. I will try to call you tomorrow okay Vince. Lartesha said as she was ending the conversation.

Vince knew Lartesha was in pain the way she hit the ground when Dirty punched her. Vince did not feel any pity for Dirty. He felt that he deserved every bit of what happened, for hitting a woman and not just any woman, the woman he wanted to have a future with.

All right Lartesha, I guess I will see you or hear from you later baby girl; I hope you get well. Vince said.

Okay Vince, thank you, I'll call you real soon baby.

When Lartesha hung the phone up, she let out a sigh of relief. She was thinking Vince would never give up. She cut out all the lights and jumped in the bed, hoping and praying that Trick makes it out of his coma.

CHAPTER 20

Hearing me out

When Carlos walked in the apartment, Marie was in the living room bundled up on the sofa, Marie gave him a look that if looks could kill, Carlos would have been dead, she knew in her mind that she could not be mad at him for long. But she sure played it off as he made his way towards her. She rolled her eyes and stood up.

Carlos, you could stop right where you're at. Because ain't no need for you to be all over me, when you're around your friends you try to send me off like a stranger. Marie said, in her mean soft Dominican tone of voice.

Marie, it's not even like that. When I told you to leave, I did that because I had all intentions on talking about what happened when I got home. I knew that if you would have stayed over there any longer, then eventually you would have fed off Lartesha's emotion and that is something I did not want. I felt that we could talk about this one on one, okay. Carlos said.

Okay Carlos, so what in the hell happened. Marie asked.

I asked Lartesha to do one simple thing. Then she took it in her own hands. That is when Jay and Young Chris had to save her damn life. It's because of her mistakes that things are the way they are now if she would have just listened to what I told her to do. Maybe things wouldn't have ended up this way... just maybe. Carlos said.

So, what is it... you asked her to do Carlos, stop beating around the bush... stop blaming one person for something? Let me be the judge of who was in the wrong. Marie said.

Okay, you want to know the whole truth... I asked her to pick her friend Veronica up, take her to the bar, get her drunk, then leave her. Veronica had to meet this clown ass nigga name Dirty, somebody we would kill. Now I guess that maybe she thought Jay and Young Chris would kill Veronica. So, she took it in her own hands to avoid that. But now look, who has to suffer because she did not do what she was told to do, because she was running off emotions. Carlos explained.

Carlos, hear me out, I'm not trying to take anybody's side. But you were very wrong for putting her in that predicament. You know how she feels about Y'all. So, you know that she would not turn Y'all down, at the same time she didn't want to set her friend up to get killed, if you want to blame somebody, then blame yourself for not doing it yourself and by yourself, take this as a big lesson learned in life; you can't take back what has already happened... All you can do is learn from it and move on, oh another thing, never think you can't talk to me about the problems you have in the streets, If you could ask me to hook you up with my uncle, then you should be able to trust me with the little problems your having in the streets. One thing for sure; you need to know Carlos. I might just look like this, But I will go all the way for my man if it means dying, then so be it. But just remember, I am here for you, so please, do not feel you must hold back from me, we have been together too long Carlos. Marie said as she walked up close to Carlos putting both her hands on his cheeks trying to get him to pay close attention to her as she spoke.

After speaking her mind, she moistened her lips and kissed Carlos passionately on the cheek. Then she turned and headed towards the bedroom, walking seductively. Carlos was loving every bit of her walk, but the way he felt made him resist the temptation. He knew he was not in the right state of mind; he knew he wasn't able to give Marie the passionate love they always made. His mind was on many other things that had happened throughout the day. Carlos watched Marie walk through the bedroom door, while he sat back down on the sofa as he reflected on all the critical decisions he made and the powerful words his girl lay down on him; he knew she was right. Carlos sat with his head looking towards the ceiling with his eyes closed, that's when Marie walked back to the doorway of the room and stood there for a moment without ever saying a word.

Carlos.... Carlos... would you come on, let's go to bed, don't be trying to fall asleep out there Carlos. Marie shouted out.

Marie, I'm coming... I'll be there in a minute, oh, I almost forgot to tell you, I need you to help Lartesha out with the funeral arrangements and don't drive your car any more take mines and get a rental car for me for two days, please Marie, do not ask why. Carlos said, as he still had his head back, looking towards the ceiling with his eyes closed.

Okay... Okay, Carlos, now come to bed. Marie spat back as she turned around and headed back in the bedroom.

Carlos… Carlos...! Marie called out.

Carlos was in a deep sleep today, exhausted from pass days of not properly resting; he had overslept and never heard Marie calling his name from the living room, telling him to come get the phone. The last past couple of days have been very hectic for Carlos with all the different arrangements and still being in the mourning stages, something he had been trying to overcome. But with Trick still in the coma, and the funeral being today, it has been hard for him. Marie came in the room cursing to herself in Spanish. Mad because the same person has been calling all morning and Carlos has not gotten up yet. This was her third time trying to get him up. When she went into the room this time, she yelled loud to be funny. Carlos rolled over and grabbed the alarm off the nightstand, then shot it at the wall. Scaring the life out of her. Then he rolled back over with a big smile on his face.

Marie, please find out who it is and tell them I'll call them back as soon as I get out of the shower, please. Carlos asked.

Shit Carlos, I already know who it is. The damn man has been calling all morning. Now get your ass up and don't never, and I mean never shoot nothing at me again! Marie said, pointing her finger at Carlos.

Yeah... Yeah... Yeah, just tell them what I said and take a message. Carlos spat back with his head on the pillow.

Excuse Me! Carlos, if something is bothering you, then you can talk to me about it. Don't let it build up and don't brush it off like there's nothing wrong. Marie said and stood there with her arms folded with a frown on her face.

Please, not right now Marie... We'll talk about it later, just see who it is then to take a message, please. Carlos said.

Shit, I already know who it is, but what he wants I don't know that, but I could assume that it's important the way he keeps calling. Marie said in a sassy tone of voice and walked off back towards the phone.

Carlos laid in bed for a few more minutes, then he jumped up assuming he knew just who it was on the phone. They had to go pick their suits up for the funeral. As he started grabbing his things to go get in the shower, he heard Marie slam the phone down.

Carlos, Bobby said, call him on his cell phone as soon as you get out the shower, it's important and he didn't tell me what it was about. Marie yelled.

Damn, Carlos said to himself, clutching down on his teeth so hard that his jaw muscles showed. He had his hands to his sides balled up in a tight fist trying to control his anger. These last couple of days he felt nothing was going right in his mind. As he got out of the shower, Marie burst into the bathroom.

Carlos, I meant to tell you I went over to take your little brother to school this morning and he wasn't there. Also, about this funeral, me and Lartesha took care of everything we talked with Jay's mother about the gathering after the burial; she said; that she would prefer it to be at her house with only immediate family and friends… So, we took care of all the food for that also; we let her know. Marie said and walked out of the bathroom.

Thank you, Marie. Carlos shouted out.

CHAPTER 21

It will catch up to you One day

Justin laid back in the passenger seat, dozing off from the potency of the marijuana smoke and the long drive Murder Black took to Watertown. Justin was in relax mode, thinking to himself that he really could get used to the hustling game. The way his cousin played it, all the moves he witnessed Murder Black make tonight. He figured working on the road was way better than dealing with the crack heads on the blocks.

Justin… Justin... Murder Black yelled out.

Huh-Huh... Justin mumbled back as he woke up. What are you trying to do, go to my apartment or you're going to the crib? Murder Black asked, as he was trying to keep his own eyes open from the long drive, and the powerful haze's they were smoking.

Your apartment… what son… I know you ain't doing it like that, so you got your own pad? Justin asked with excitement.

Yeah, my pad nigga... what? So, you think a nigga can't afford no bullshit apartment nigga, shit I grind hard enough to don't I. Murder Black said, looking at Justin with a frown.

Nah... Nah... I ain't saying it like that, fam… Justin said, as he was sitting up in the passenger seat.

Anyway, what you going to do nigga, if you're going to my crib, I'm about to get off the highway right here on Adams Street nigga. Murder Black said.

All right, then that's what's up nigga. Justin said, leaning back in his seat.

Yo, I'll take you home tomorrow afternoon, I'm about to hit the sack when I get in the crib, I will be out you better believe that. Yo, how much money you made tonight, Justin? Murder Black asked.

I made about four hundred tonight. But I already had a couple hundred, so all together I got about a thousand. Why, what's up? Justin asked.

Nah, I was asking because I might make this move down to New York city. I know you remember our cousin Mike who lives in Brooklyn, that's who Carlos be connecting with. I spoke with him the other day and he told me to come down. I heard he had a mean connection. So, if you are trying to come up, then I will take your money down with me. But only under these circumstances you do not tell anybody who you got it from. Is that a deal... I mean nobody? Murder Black asked, as he was pulling up in his apartment complex on the North side.

Shit, that's what's up, my mouth shut, you ain't got to worry about me. Justin said.

Justin and Murder Black had been hanging out real tight, these last couple of days. Instead of going to school, Justin would get up, grab his book bag, making it look like he was catching the school bus. Instead of getting on he would let the school bus pass, then jump on the city bus, to go over his cousin Murder Black's apartment on the North side. Ever since Murder Black gave him the ideal about working off the beeper, Justin went to buy hisself a beeper, then he passed the number out to a few dope fiends. From time to time Murder Black would let him drive around. That was something Justin was loving about his cousin. He did not act funny toward him; they could kick it about everything. Today Justin was ready to make some real moves, because all he's been doing is stacking his money ever since Murder Black took his first thousand and brought him back two-and-a-half ounces, when he went down to see their cousin Mike. Today Justin was ready to re-up with more because the money he was making was just motivating him more. But this time he wanted to be in on the move, not send his money. He had a real tight grip on his five thousand and not because he did not trust Murder Black, but because he put in too much work to get where he was at. While Justin was waiting for the bus to stop where he needed to get off, his cell phone rung. Justin sat and looked at his caller I.D. wondering who in the hell was calling his cell phone so early in the morning. He started debating if he should answer it or not. As he put the phone to his ear slowly with the gut feeling of who it was, he pushed the send button.

Yeah, what's up? Justin said.

Yo nigga, what's popping. J-Love said hyped.

Shit, it's you the one who's calling all early in the morning, you tell me what's popping nigga? Justin asked.

Aye yo, I called because I knew you were up; I haven't heard from you since I got out of jail nigga. I heard that you were making some big moves with that kid, Murder Black. I know he probably already told you I am not feeling him. But later for that, I need some help. Where you at, I'll come and pick you up. J-love said.

Hold up, let us go back to the part where you said; that you were not feeling my cousin. Yeah, I stated my cousin. Because anybody who is beefing with my family, they got problems with me. I do not care if it was my close ... close friend, oh for the making moves part, whoever told you that lied, they need to get their story right. That is how nigga's catch cases. But anyway, I'm on the city bus headed somewhere. Justin said.

Yo, my bad nigga… I did not know that he was your peeps. So, you're busy right now? J-Love asked.

Yeah, I'm busy. Why what you need help with nigga. Justin asked.

Well, when you get a chance, then hit me back on my cell and I'll come pick you up so we could talk about it. J-Love said.

Man, why can't you tell me, son. Justin asked.

Justin was so busy talking to J-Love he almost missed his stop, but luckily somebody was getting off at the same stop. He made his conversation with J-Love real brief after he said how he felt about Justin's cousin. Justin was not feeling him anymore. As he was walking off the bus, he told J-Love he would call him on the cell later with a smirk on his face. As he was walking to Murder Black's apartment complex, he started thinking about what J-Love needed help with and what he needed to talk about. What if he was trying to set me up to get knocked or to get some time off? Justin was thinking, because he said he heard I was making some big moves; that's when Justin made his mind up to stay far away from J-Love as possible. When Justin got to Murder Black's apartment, he stood there knocking for a few minutes; while he was waiting, he heard somebody coming towards the door. When Carmen opened the door, Justin just stood there, staring and smiling in amazement at the sight of her beautiful features. Because with the tight cut off t-shirt and the panties she was wearing, showed it all.

Aye yo Carmen, where my peep's at? Justin asked as he was entering the apartment.

He took my car; he said that he would be right back. He had to make a run somewhere. He said you would come, that is why I let you in, here you go, he told me to give you this. Carmen said, as she walked up to Justin handing him marijuana as she stared him in the eyes.

Justin took his shoes off at the door then walked into the living room behind Carmen saying to himself, damn, I know my cousin do not know this girl is walking around his apartment like this, is she some kind of freak, because the way she was walking, Justin could not help but stare at her curvy features in those boy shorts. When she turned around and smiled at him, is when he really made himself comfortable flirting, not knowing what he was getting himself into.

So, Justin, How Old Are You? Carmen asked as she was sitting down and reaching for her glass of water with the flick of a pill in her mouth in the same motion.

I'm sixteen with all the qualities of an intelligent grown man and that's in any position I'm in baby girl. Justin said, as he was rolling the weed and licking his lips with his last words.

Huh, so that's what you say! Well, my girl Jazzy told me you were 15, but I told her that age does not matter because shit, you look good. Carmen said; opening her legs and playing with her cup, using her tongue at the same time.

Yeah, I was 15 but days passed by and birthdays come. Justin said, telling Carmen a quick lie with a straight face.

I hear that! Carmen replied, then laughed, letting the pill take its affect.

Damn baby girl, are you all right... What type of pill did you just pop in your mouth? Justin asked as he was lighting the weed up and watching Carmen.

That's a funny pill, it has a quicker affect than weed; every time you drink water, you stay with the same high. It also feels good when you're having sex with it because you can go much longer. I am getting hot just talking about it. Would you like one... Here, take one, believe me, you'll love it. Carmen said, taking off her T-shirt, then she tried to get Justin to take the pill.

The sight of Carmen sitting next to him in her bra and panties caused his manhood to form a print in his pants. Justin was nervous; he didn't know how to take control of the situation, so he played along with

Carmen's plan and took the pill. For Carmen, the pill she took already took effect she was in Justin's pants having her way until Justin busted all over her hands. Carmen looked up at him and smiled.

Damn baby, I ain't even get started yet. This must be your first time. Carmen asked, wiping her hands off.

Yeah, it feels good too. Justin said as the pill took its effect on him.

Justin had his head threw back with his eyes closed, enjoying everything Carmen was doing. He was so into it, he never notice her taking his money out of his pocket. Carmen was not new at what she did; it was just that she knew when to do it and who to do it to. Being that Justin was inexperienced, she took full advantage of him. Justin was enjoying it so much that he did not know it was costing him at the same time. It all lasted for about a half an hour until Murder Black came walking through the door. That is when Carmen rushed to pick all her clothes off the floor. She ran to the bathroom to get dressed. When Murder Black walked into his living room and saw Justin with his pants down and his head thrown back playing with himself calling Carmen's name. He became enraged, so he yelled out Justin's name, trying to get him to stop doing what he was doing; but Justin was so far gone off the ecstasy pill. When Carmen came out of the bathroom, she appeared like nothing happened with an innocent facial expression, as if she had full control over the pill she took. She walked right up to Murder Black and told him a straight face lie.

Don't ever.... ever tell me to open the damn door again... For anyone... shit that boy right there is a sick pervert. Just look at what he is doing. I had to lock myself in the bathroom until you got back because of him. I do not know what type of drugs he came over here on, but you need to do something about that. I'm leaving; give me my keys, please. Carmen said, as she was reaching her hands out so she could hurry and get her keys, then leave with the money that she had stolen.

Justin... Justin! Murder Black yelled out as he was walking up on him.

What's up, son? Ha... Ha... Ha... Where's that freak Carmen? Justin asked as he stood up laughing and smiling, not even realizing what he was doing.

Nigga if you don't pull your mother-fucking pants up nigga, I'll drop you right where you stand. Murder Black said.

Calm down... Where is that chick at... She gives some mean throat man? She turned me on to this pill that got me hornier than ever... That's my word... I feel good... Ha... Ha... Ha. I feel good. Justin said.

Yo nigga, you need to just go lay down and let that shit wear off. Carmen, why you? Murder Black said as he turned to comfort Carmen; she left quick.

That made Murder Black even more mad, for her giving his little cousin some ecstasy. He was only fifteen. Murder Black said to himself. That it was bad enough that he's selling drugs, smoking marijuana and skipping school. Now this bitch is trying to get him hooked on some damn pills. Murder Black was furious with Carmen.

CHAPTER 22

Wish on better days

Carlos jumped out the shower mad at the fact his little brother did not listen to him. Not only that, he knew that if Bobby was calling all morning, that it was not good news. So, the stress was building up, with the anger and the way he felt, he just wanted to catch his little brother skipping school and give him an old fashion ass whipping. Something his aunt used to say to him a lot when he uses to be over her house, while his mother worked late at night. Just thinking about his aunt made a smile come to his face. Because from all the whippings and all the harsh curse words, he could look back and see that it was nothing but tough love. It was her way of trying to discipline him and not being soft about it. That thought just really tickled him; because he knew his aunt still used the same tough love with her own kids, to this day and through the years, their relationship was tight. As Carlos was smiling from the memories of his aunt, Marie came into the room breaking him out of his thoughts.

Carlos, what's the smile for? What's on your mind? Marie asked, walking over and sitting on him.

Nah Marie, it's nothing, just old memories, that's all. Carlos said.

Carlos, what the hell did I tell you about holding shit back from me, I don't care if it's little. I want to know. Marie said, folding her arms.

Marie, please don't start... I was just thinking about my aunt and the things she said and did, that's all, some good old memories. Carlos said as he got up, then walked over to the closet.

Carlos I'm sorry. Marie said.

Marie, it's all right, do me a favor and go get the cordless phone so I can call Bobby back to see what's up with him. Carlos said.

Marie got right up to get the phone quickly and came right back.

Here you go, Carlos... I'm about to jump in the shower to get myself ready. Marie said, handing Carlos the phone with a kiss on the lips.

Carlos started dialing Bobby's number quick, letting it ring for a while.

Hello Bobby... What's popping my nigga, did something happen? Carlos asked.

Hell, yeah something happened... I was on my way back to the shop this morning, so I could get my wallet, because I left it here last night. And I caught three young dudes busting the windows out of the Mercedes Benz truck that you put out on the lot the other day. When I jumped out, they ran, but I caught one of them and held him at gunpoint until the police came. Yeah, I called them in case you need a report for the insurance before they took the kid to jail. He had a gun on him, but too bad he did not have the chance to use it. That is all I wanted to let you know. I'm about to get dressed so I can go to Jay's funeral, see you later. Bobby said.

All right, thanks for keeping me up to date on shit Bobby. I'll see you soon, my guy. Carlos said, hanging up the phone.

After Carlos got off the phone, he went to put his Polo outfit on that he got from out of the walk-in closet, Carlos then smiled to himself thinking about what Bobby had just told him; he couldn't wait to see the police report because he wanted to know the name of the little coward Bobby caught. By the time Marie got out the shower, Carlos was sitting on the edge of the bed, going through his e-mail messages on his T-Mobile. As he roamed through the messages, he noticed that he was missing out on some real important money; he usually had his real important customers hit him on the T-Mobile by text in code. But one message he came across was his cousin Mike giving him the lowdown on the prices of cocaine in their code, at the end of the message he told Carlos to get at him as soon as possible because it was not looking good. Carlos said to himself, '26 a gram, shit, and it might go higher.

Then he closed his T-Mobile, then shook his head at all the things that were happening. Carlos was wondering why the cloud was so dark over him. Then Marie walked in.

Carlos, what's wrong? What did bobby say? Marie asked as she was putting lotion on her body.

Oh, he said; when he went to the shop this morning, he caught some young punks busting the windows out of the cars. He said they tried to run, but he caught one of them and called the police. Carlos explained.

Well, that's good that he caught one of them. But does your insurance cover what they did to the car? Marie asked while putting her dress on for the funeral.

Shit, I hope so Marie. Carlos replied while standing up.

I'll check into that if you want me to Carlos. Marie asked, walking over to the mirror.

Nah, that's all right, I'll take care of that, but what's up, you going to ride with me? Because if so, I must hurry and go pick my suit up. Oh yeah, before I forget, what is up with your uncle... Have you heard from him lately? Carlos asked.

No, I will ride with Lartesha, no I haven't heard from him, I already told you how he was, so just because he told me yes, that doesn't mean he will move right away, he's very stubborn. I can't see how my brother used to work for him. Marie said, as she was putting on some lip gloss.

Well okay Marie, I'm about to be out. I'll see you at the funeral. Carlos said, walking out.

Lartesha was just getting out the shower when her doorbell rang the first time. She did not pay any mind. When the person pressed it three times in a row is when she became annoyed, she rushed to her shorts and t-shirt, then went to the intercom, pushing the speaker button aggressively to let the person know a few things.

Whoever the fuck is down there ringing my fucking bell like that… it better be mother-fucking important. Lartesha yelled.

When a soft voice came over the speaker, Lartesha did not recognize put her in a paranoid state making her change directions she rushed to grab her baby 9mm out of the dresser drawer, then she slowly walked back to the door putting her sneakers on with a tight grip on her gun.

Excuse me, miss, but I have a delivery for apartment 307… would you mind coming down to sign for it, please? The Delivery man said.

Yes, I mind, what kind of delivery is it first. Lartesha yelled back.

Oh, I'm so sorry for not telling you who I was… that's vulgar of me. I'm from the flower shop, Ms. Brown, that is your name. The delivery man said.

Lartesha said; to herself, oh he's good reading my last name off the doorbell panel, okay this person must think I'm stupid or something. Well, shit, I ain't scared, so he is playing with the right one. Because this time I ain't holding back. I'm letting off shots, asking questions later. She pushed the button again to tell the person she would be right down. When Lartesha made her way down to the last flight of stairs, she thought damn, what if he's not alone as she walked to the door giving a quick look out the door window feeling real low and ashamed of herself for having all those bad thoughts? When she opened the door, she kept her guard up as she was gripping the baby 9mm tight behind her back as she apologized. The delivery guy looked at her strange not knowing what in the hell she was apologizing for not knowing if he was not who he said he was, she had plans on making him another statistic. As Lartesha grabbed the roses, she was smiling at the Guy and saying in her head, only if this nigga knew how close he was to death. Then she closed the door, then rested her back on it and started laughing to herself some more. Then she let out a sign of relief. Knowing how crazy the last incident with Dirty made her, she said; to herself, never again would I let my guards down. Then she ran back up the stairs to continue with her day. what she was doing because she knew she had to hurry get dressed so she could go pick Veronica up then Marie, before sitting her flowers down Lartesha took the envelope off to see who sent them, seeing the name made her smile saying to herself, he's not giving up I see then her phone rung. Lartesha looked at the caller I. D and saw who it was, then she picked up quick.

Hello... Aw, thank you Vince for the flowers, they're lovely. Lartesha said as she picked up.

I was hoping my love reaches you…. before my call baby girl… How are you feeling? Vince asked.

That is so sweet of you Vince… I'm all right, just in a rush as usual? Lartesha said.

Well, don't let me keep you… I have some things to do also, maybe we can get up later or something. Vince said, working his plan out to the fullest.

That's fine with me, call me all right. Lartesha said, hanging the phone up.

CHAPTER 23

Thought you were smart

Justin... Justin! Murder Black yelled as he was shaking him to get up.

Murder Black was getting restless. He did not like missing out on his money sitting around waiting for Justin to get up off his ass. He had already let Justin sleep for two hours now. Murder Black knew that his little cousin did not take the pill on his own. He felt stupid letting Carmen pull one off on him like that. When Justin woke up, the facial expression he gave off showed the pain he felt grabbing his head as he sat up straight.

Aw... man, my fucking head is spinning. Where is that dumb bitch at? Yo, I cannot see how J-Love could be mad at you, for something like that... Aw... damn my head is spinning. Justin said, as he was attempting to stand up.

Man, that bitch bounced as soon as I walked in the door. She said you were all over her when she opened the door; she said that you came over here like that. Now you are saying something different, what makes you say what you're saying, Justin. Murder Black asked with a curious look on his face.

Son, I know you not believing that bitch. She is the one who gave me the damn pill, then she started doing all kinds of nasty shit to me; man, the bitch is a freak when I came to the door she was wearing her panties with a cut off t-shirt. Is that how you left her here… Then she gave me some weed and told me it was from you… come on nigga, do not come at me with what the fuck she said this is from your family, that bitch is a hoe. Now I came to make some money. Justin said, stopping at his last words as he was pulling his money out of his pocket.

Something was not feeling right to Justin because he knew how much money he had and how it felt.

Man, I knew all along something wasn't right, just how everything played out… when I came to the door, I heard somebody's footsteps… Yo Justin do not worry, I will get her back. I got just the plan for her too… how much did she get? Murder Black asked.

While Murder Black was talking, Justin was focusing on the money he was counting when he came to the last bill, he sat back down on Murder Black's new leather sofa with the money balled up in his fist, looking at his cousin with a serious expression on his face, that was all understood because he knew how his little cousin felt. So as Murder Black was about to turn around and leave out of the living room, he said a few words to comfort Justin.

Aye yo my nigga, you can't let that little shit break you. Shit like that comes with the game; everybody takes a lost, all you got to do is just capitalize off it, don't let it get the best of you. Murder Black said, as he was leaving out the living room.

Well… shit, that was my re-up, she got me for damn near half of it. I did not leave any money in my shoes box. I brought everything I was saving nigga… I put too much work in for this… Take me to that bitch crib right now. Justin yelled as he was getting up, walking behind Murder Black.

Just chill, I told you, we will get her back; you got to have patience. Let her think she did something then that is when we get her back. But later for that. Mike called me yesterday talking about prices is about to go up, so I need to get down there. How much are you working with? Murder Black stopped and asked.

Well, shit, I had my whole damn stash hoping to make a major move. I had five thousand, but now I only have twenty-eight hundred. You might as well say twenty-five hundred because I'm holding on to three hundred, I want to go with my money this time. Justin said, holding up the money.

What nigga, so now you don't trust me with your money or something. You should have had your guards up with that bitch... Not me, I am family... I want to see you blow up nigga. Murder Black spat back, changing his voice level as he spoke...

Nah... Nah... Nah, it's not even like that... I feel like I should make some moves to, you feel me. So, do not take it like I do not trust, you. Justin said.

Son, how long have you been hustling... And now you ready to step up and make trips. I am telling you nigga this life ain't all fun and games. This shit here is real for real; you think she got you for a couple hundred. You got niggas taking lives. You ready for that... Are you ready to sit behind bars and keep your mouth shut if you get caught? When the people throwing your freedom in your face are you ready, huh, huh, tell me, tell me. Because if so, I'm all for that nigga. We can jump on this highway now, nigga! Murder Black said, walking back towards Justin real hyped.

Shit, you ain't said nothing, I can hold my water... yeah that bitch got off on me, but she will pay like she weights. Justin said, pulling out his .38 he brought from J-Love holding it up.

Oh, now you a killer huh... Man quit the games nigga. Put that shit up. I see I got to put you on some more because you are already thinking wrong. This is not some shoot them up bang, bang game. This is a thinking game you have to know how and when to make the right moves. Murder Black said.

As Justin was putting the gun back
Black was just shaking his head, sa
somebody one day. Justin was walk
in his thoughts with his chest all pok

Huh, I trust you all right. Justin said, h

Nah, keep your money, just hold it, we
Let me get situated, then it's on. Murd
hand back then running to his room.

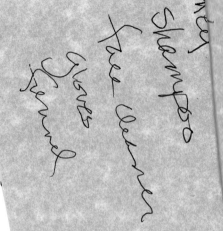

CHAPTER 24

Keep it moving

Coming out the store after picking his suit up, Carlos knew he was running short on time. He was making his way towards the escalators when he spotted Mack, Terry and Buns coming up the opposite side of the escalator. Carlos caught the expression on Mack's face, Carlos kept his eyes on them, and never got thrown off by the fake head nods. Carlos did not greet them back, he kept eye contact directly on the dude Mack, wanting him to try something funny. Jumping off the escalator making his way towards the exit, he started wondering was Mack shooting at him and did he know that was him who shot the young boy like that. Carlos had many thoughts running through his mind. Then he stopped at the exit door and said to himself, the nigga I had on the wall, that's who saw me. Then he laughed to himself walking out the mall. As Carlos approached his rental car, he remembered what else it was he had wanted to grab for Young Chris. So, he threw his suit in the back seat, then grabbed his gun from under the driver's seat, tucked it in his waistline.

I'd rather be safe than sorry, I don't know who this little ass nigga think he's fucking with, I will not play the staring and mean mug game with him, if I see him again fuck them nigga's he's with, they could get it too. Carlos said.

When Carlos said that to himself walking into Footlocker's, Mack, Terry and Buns were at the cash register with their backs turned.

Carlos walked up to the counter so they could see him, the expression on Mack's face tickled Carlos, he had the look as if he saw a ghost, even his friends had the same reaction, when they saw Carlos reappear. After he made his presence known, he called out for one of the sales representatives to assist him as he was walking towards the wall where the shoes were, giving Mack a devilish grin at the same time still paying close attention to his surroundings while telling the sales representative all the things he would like to purchase. Mack, Terry and Buns made their way towards the entrance, Carlos made a quick glance and saw Terry whisper something in Mack's ear then stop at the entrance as if they were debating on doing something, Carlos then saw Mack whisper something back with the shaking of his head. They then walked out the store, Carlos was watching their every move he did not see the sales representative walk up on him, so when he tapped Carlos on the shoulder, it startled him a little on the inside, but he played it off by laughing, then Carlos cell phone rung. As he was looking at the phone screen, he was walking to the counter to make his purchases. He saw it was Rell calling, so he picked up.

What's really popping Rell? Carlos asked.

Shit, what's popping... where the fuck you at? Rell asked.

I'm at the mall picking my suit up and I stopped in Footlockers to get Young Chris a few things. I'm on my way out right now. Yeah, I ran into some fake ass tough guys, Mack, Terry and Buns... That nigga Mack was mean mugging real hard... He probably found out, but oh well, fuck him. I know some young boys came to the shop this morning, broke the windows out of the Benz like some cowards... I'm like don't get at the car, get at me, nah mean. Carlos said, as he was walking towards the car.

Yeah, I feel you, but man fuck them pussy ass niggas, they're only rolling together like that because of them niggas on the 110th. Be putting the pressure on them, we'll handle that on a later note nigga. That suit was ready the other day. Because we all ordered our suits at the same time the shit you were getting for Young Chris was not going anywhere, that shit could have waited. Me and Rock just took the little nigga something, anyway. He is living better in jail than he was living out here… Nigga the funeral starts in two hours. You were already late for the wake yesterday. Get it together, nigga. Rell said.

Nigga I don't need no mother-fucking counseling… I was late yesterday because I was handling something important for your information and anybody else that wants to know nigga. So, I will be there. Carlos said, hanging the phone up on Rell, as he was getting on the highway.

CHAPTER 25

Missing you for life

Lartesha was in Jay's room cleaning up things; something his mother asked her to do when they arrived. Jay's mother knew how close of a relationship Lartesha and her son had. That is why she asked Lartesha by pulling her to the side and telling her she has not entered her son's room yet; She hasn't had the strength to. And she told Lartesha that she knew he probably had clothes all over the place. That was true, Lartesha came to find out when she stepped in Jay's room. She picked up all kinds of designer clothing that still had the store smell to it, as if he tried it on and took it right back off then threw it on the floor. Lartesha's eyes were getting wide from some clothes she was picking up with the tags still on them; like the Bathing APE Varsity jacket that laid by the foot of the bed with a price tag that said $1,140. She picked the jacket up, then she put it on and continued cleaning up other clothing. Lartesha saw if there was any room in Jay's closet, but she came to find that the closet was full with clothes she never thought Jay would wear and they still had the tags on them, Lartesha was smiling to herself as she went through the closet, because she couldn't imagine Jay rocking Prada suits or anything having to do with dress clothes. As she kept looking, she saw that he was not a slouch, and that there was not any room; so Lartesha headed over to his dresser, where she looked in his jewelry box. She came across an Iced-out Jacob's watch with the tag still on it that read $20,000 Lartesha said to herself. Damn, when it was time for everybody to shine, Jay was not playing games. Then she smiled to herself again as she started going through the drawers, seeing if the clothes would fit. As Lartesha was taking the clothes out to pack them in other drawers properly, a sock fell out, Lartesha picked it up, she could see that something was in it and knowing her she just had to see what it was. As she poured the items out the sock, she said, nigga's had Jay fucked up, this nigga was about his money. Lartesha started counting the hundreds he had rubber banded tight. Then a letter dropped out, and she picked it up and started putting the money back how she found it. Then Lartesha walked over to the edge of the bed to read the letter. When she opened the letter and saw who it was for, she closed it for a moment holding it to her chest tight, hoping and praying it wasn't what she thought it was. Tears fell down her cheeks. She opened the letter and read.

'Dear Mom,

This is your baby boy. I just had to sit down and write this letter because of the things I'm into in the streets doesn't last forever. Please believe me when I say this; I love you and did not mean to hurt you or cause you any pain. Mom, I know you wanted the best for your baby boy, and whenever you find this letter, think of your baby boy being happy. Because I am happy, happy to have somebody like you. Mom, I know this money is not a lot, but it's something to get you by. Spend it wisely. Smiles. But before I end this letter, I would like all my clothes and shoes to go to Young Chris. Ask Carlos who he is, and the watch also, he's like a little brother to me and no this isn't a suicide letter, this is a letter to you just in case I don't get to tell you how much I love you because we hardly see each other because I'm always in these crazy streets and before I end this, tell Carlos, Black, Rell, Trick, Rock, Young Chris and my lovely friend Lartesha, that I love them.

P.S.
Your baby Boy

Lartesha hurried and folded the letter back up when she heard footsteps coming her way. She got up and walked over to the dresser to put the letter and money back where she found it, then she hurried back to the edge of the bed with tears still falling from her cheeks. As she sat there, she let her head drop in her lap. Lartesha knew she did not depart on good terms with Jay. It was eating at her conscious because she yelled at him, then pulled a knife out. With that thought, Lartesha wanted to take that day back, especially her big mistake. While Lartesha was so busy thinking, she never saw Veronica walk in. When she stepped in the doorway, she stood there for a while looking at Lartesha, then taking a quick glimpse at the pictures on the wall.

Lartesha girl... You okay? Veronica asked, walking towards her.

You know Veronica... No, I'm not all right... Me and Jay did not depart on good terms. We had a petty argument before we went out that night, and it's eating at my conscience. I never got the chance to say I am sorry, or I still love you, nothing like that and he saved my life... was my life worth that much for him to just die? Was it... huh... huh... huh, was it? Lartesha shouted as tears dropped.

Lartesha, you really need to calm down and stop thinking about the negative events that happened with you and Jay... He knew you loved him, he loved you back... I saw it in his eyes when he shot that guy Dirty... when he ran over and tried to wake you up, so just believe me girl, please just look at the good times Y'all had together, like look right there on that wall, Y'all look like Y'all was having fun, wasn't Y'all? Veronica said pointing to one of Jay's pictures on the wall, then putting her arm around Lartesha's shoulder.

Yeah, we all had fun that day. It was Jay's ideal to go visit one of them Rides Car Show he was so caught up on the car thing. We all tagged along, I must admit girl, he knew his thing about automobiles... believe me; I know for sure when it was his time to shine; he was not playing no games. Lartesha said as she was looking at the pictures with a slight smile.

156

Lartesha and Veronica sat on the edge of the bed for a while; both in their own zone. Veronica was staring at the pictures on the wall, especially the one with Jay and Young Chris, then seeing Young Chris's face made her get a closer look.

This.... this... is.... Veronica was stuttering and pointing at the same time.

Lartesha interrupted her because she knew what Veronica was about to say.

yup... That's Young Chris and yeah, he was with Jay... that was his little man, Jay loved that little dude and yeah, the little nigga is crazy. I've heard plenty of stories about him. Lartesha said as she was wiping her face.

While Veronica was looking at the picture Lartesha was talking. After Lartesha finished talking, Marie walked in the door and stood right in front of Lartesha.

Girl... my feet are killing me... When we ordered the food, we sure should have called some catering service or a damn maid, because these heels are not for standing up all day in. What's wrong girl, are you all right? Marie asked as she was sitting down next to Lartesha.

Yeah, I guess so... I'm thinking about Jay and taking in the moments, when they say you never really miss a person until they're dead or they're gone, I'm believing that... I haven't lost a person this close before. Lartesha said.

I know how you feel because that feeling stays with me every day. I wake up thinking about my family; it hurts. I know; believe me. But we have to stay strong, girl. Marie said.

Veronica was so caught up in the pictures on Jay's wall that she never noticed Jay's mother walk into the room and stand beside her.

157

That's my baby... yeah, that' my baby. Jay's mother said, as tears rolled down her cheeks.

Veronica looked to her side, not knowing what to say for a slight minute; she then reached out and hugged Jay's mother tight.

We just have to stay strong because I'm sure that is what he would have wanted. Veronica said, as she pulled back and looked in the eyes of Jay's mother.

Jay's mother shook her head in agreement with Veronica's words, then she walked over towards the bed where Lartesha and Marie were sitting to take a seat.

Lartesha, thank you very much for cleaning my baby's room like this... I don't know what I would have done without Y'all... I can say this though, it's a blessing my son has friends like Y'all, I know without Y'all, I probably would not have the strength to come into this room. Jay's mother said, as she was sitting next to Lartesha, letting her eyes scan the room as she spoke.

Oh, it's nothing, I love Jay very much. Lartesha said.

Oh, before I forget to let Y'all know the fellas called, they said; they're on their way. Jay's mother said.

Did Carlos call? Marie asked.

Well, no, he was the one who hasn't called yet. Jay's mother said.

Lartesha thought about the wake and how mad and annoyed she was getting when she sat in the front row watching people who she consider as a bunch of fake people who came in to look at Jay's body like they cared. She knew some of them did not like Jay and what made it worst was the people who stood around outside, like it was a fashion show, the young ladies were wearing their best outfits just to catch a guy for the night. She saw people wearing their rest in peace Jay t-shirts and some of those people did not know him. Just thinking about the expression that Carlos had on his face, she just knew that he was fighting back the urge; to let a few people have it. But remembering who he was in the presence of and all the respect that they had for Jay's mother, they stayed cool. While Lartesha was in her thoughts, Jay's mother was sitting beside her looking her in the face. She did not know until she tapped her on the arm.

Girl you, all right? Jay's mother asked.

Yeah, I guess... I was just thinking about the wake yesterday. Lartesha said.

Lartesha, I know how you feel because I was saying to myself; I know like hell my baby did not know half of these ignorant ass people. That's why I wanted the gathering to be strictly for immediate family and close friends. But I need you to stay strong because I get my strength from Y'all. Because like I said, I know if Y'all were not in this room, then I probably wouldn't be standing here either. Jay's mother said, as she was rubbing Lartesha's back while talking to her.

Everybody was in their own thoughts; Veronica was in her own little world staring at the pictures on the wall. Marie was listening to Jay's mother talk, but she was wondering what was taking Carlos so long. When they heard the doorbell ring, everybody looked at one another without making a move.

Well, everyone, let's not all move at once. Jay's mother said.

I'll go get it! Veronica said, as she was walking towards the door.

Thank you. Jay's mother replied.

CHAPTER 26

Remain focused

Carlos walked in the apartment with Mack still on his mind until he came across an envelope that was staring him in the face, on the floor as he was walking in the door as if someone slipped it underneath. Carlos dropped his bags he was holding in one hand, bending over he kept his suit in his other hand as he picked the envelope up, thinking to his self who could it possibly be for and how did the person enter the building to slip it under the door. Many thoughts started running through Carlos' head because he knew the door downstairs was always secure. Especially after anyone exit the build because the door automatically locked by itself. Carlos mind was even more boggled when he looked on both sides of the envelope and there was no name; so, the curiosity made him opened the envelope. Carlos did not waste anytime either, he ripped the envelope open quickly took the small piece of paper out as he was walking towards the bedroom, but before he could enter the room, he suddenly stopped walking captured in the words of the note he was reading. Carlos was so deep into reading the note, he started thinking in the mist of reading I don't do business without seeing what I'm buying. Carlos did not like how Victor was going about setting the transaction up. As Carlos walked into the room, he said; to himself, why wouldn't he want to take my money from me personally. Then before Carlos tossed the note on the nightstand; he read it again,

Leave the money under the passenger seat at 12:00 midnight with the key to the rental car.

After Carlos was finish reading the note, he tossed it on the nightstand still not understanding why Victor wanted to handle business without meeting in person. Carlos sat on the edge of the bed thinking, but the first thought came to his mind was how in the hell did Victor get in the building. How does he know I have a rental car? Carlos said to himself, Marie, now why would she tell him what I was driving, then the words Marie stated started coming back to him, Carlos my uncle takes his business seriously. After that statement hit him, he shook his head got up saying to himself, I always took this shit seriously too, so I hope he knows that I play for keeps about mine. He then started getting dressed because he knew he was running late. After Carlos slide his pants on, he walked over to the full-length closet mirror then buttoned his shirt up. Carlos was watching himself get dressed, when the thought struck him like a sharp pain to the stomach which made him nauseous. Carlos hurried to the edge of the bed, the thought of carrying Jay's casket made him weak, as tears being falling down his cheeks, he knew he had to get himself together. He knew Jay expected Him to be the strongest one of the crew. As Carlos stood, his cell phone rung. He grabbed it off the nightstand. And looked at the screen.

Hey Marie. Carlos said.

Carlos what is wrong, why do you sound like that, where are you? Marie asked, sensing sadness in his voice.

I'm at home getting ready to walk out the door. I will be right, there is everybody there, yet? Carlos asked.

Yeah, uh huh, everybody's here... But why are you avoiding my question Carlos; is something wrong? Marie asked again.

Marie, I'm all right, okay... I'll be right there. Carlos said.

Okay, Carlos bye! Marie said.

All right... Bye...! Carlos replied.

CHAPTER 27

Let me school you

Murder Black was in his room for a few minutes looking through his closet before calling Justin, when he shouted Justin's name, he stepped in Murder Black's bedroom in amazement saying to himself, damn, Then he walked towards the closet where Murder Black was standing.

Aye yo nigga, what size kicks do you wear? Murder Black asked Justin.

I wear a size eight... Why, what's up? Justin asked.

Huh nigga try these on.... Murder Black said, handing Justin a pair of beef and broccoli field Timbs.

While Justin was busy trying the boots on Murder Black was in the closet picking an outfit out for Justin.

Yeah, they fit. Justin said.

Now try these pants on. Murder Black said.

Man, what's this all about? Why am I changing? Justin asked.

What's going on is when you are with me, you will dress more presentable... Not like you about to go on the corner and hustle with all that damn Army fatigue you got on... We for sure not trying to draw no attention, nah mean. Murder Black said, as he was handing Justin some Polo denim jeans.

As Justin was taking off his Army fatigue pants, he glimpsed at the jewelry sitting on Murder Black's dresser.

Aye yo, I'm surprised that bitch didn't rob your ass nigga. Justin said.

Shit, I ain't stupid. Murder Black spat back, holding a key up in the air so Justin could see it.

Oh, so you knew about her already. Justin asked.

Nah, I just don't trust a bitch that's all... Now put this shirt on huh, you can have this jacket too nigga see this is a gun; click.... click. Murder Black pulled his 9mm out and cocked it as he was talking.

Shit, I know what that is nigga. Justin said.

I'm glad. Put that six shooter away... you can get it when we come back... Put it over in that dresser drawer right there and hurry because I'm trying to catch this bus. Murder Black said, while he was standing in the room's doorway.

I thought we were driving down there. Justin said.

That's what you get for thinking... Now come on we ain't got all day nigga. Murder Black shouted.

Justin quickly stuffed his gun underneath the clothes in the drawer because he saw how his cousin was in a rush. After Justin caught up with Murder Black, he had butterfly's in his stomach being that this was the first time making moves out of town, just hearing about things that happen to people in bad transactions made him a little weary of what he was getting himself into. The way Murder Black carried himself, Justin could tell he had confidence in what he was doing. When they jumped in the car, Murder Black tossed the backpack he had in the back seat then looked over at Justin with a slight grin on his face.

You ready, baby boy. Murder Black asked.

Hell ya...! Justin replied.

All right, first we got to go pick up this girl, then everything is everything. Murder Black said.

Why are you going to pick her up? Justin asked.

Damn nigga...! You got to stop asking so many questions, sit back and listen, pay close attention, because everything I do is for a reason, ya heard. Murder Black said.

CHAPTER 28

Smile just to keep from crying

Carlos was turning the corner to Jay's mother's house, but throughout the entire ride, he had things on his mind. The things he saw at the wake yesterday were bothering him as well; he was holding back his anger to be respectable to Jay's mother, Carlos knew that some people were faking, and he did not want to see that today. So, as he pulled in front of the house, he could see that the limos were there and ready. Carlos sat in the car for a minute when Marie walked up and knocked on his window. It was as if she scared him half to death from his expression. After adjusting himself and seeing who it was, Carlos was a little embarrassed because by the big smile Marie had on her face, he knew she saw the way she startled him. Carlos played it off, laughing with her as he got out of the car.

Ha… Ha… Marie, where is everyone? It's time to go. Carlos asked as he laughed.

They're coming out now… They were getting restless waiting on you… you look good in that suit, dress up more often. Marie said while poking him in the chest playfully.

Ya... Ya... Ya... Ya… Let's go get in the limo. Carlos said as he was smiling and laughing.

Boy's ride with boys and lady's ride with lady's, so see you...! Marie said, walking towards the limo and smiling back at Carlos.

CHAPTER 29

Stick to the script

Murder Black was on his way to pick Peaches up so she could drop them off. But before he got to her house, he knew he had to call his cousin Mike to let him know they were on their way. Murder Black did not like too many people in his business, especially women he did not have any problems telling one a quick lie. When he pulled up in front of Peaches house, he sat in the car talking to Mike before blowing the horn.

Aye yo Mike, I need you to be right out front of Port Authority; because I'm not trying to be waiting around with all those damn police out there, nah mean? Murder Black said.

Hold up... Why are you going to Port Authority, why you won't just get off in New Jersey where you were getting off? Mike asked.

What's with all the questions nigga? Are you going to be there or not? Murder Black spat back.

Man, why I said; New Jersey is because I just moved out here. But if you insist on the Port Authority, then I will be there. Aye yo, be looking out for an eggshell Denali. Ya, I just copped it so don't ask. Mike said.

All right, I got someone with me, but don't worry, it's family. Murder Black said.

That's on you, I'm out... I'll see you, one. Mike said.

After Murder Black got off the phone, he started blowing the horn for Peaches to come out. Peaches was older than Murder Black, a lot more experienced than he thought. But that came from all the hustlers she has been with throughout her life and all the broken promises she has been told. Peaches had a special place for Murder Black in her heart. But he refused to put his guard down with any women. Murder Black saw and heard how women did dudes who got caught up in the game and he could never trust them no matter what. But he never disrespects no women in their face. He played the same game they played, something for something. Murder Black knew that he was young and if he had nothing, he wasn't getting anything. When Peaches stepped out the house with her tight Capri jeans, Giorgio Armani top with open toe heels, with a resemblance of Melissa Ford, with a little more curves in her 5'8 frame with her 24 years of living, she knew how to work it in every way. Murder Black, he never allowed his dick to do the thinking. So, all the good sex he got did not matter; he stuck strictly to the M.O.B. code, something taught at an early age from an old head name Smokie. He stayed schooling him about the game until the day he died. Murder Black used to sit in his weed spot from time to time, it was around the hood; it was this one day that Murder Black did not make it to his house and that's the day Smokie lost his life from bullets through the door some dudes in the hood say a wino tried to rob him, no one would ever know the truth, because nobody never got arrested for it. Murder Black said if somebody were to get charged, he had sure enough plans to put something on their head, because he had much love for Smokie and he thanks Smokie to this day for the game he put him up on. When Peaches got close to the car Murder Black told Justin to make her get in the backseat, Justin looked at Murder Black in shock.

Nigga, she's bad...! You sure. It will be a little tight back there. Justin said.

What I tell you about the question's nigga? Murder Black asked.

Peaches approached the passenger door. Then she stood with her arms folded like she had an attitude. Murder Black quickly reached over Justin and opened the door.

Would you get in; we don't have all day. Murder Black said.

Well, tell him to get in the back seat. Because I'm not trying to mess my hair up by climbing in that back seat. Peaches said, pointing her finger and snapping her neck back and forth.

Pulling up to the bus station, Murder Black sat in the car breaking things down to Peaches, letting her know what to do and what not to do. Justin was not trying to hear him, and Murder Black was mad that Justin got out the car because he wanted Justin to listen and learn how to handle a lady. After he was finish filling Peaches in on everything, he told her a quick lie on where he was going; he knew what people did under pressure, that's another reason he kept everything in somebody else's name, he did not like too many people knowing his business. Peaches called him Black because she told him the name Murder Black sounded too scary. So, he did not mind with her, for everybody else it stayed the same.

I'm about to take my little cousin to Boston to see our grandma, I'm expecting my other cousin to call sometime tonight because she will need a ride from this bus station right here… She's coming from college all right. Murder Black said, as he was reaching over to go retrieve his cell phone out the glove compartment to give to Peaches.

Peaches was shaking her head in agreement with everything Murder Black said. Justin ran up and knocked on the window as he heard their bus being called. Murder Black grabbed the backpack from the backseat, jumped out the car then rushed straight to get their tickets.

CHAPTER 30

The funeral

After watching Jay's casket go down in the ground, Carlos could not find the strength to move. Rell had to put his arm around Carlos' shoulder to walk him away. Lartesha started making her way towards the limo holding on to Veronica with tears flowing from her eyes; when Vince appeared out the crowd of people that were walking to their cars; Lartesha had a frown on her face as if she was curious. Vince extended his arms out for Lartesha to come to him so he could hug her and to tell her it will be all right. While Vince was hugging Lartesha real tight, Veronica was standing quietly looking at Vince strangely because she did not know his name; Lartesha never mentioned him before, she said to herself, that she knew the eyes and that voice. I know him from somewhere. While Veronica was thinking this, Vince brought his head up to meet Veronica's eyes. Then he greeted her and said his name, but she was so far gone in her thoughts she did not catch what he said.

Excuse me... But what did you say your name was? Veronica asked.

I said my name is Vince. Vince repeated.

When Vince said, the word, hi again; Veronica said; to herself, I know him from somewhere; I know that voice and the eyes because his words give me the chills, right along with those eyes. Veronica rudely greeted Vince, then asked Lartesha was she all right, then she walked off giving Vince the evil eye.

Vince walked Lartesha to the limo she rode in. He was hoping in his mind that move he just did would get him a little closer to Lartesha and the crew. While he was walking her to the limo, he explained to her how he knew Jay, Vince felt that everything was going as planned for him; He now had to convince the fellas to how he and Jay met is what he was thinking. When Lartesha got to the limo, Vince gave her a kiss on the cheek, then told her he would call her. Then he walked away. But Lartesha shouted for him to follow them to Jay's mother's house for the gathering of close friends and family. He agreed then got in his car smiling to himself. He felt that Lartesha was in his pocket. But before pulling off, he said to himself; I know where I saw that girl from; but damn, I hope she didn't recognize me, because she could hurt this investigation and me too. But what the fuck, I had my mask on when we raided that house. Many thoughts were running through Vince's mind. After the limo pulled off, Veronica asked Lartesha who Vince was, then she said that it was something about Vince that gave her the chills.

What...! What Veronica huh...! why you say that. Lartesha asked, trying her hardest to keep her cool.

It's something... I cannot point my finger on it right now... But it will come to me soon. I'm telling you, watch. Veronica said.

While Lartesha and Veronica were busy in their conversation that was heating, Marie and Jay's mother were staring at them strangely because they did not know what they were talking about and Jay's mother did not care anyway she still had her mind on her son. Marie knew she had to put an end to the madness before it got out of hand. She knew now was not the time for what they were conversing about.

Ladies... Lady's. Now isn't the time for that, please. Marie yelled out.

But Marie, I'm telling her it's something funny about that guy, that's all. Veronica said.

Yeah, I want to know what… Because if you do not know, then maybe you should have kept your mouth shut. Lartesha said.

Well, whatever, maybe I should have; but I didn't. Veronica said, in a harsh tone of voice.

Okay, that is it… that is it… I can't take anymore. Jay's mother yelled.

After the limo pulled over, Carlos asked everybody to hold up before they all got out. He wanted to break the news about the connection; he wanted to know how they felt about him doing what the note said.

All right Y'all… I know everybody is down and out because I feel the same way… But I wanted to let Y'all know that I heard from Marie's uncle and it supposed to go down tonight… But here's how he wants to do it. Carlos said.

As Carlos was explaining what the note said, he was looking around to see if there were any changed facial expressions, because he wanted everybody to have some say so, but when nobody spoke up, he had the impression that everyone agreed.

So everything is everything. Carlos asked, giving everybody another chance to speak their own minds.

Shit, if you trusted it, then we trust it. Taking chances is part of life, so fuck it, do it. Black said while Rell and Rock were shaking their heads in agreement with what Black was saying.

When they got done talking everyone got out the limo and went up in Jay's mother's house to join the gathering Jay had a good number of relatives that attended; some Carlos never met. He was making his way through the family gathering when he spotted one of Jay's cousins who Jay disliked; and did not care for either. Carlos knew plenty of times when they were together, and they saw Rico; Jay wanted to jump out and do physical harm to him. For whatever reason, Jay never said; but Carlos was with Jay right or wrong and that was Carlos reason for not liking Rico because his boy didn't, so when he saw him Carlos kept his eye on Rico's every move. Carlos stood close to the wall with an excellent view of Rico and he was staring at him hard, hoping Rico saw him, just to shake him up inside. But it did not work. When Rico looked, he gave Carlos a slight grin then continued with his conversation. Marie walked up on Carlos with two cups, handing one to him, while wondering what he was staring at like that, she tapped him on the arm.

Carlos, you all right? Marie asked.

Yeah, I'm just trying to understand why that bitch ass nigga over there; came and he knows Jay didn't like him. Carlos said, as he nodded his head towards Rico so that Marie could see who he was talking about.

Well Carlos, that is his family, right? Maria asked.

Yeah... but fuck that nigga. Carlos said.

While Carlos and Marie were talking, Lartesha walked up with Vince to introduce him to Carlos, after they exchanged names Carlos inquired on how him and Jay came about. Vince tried to laugh it off like that was an interesting question. But Carlos just stood there without even a smirk on his face.

Me and Jay came about a few years ago when he saw me at the car wash. I had this car he liked; we have been cooling ever since. We would chill from time to time and smoke some weed. I like that young nigga we would do business sometimes. I will miss him. Vince said.

When Vince was telling Carlos everything, Lartesha was a little shocked to hear that Vince was buying from Jay. She thought Vince had baller money; she knew Jay was not selling heavyweight, but she said; to herself, damn he looks good in that suit with his waves spinning and the smell from the fresh haircut.

Vince was not paying Lartesha any attention because he was trying hard to win Carlos over with small talk. Carlos was listening. Then he started looking around for Rico.

Marie, did you see where that nigga went? Carlos asked as he excused himself.

Yeah, I saw him go up the stairs a few minutes ago. Marie said.

Who is Y'all talking about? Lartesha asked.

That nigga Rico, Lartesha. Excuse us Vince but Lartesha, go tell Rell, Rock and Black to meet me upstairs. Carlos said.

Yo, I'll go with you... Is it a problem that you need handled? Vince said, poking out his chest.

Nah, it's all right... we got this. Carlos said as he walked off.

Lartesha hurried over to where Rell, Rock and Black were standing and told them what Carlos said. When they got up the stairs towards Jay's room, they heard some noise coming from that way, so they picked up their pace. When they got to the room, Carlos was pushing Rico down and pulling his gun out. Rico was sitting on the floor with his back against the dresser drawer with his hands up, pleading and begging for his life. Rell ran over to Carlos to remind him where they were. So instead of Carlos shooting him, he slapped him so hard in the mouth with the gun that blood splatter flew everywhere.

Look, I saw this nigga putting this in his pocket. Carlos said holding up Jay's iced out Jacob's watch.

Everybody looked at Rico as if they wanted to shoot him themselves. Lartesha grabbed a towel and threw it at him.

Nigga clean yourself up and get the fuck out of this house and put this t-shirt on. Don't wear that bloody ass shirt downstairs. Lartesha said, throwing Rico a towel and t-shirt before spitting in his face.

Rico grabbed the towel holding it over his mouth letting the blood soak it up as he got off the floor. Lartesha went over to the dresser drawer to make sure the money and the note were still there. While Rico was putting on the t-shirt, she pulled out the note and took it over to Carlos for him to read because she wanted him to be the one to give it to Jay's mother.

Lartesha, what's this, how you know about this? Carlos asked as he took it.

I found it when I was cleaning up in here... read... read it! I didn't know what to do with it, so I put it back. Lartesha said.

As Carlos was reading, he could not believe what Jay wrote before his eyes. Carlos had a mind-blowing expression on his face. All he could do was shake his head. Then he set on the edge of the bed in his own world, shaking his head. When he looked down and realized he had money in his hand, he started counting it. Everyone stood watching as he was counting. Marie walked right in while Carlos was counting.

Is everything all right in here... I saw that guy rushing out the house with a towel over his mouth. Marie asked as she walked in the room.

It's $25,000, did you already know Lartesha? Carlos asked, not paying attention to the question Marie had just asked.

No, I didn't know because I didn't count it. After I read the letter, I put everything back. Lartesha said.

Could somebody tell me what's going on, is everything all right. Marie asked again.

Yeah, Marie, everything is straight. Rock said.

Marie, go downstairs and tell Jay's mother to come here. Carlos said.

What...! I know you not giving that to her right now. Lartesha asked.

Shit, what you want me to do, just put it back... Are you crazy and let her find it one day when she is here by herself? I don't think so Lartesha. Carlos said as he stood up.

CHAPTER 31

New York City

Walking through Port Authority, Justin was nervous about seeing the police with dogs walking around. He could not wait to get out of the building. When they stepped outside, Murder Black spotted Mike's truck quick, then him and Justin walked over towards Mike jumping in the truck all smiles.

What's up son, son? Mike asked.

Damn nigga, you didn't say that you had big rims on the truck. What are those 24's? Murder Black asked.

Nah... 23's son... Why they big, huh? Mike asked.

Hell yeah, and they are looking good on that eggshell white. Murder Black said.

Aye yo! what the hell, I know that ain't Justin with you? Mike said, all surprised.

Yeah, and it's not Little Justin anymore, it's Justin all right. Justin spat.

Wow... he is all grown up. How old are you, little nigga? Mike asked.

I'm 16, why? Justin spat with his chest poked out.

Nigga, Carlos will kill you for bringing his brother down here to buy drugs. Are you crazy? Mike said.

NO… he will not know, because you will not tell him, right? Murder Black asked with a serious face.

Nah, I won't tell on my family, but if something was to go down, it's all on you… Because I don't want no parts of it… Now come on, let's be out. Mike said.

Aye yo, Mike, let's go straight to take care of this business first, I got someone on standby, nah mean. Murder Black said, as he got in the truck.

Mike was cutting in and out of the afternoon traffic in downtown Manhattan, headed uptown to see his longtime Dominican friend, Jordan. Mike always took people to Jordan for years now. It was to where if his man Jordan was out, then he would tell everyone who would want to come from out of town to buy he did not know anyone else, because he only trusts Jordan. Jordan had lots of cousin's who he did not mind them selling their packages around his pool hall, Jordan understood Mike's loyalty towards him and that was something he respected. That is why Jordan brought Mike truck and gave him money to move out to New Jersey. While Mike was driving in and out of traffic, he grabbed his cell phone off his hip, after dialing some numbers he started speaking in Spanish, that is something else he picked up from Jordan; he was not very fluent with the language. After Mike hung up the phone, he nearly ran someone off the road as he was getting off on 125th Street. Murder Black looked over at Mike with a puzzle frown on his face, wondering why he took the exit.

Aye yo nigga, just because you live in this crazy city, doesn't mean you have to drive crazy. Murder Black spat tilting his head giving Mike an evil glare.

Mike looked over at him and smiled. Justin was in the back seat, laughing and looking out the window. Mike pulled over a block away from the pool hall, then asked Murder Black how much he was spending. After Murder Black told him, he jumped out the truck telling them to wait a few minutes. Justin scooted up between the armrest to see where. Mike was going. Then he asked; Murder Black, why they could not go with him that question made Murder Black mad. Justin saw it in his face. So, as he sat back in the seat and watched the pool hall door, Justin was watching the young Dominican boy come running out of the pool hall, then jumping on his scooter with a walkie talkie in hand. Then Mike came out right behind him, which made Justin say to himself, why did that boy just run out like Mike was chasing him? As Mike was making his way towards the truck, another guy came walking out the pool hall; this guy stood out as the big man. With his tank top, black slacks, Gucci loafers and a Cuban link necklace with an iced out cross with diamonds gleaming from the sun reflecting off it. Justin heard Murder Black mumble the name Jordan, Justin said to himself. So, he must be the man, damn he looks young. Jordan was only 27 holding the business down for his uncle. Not too many people do business with Jordan. He was 5'11, light skin very muscular with wavy hair, brown eyes. When Jordan stood outside, he kept looking both ways down the street, absorbing his surroundings. Then he waved over to the truck after Mike got in; being that Mike had tints, he was not looking while he was getting in the truck, Murder Black thought Jordan was giving Mike some secret code.

Aye yo Mike, look that dude over there is waving at you. Murder Black said, as he tapped Mike on the shoulder.

Oh nah, that's Jordan, he's waving at you. I told him some good things about you, that's all. Mike said.

Justin was looking out the window, taking in everything that was going on outside when he saw the young kid coming back down the street on his scooter. He said to himself he must be the runner for Mike, so he kept his eyes on the kid that was coming in their direction. Justin was watching the young kid even more. When the young kid leaned his scooter against the pool hall wall making his way towards them with a paper bag in his hand.

Aye yo, Mike, he ain't worried about the police? Justin asked.

What...! Man, his uncle got the area on lock. Mike said.

When the Young Kid approached the truck, Mike quickly rolled his window down as the young kid dropped a bag in the window. Then he rushed to his scooter to pick it up, then he quickly rode off yelling in his walkie talkie. Mike tossed the bag on Murder Black's lap, telling him to check it out. As Murder Black was absorbing the package, Justin's eyes were on the Young kid's every move while he sped off. Then another guy appeared from out of the pool hall, joining in on the conversation. While he was talking, he was looking over at Mike's truck like he was mad about something. Murder Black looked at Mike with a head nod, approving him on the package. He noticed the guy who was talking to Jordan, staring in their direction, like he was mad about something. Mike notice who Murder Black was looking at, then he started laughing.

Ha... Ha... Ha...! Mike laugher carried on as he looked out the window and back at Murder Black.

Aye Yo, you see him, that's Roberto. He stays mad about everything and yeah; he does not like me, never did, but fuck him, that's Jordan's older brother. He is too aggressive and serious and not too many people like doing business with him and I advise you and whoever else not to do business with him. Mike said.

Shit, he is looking over this way like we were about to pull off with their shit. Justin said, as he was watching Roberto.

Man, fuck that nigga Roberto... Yo let me get that money and the package so Jordan could get it where it's going. Oh, he told me to tell you that prices went up from 16 to 26, but being that you came just in time, he said; he would give you a deal. You need $2000 more though, with what you said; you had. Mike said.

Aye yo fam, I'm good for it. I'll Western Union that shit right back, word. Murder Black said as he was giving Mike the backpack and package. Mike shook his head in agreement with Murder Black, then he grabbed everything jumped out the truck made his way towards the pool hall.

CHAPTER 32

Feeling the pain

When Marie and Jay's mother appeared in the doorway, Carlos stood up, but could not look Jay's mother in the face. He already knew the pressures she was under from seeing her baby in the casket. And for her to receive a letter like that, he knew it was not making the situation any better, that is why it hurts him inside, Carlos did not want her to be alone than find it. Lartesha was still sitting on the edge of the bed, slightly rocking back and forth with her arms folded across her chest as the tears were flowing down her cheeks. Veronica did not want to know or see what happened when she peeked in the door; she saw all the long faces, so she turned around to walk back downstairs. As Carlos was handing Jay's mother the envelope, she gave him a strange look as she was looking at all the long faces and seeing Lartesha the way she was, Jay's mother knew it was not good news.

Baby, what is it? Why is everybody looking like this? Don't be so down and out, my son is resting in peace, he's in a better place. Jay's mother stated as she was looking around at everyone and taking the envelope from Carlos.

Ms. Williams, I came across this envelope after I caught Rico up here trying to steal. I really think you should read it. Carlos said, as he was handing the envelope to her.

That damn Rico, where is he now? Is he downstairs? Jay's mother asked.

Well, no, I made him leave. Carlos said.

Thank you ...! Let's see what this is, if Y'all don't already know. Jay's mother asked, as she was walking towards the bed to sit down.

After pulling the letter and money from the envelope, she scanned the room taking in the sad expression on everyone's faces trying to get a sign without reading the letter. But seeing no changes in the faces that surrounded her, Jay's Mother cautiously opened what she had at hand, Marie sat down close to her because she could see the hurt and pain in Jay's mother's face. Marie did not know what was going on. She sat rubbing Jay's Mother back in the attempt to soothe her as she was reading. After Jay's Mother took in the words from the letter, all the strength left her body the way she fell in Marie's arms as she kept asking.

Why... why... why... Ms. William asked pleading with her hands.

Carlos walked up to her and kneeled in front of her, then tried his hardest to look her in the face.

Ms. Williams, I know how you feel because we all loved Jay ourselves, but we also have to stay strong okay. Carlos said, as tears were rolling down his cheeks while he was trying to choose his words wisely.

Lartesha scooted over towards Jay's mother on the bed after seeing how much pain she was in from reading the letter made her feel awful, that was why Lartesha kept giving Carlos an evil glare, with the shaking of her head saying in her mind he knew he should have waited, he knew he should have waited. Lartesha joined Marie in rubbing Jay's Mother, Carlos was kneeling in front of Jay's Mother attempting to soothe her with words.

Baby...! I know Y'all meant well by this and I'm glad that Y'all brought it to me, I know my son was unpredictable he was always full of surprises, I will miss him that is why it hurts so bad. Jay's mother said; as she sat up and started wiping the tears away from her eyes.

Ms. Williams we're here for you and we will miss him too, like Carlos said, we have to stay strong because I'm sure that is what he would have wanted. Rell said.

All right, all right... Y'all I know everyone downstairs is probably wondering where I went, so we have to get back down there, so let me have a few minutes in here and I'll be right down okay. Ms. William asked, as she got the strength to stand up.

Carlos stood up looking her in the eyes as if he were trying to read her mind then he leaned forward and gave her a soft passionate kiss on the cheek, along with everyone else to follow. Marie was the last to step up, so when she did, she stood in front of Jay's mother, staring at her for a while revisiting the moment that she had to experience in her life with the death of her loved ones, she knew how bad Jay's mother was hurting inside. So, before she stepped off, she gave her an emotionally big hug and whispered to her she was always there for anything. Then she turned around to walk out, but Jay's mother stopped her in the doorway.

Just one-minute sweetheart... What is your name? Because after all this time, I did not know it. Ms. William asked, walking up to Marie.

My name is Marie, Ms. William. Marie said.

Well Marie, I really truly... deeply appreciate everything. That hug you laid on me was some hug, it felt like you have experienced someone close to you passing away. Jay's mother asked, as she was standing in front of Marie staring in her eyes as if she was looking through her.

Marie could not stand the stare because she knew Jay's mother was speaking the truth, and that was something she would rather not talk about, so she was trying to dodge the stare and the question.

Well like I said, Ms. William, I'm here if you need anything, okay I have to get back downstairs before Carlos comes back looking for me. Marie said, walking out of the room.

Okay, sweetheart... I'll be down in a minute. Jay's mother said.

CHAPTER 33

Making moves with family

After Mike passed Jordan the bag, Roberto approached Mike aggressively shouting at him speaking Spanish. Mike looked Roberto in the face, laughed, then walked off. Murder Black had his hands latched onto the door handle with his eyes on Roberto's every move. Murder Black was not trying to hear anything happening to Mike. If it was on, then he was with it. That is how he felt for his cousin. Mike turned and headed back towards the truck; Murder Black fell back in his seat. Justin was in the back watching everything. His heart is bigger than his brain thinking he could take on the world. Mike jumped in the truck laughing, breaking Justin's thoughts by expressing the rage he felt for Roberto.

Aye yo son! What was that about? Murder Black asked.

Son...! you saw that stunt that sucker just tried to pull. Son, one of these days, I will give him what he's asking for. He is lucky Jordan is his family. Mike said, as he was cutting in and out of the Broadway traffic heading for the highway.

Yo.... Yo... Yo... before you drop us back off, stop at that one spot coming up right there. Murder Black said, pointing at a bodega on the corner, with a few dudes standing out front.

OKAY... nigga...! Mike shouted.

Aye Yo...! You going to straighten that dude Roberto out before he tries to get at you. Murder Black said.

Who you telling? I know I can't keep giving him a pass, that's why I said one of these days. Mike said, as he was pulling over by the bodega.

Aye yo grab me something to drink while you're in there and a bag of chips. Justin yelled out as Murder Black got out of the truck.

Shit, what's wrong with you? You better get out and get it yourself. I might forget I'm on something different nigga. Murder Black turned around and yelled back.

The New York City streets were busy with cars speeding by like they were in a rush. People filled the sidewalk, rushing to their destination. Murder Black mind was on one thing and one person, that was in his view. While the young kid Pedro was busy talking to the rest of his boys on the corner, Murder Black walked over towards him. As he was approaching one dude gave Pedro a heads up signal quick like Murder Black did not see what he was doing. Murder Black and Pedro became very familiar with one another throughout the times that Murder Black would come to New York City, whether it was to shop, buy drugs or chill, he would make it his business to stop around where Pedro chilled at, Pedro had exotic weed. He would try to offer him to buy heroin, Murder Black liked his style. Pedro was Dominican and Black, Short and Stocky with a light brown complexion. Brown eyes, a goatee, he kept his head bald. Pedro stayed dress in the finest and being that the weather was nice, he was rocking the Sean John denim shorts, with the white t-shirt on his feet were the brand-new construction Timbs. As Pedro turned around and saw Murder Black was making his way towards him, he was all smiles with his eyes hiding behind some transitional Cartier glasses. When Murder Black approached him, Pedro shook his hand then embraced him like they knew each other forever, it was how Pedro was too many people he liked. After Murder Black pulled back, they looked each other up and down playfully, then started laughing. Justin made his way pass them both, looking at his cousin strangely; wondering how long he knew this guy and who in the hell was he, not wanting to ask Justin kept it moving. Murder Black and Pedro was deep in conversation like every time they met up.

Hey, my friend...! What's happening, you know the prices went up. But me, I got good prices for you, good! Pedro said.

Nah, I'm straight on the cocaine, Pedro. But I need something else. Murder Black said, looking around as if people were listening to him.

I know... I know... my friend. You want to smoke, right? Pedro asked.

Nah, it's not that, but I can use some of that too... But I really need a cap of that water if you got some. Murder Black said, referring to the drug PCP.

When Murder Black told Pedro what he needed, Pedro called over to a young Spanish looking kid who was sitting on some milk crates talking to the other group of boys out on the corner, after Pedro gave him a head nod, the kid walked in the bodega.

Follow my friend. Pedro said pointing to the kid walking in the bodega.

As Murder Black was walking in the bodega, Justin was coming out.

Aye yo, tell Mike I am on my way. Murder Black shouted, as he was passing Justin.

All right. Justin said, as he kept it moving.

Murder Black followed the kid to the back of the bodega, then he turned and put his hand out as if he were telling Murder Black to give him the money first. Murder Black threw his hand out back at him.

Let me see first... I want one cap of that water and 10 bags of that purple haze. Murder Black said.

Okay, wait right here. Young Kid said then walked off and grabbed a bag.

When the kid came back with the stuff, Murder Black quickly paid him and walked out the bodega to where Pedro was standing. He gave him small talk until Mike started blowing his horn crazy.

Pedro, I got to be out… I'll get back up with you, all right. Murder Black said, as he was back peddling towards the truck.

Okay, my friend, but just remember, I got good prices for you. Pedro yelled out.

CHAPTER 34

So much anger and stress

Carlos was sitting in the chair thinking about the letter, hoping he did not have to go through another death no time soon. He was hoping and praying his boy Trick makes it out the coma. Then Vince walked up.

Aye Carlos, is everything all right? Vince asked as he walked up in front of Carlos.

Yeah, everything is cool. Carlos said, looking Vince in his eyes.

Well, here you go take this if you need to talk to somebody. I'm here, Vince said, handing Carlos a card with his phone number on it.

I'm about to go, so I'll see you around. Vince said and turned around and walked over to where Lartesha was standing.

While Carlos and Vince were talking, Rell was over on the other side of the room talking to Veronica, from time to time Rell would catch her turning her nose up in someone direction with an evil frown on her face like she disliked someone in the room, when he turned around to look for himself, he could not figure it out, Rell did not pay it no mind until she did it again this time, Vince was walking over towards Lartesha and she was not that far away from where they was standing. This time he caught who she was giving the evil look too.

Aye, baby girl...! You know that, guy? Rell asked.

No... well I do not know, it's something that is telling me I do and not from a good encounter. I've been through a lot throughout my life with men. Veronica said, looking Rell in the face.

Well baby girl, I'm not here to give you any problems. I'm trying to get to know you. Rell said, turning his head in a different direction as if he was a shy individual.

Huh... oh so that's right... well, what about Kelly? What you think she got to say about us getting to know each other? We know she is a little possessive, and that is some problem's you guys bring along with Y'all. Because Y'all tell us ladies one thing and it is the opposite, then when everything comes all out, then Y'all start telling a million different lies. Veronica spat back.

Rell stood blank face not knowing how to come back with an answer. After Veronica mentioned Kelly's name then said; what she said about men, he knew that he had to come correct. He saw how badly she had it out for men. While he was standing speechless with a loose four words, he started looking around as though he lost interest in the conversation.

What's wrong with Rell? Did I say something to offend you? Veronica asked sarcastically.

Nah, nah, I was just thinking that's all. Rell said as he was still looking around.

Well, why are you acting like you don't want to talk anymore? Is it what I said about your girlfriend? Huh? Veronica asked.

No, and she's not my girl anymore, and how do you know about me and Kelly in the first place? Who told you? Rell asked.

I have a cousin who lives down in the Pioneer Homes Projects, right around the corner from you. She talks about you and Kelly a lot; she said why is he with her she is not attractive... She said you could do so much better than her because you look good. Veronica said, smiling at him as she was talking.

Carlos was sitting around contemplating on leaving his self until Jay's mother came downstairs and made her way over towards him.

Hey, baby! Are you okay? It looks like you need something to do. I think it would probably keep your mind off things. Why don't you just come and help me with the kitchen? It looks like everyone is leaving. Jay's mother said, as she was standing over Carlos.

Lartesha was making her rounds to let everyone know she was leaving with Vince. She wanted to make sure that everyone was all right; stopping over where Rock and Black were standing. They hugged her and told her to be safe, then she started making her way over towards Veronica and Rell. As she was walking up, she could tell by Veronica's facial expression that she had something smart to say.

I suppose your leaving with him. Veronica asked as she nodded her head towards Vince.

Yep, you supposed right. Now do you need a ride or what? Lartesha asked in a smart tone of voice.

That's all right; I'll get a ride from Rell. Veronica said.

Rell was looking back and forth at them both. He saw and felt the tension in the air. He could not understand why they were acting this way towards each other until Vince started making his way towards them.

Rell are you about ready because some people give me the chills. Veronica said, as she saw Vince making his way towards them.

When Lartesha realized that Veronica was talking about her friend Vince, it made her even more furious.

I'm tired of this shit...! Veronica, you got something on your mother-fucking mind because you sure keep making these crazy ass comments every time Vince comes around. Lartesha said as she walked up in Veronica's face.

Rell quickly stepped in between them both because he saw where the argument was going.

You both need to calm down up in here... do you both realize where the hell you are at? Lartesha, you know better! Rell said as he held his arms out low, not trying to draw attention.

Vince had just walked up as Rell was in between Veronica and Lartesha. He heard Rell telling them to calm down, and Vince saw and felt the tension between the girls.

Is everything all right over here? Vince asked.

Yeah, everything's cool. Rell said, Rell, this is Vince, mine and Jay's friend. Lartesha said.

While Lartesha was introducing Rell to Vince, Veronica was just staring Vince in the face, trying to remember where she knew him from, but Lartesha had her eye on Veronica, watching her at the same time.

Rell, I'm about to go tell Carlos and Jay's mother that I'm about to leave. I got to see if Marie's straight, so I'll be right back, Vince wait here for me. Lartesha said; looking at Vince, then looking at Veronica, cutting her eyes at her before she walked off.

Carlos was wiping down the table, thinking about the move he was about to make with Victor. He stopped dead in his tracks, as if he were in a daze for a minute, and then said; to himself, How the fuck am I supposed to know the damn prices? He started back wiping the table again while Jay's mother was putting the food away. She was also watching Carlos. As he stopped, then started cleaning the table again, she shook her head then continued to do what she was doing. She knew Carlos was going through a lot and dealing with much pressure.

As Carlos was finishing up the table, his cell phone suddenly started ringing. He looked at the screen but already knew who it was.

Hi Mom. Carlos said as he answered.

Hi Carlos, I don't mean to interrupt you, but have you spoken with your brother lately? Ms. Johnson asked.

No, why do you ask? Did something happen that I should know about? Carlos asked with a worried look on his face.

Well, I have a letter from his school that says he has not been going; I have some messages on my answering machine from his principle. I have been calling his cell phone and the damn boy has not answered yet. If you hear from him, please call me okay? Ms. Johnson said.

All right, Mom, I'll get on that after I leave Jay's mother's house. I'm helping her clean up. Carlos said.

Okay baby, tell her I said; hi and I send my deepest condolences. Ms. Johnson said.

Okay Mom, I'll call you okay? Carlos said as he was holding in his anger.

They said their goodbyes and hung up.

As Carlos was getting off the phone Lartesha was walking in the kitchen. He aggressively pushed the button to hang up the call as soon as she came in, she quickly noticed Carlos attitude. She knew right off hand that he received some bad news. She stood there in the doorway for a minute without even being noticed. Carlos was busy staring down at his phone in hand deep in thought then Jay's mother had her back turned she was still putting food away neither noticed Lartesha standing there. As soon as Carlos lifted his head up and saw Lartesha staring at him, he quickly changed his demeanor.

Hey Lartesha, you all right? Carlos asked as he set his cell phone in its casing on his waist.

Yeah, I'm all right, but the question is, are you all right? Lartesha asked.

I'm straight; it's just that my little brother is so damn hardheaded. He never wants to listen, but I will straighten him out though. Oh yeah, Ms. William, my mom sends her condolences and said she's sorry she could not make it. Carlos said.

Well, Carlos, I'm about to go. You need me to do anything before I leave? Lartesha asked as she was walking towards Jay's mother.

Nah, I'm straight. Oh yeah, are you going home, I will stop by after I'm finished here? Carlos replied.

Yeah, I'm going home. Lartesha said as she was giving Jay's mother a hug.

I'll call you when I'm about to leave, all right. Carlos said.

Okay… Ms. Williams, do you need me to do anything? Lartesha asked as she stood in front of Jay's mother.

Now I'm sure that I can handle it, baby. Ms. Williams said.

Well, here are my numbers, call me if there's anything you would like and I don't care if it's for some conversation, please call. Lartesha said, then she leaned over and kissed her on the cheek while she was giving Jay's mother her numbers.

CHAPTER 35

Cannot lie forever

Riding on the bus back home was taking forever for Murder Black. He had so many things running through his mind ever since Mike dropped him and Justin back off at Port Authority. Now the bus ride was annoying him. Justin was sitting by the window, staring out, watching the day turn to night. Murder Black kept looking over at Justin, from time to time hoping he did not say a thing because he was very annoyed already. When they pulled up at the bus station, Murder Black's car was not in sight, which made him furious. Justin glanced at him but never said a word, he saw the expression on Murder Black's face, as they were getting off the bus Murder Black was calling the cell phone he left with Peaches. After letting it ring, then hearing the answering machine, made him continue to call repeatedly.

Man... Peaches, where the hell you at? Murder Black yelled through the phone as she picked up.

I'm around the corner, pulled over by the damn police. They said I was speeding and yeah; I heard the phone ringing, but I could not answer because the police were asking me too many damn questions. Hold up... here he comes with the ticket in his hand. I'll be right there... bye. Peaches said, looking through the rearview mirror as she got off the phone before the police got to the window.

All right, hurry your ass up! Murder Black yelled before hanging up.

Murder Black was slightly mad and embarrassed at the same time he did not want Justin to get the impression that he did not have his game tight or have his girls in check. When he turned around to face Justin after hanging the phone up, he played it off like he had everything under control.

Aye yo… what's up with your chick? You need me to call a taxi for us or what? Justin asked.

Nah, here that bitch comes right now. Murder Black said, as he saw a car headlight coming in their direction.

Justin took his cell phone out of his pocket, turning it back on. He had it off all day as soon as he saw all the messages his mother left; he knew he was in trouble. He started thinking, as he was staring at the phone, then he looked up and said to himself, maybe that stupid-ass nigga J-Love called my house because my phone was off and blew my spot up. Justin was deep in thought, trying to make up a quick lie to tell his mother he kept looking through his messages, he also saw all the times his mother called, and he knew she was on to him. When he finally got to the last person to leave a message, it felt like a sharp pain of fear going to his gut. It was his brother's number. His brother call was not long away from his mother call, so he knew that they both were on to him. Murder Black was heading towards his car when he turned around to tell Justin to come. He noticed the worried look on his face. Murder Black shouted for Peaches to wait a minute. Then he rushed to where Justin was standing, looking worried and stuck.

Aye yo son! What's bothering you? What's the look for? Murder Black asked as he walked over towards Justin.

Man… man! Justin said, as he was looking towards the ground and shaking his head.

Man, what nigga? What happened? I don't have time for games! I'm already fucked up with this bitch, so what's up? Murder Black said, while pacing back and forth in front of Justin.

Nah, it's just my Mom's and Carlos. I think they are on to me with the skipping school. My mom's been calling my cell phone crazy and now Carlos is calling too, he supposes to be out of town. She had to call him. Damn… or probably Marie. Justin said, as he was talking to Murder Black, he had remembered that Marie was go to be picking him up.

What about Marie, Justin? Murder Black asked.

She supposed to be picking me up and dropping me off to school, she might have told Carlos on me! Damn! What should I say? Justin said.

I don't know but keep my name out your mouth; you weren't with me and nigga don't start getting soft now. You, the one who wanted to sell drugs like a man and live the fast life, so stand your ground. Now let's go, I got a bitch to check nigga. Murder Black said, as he turned around and heading towards the car.

Justin cut his phone back off then put it right back in his pocket, thinking to himself, oh well, then heading towards the car right behind Murder Black. Justin could not help but ask himself why Murder Black was not manning up, why was he being so soft and why couldn't he just face his consequences? Justin got in the car; Murder Black got in the driver seat and noticed Peaches roll her eyes at him.

Aye yo! What's your problem, girl? Murder Black asked.

You, my mother fucking problem nigga! You think I'm some dumb ass bitch that will fall for anything, huh? Huh? Huh? You tried, but you will not get that one off on me! I hope your other little bitch makes it to the nearest hotel safe, who you probably told I was your cousin! Peaches yelled as she was getting hyped with her words.

Murder Black sat staring at Peaches with no expression on his face. Then he snatched the door handle with extreme force, pushing the door open. He jumped out, rushed around to the passenger side and yanked the door open in a rage and grabbed Peaches by her hair.

Ah… stop… ah! Peaches screamed.

Bitch! You had a better chance of making your momma walk instead of that girl! Murder Black yelled as he was pulling Peaches out of the car by her hair.

AYE, YO…. police going to come! Do that shit somewhere else, not right here! Justin yelled.

Ah… police! Ah, somebody help! Peaches yelled.

Man, fuck the police! Murder Black shouted.

Shut up, bitch! Nobody helped your ass make that girl walk! Murder Black yelled as he yanked Peaches to the ground by her hair, then smacked her.

I'm sorry…. I'm sorry… I'm so sorry, please…. Peaches begged.

Murder Black stood over Peaches watching her beg, then he turned around jumped back in the car still in rage he reached over and grabbed the passenger door to close it, but Peaches was faster than him. It was like a tug of war until Murder Black finally got tired. He kept pulling with his right hand and used his left hand to put the car in drive. He then tapped on the accelerator, making Peaches fall backwards with her last tug, and then slammed the door.

Murder Black's tires were the last thing Peaches heard because Murder Black made sure of that when he zoomed out of the parking lot. He was heading towards the closet hotel near the bus station, but as he got a little way from the bus station, he pulled over and had Justin get in the front seat. Not knowing why his cousin just wild out on Peaches like that, Justin got in the front seat looking at Murder Black strange.

Son! Why in the hell are you staring at me like that? Murder Black said.

Because I'm trying to figure out why in the hell did you just flip out like that? Justin said.

What! Why, I just flipped out like that... nigga! You did not hear that bitch back there? Man, that bitch made the chick that brought our package back walk back to the hotel, because she assumed that I was fucking the chick. Man, fuck that bitch! It's M.O.B. with me anyway, nah mean? That's what's up! Now I just hope this bitch didn't hop her ass back on the bus. Murder Black said, as he was pulling in the hotel parking lot.

Aye yo! Do you know the chick's name and how she looks? Justin asked.

Yeah, I know! Later for the 50 cent, 21 questions shit because now is not the time word....! Murder Black said, with a little anger in his voice.

Nah! I'm just saying call Mike and see if she got back at them yet, that's all. Justin spat back.

Well Damn! It's about time you use your brain nigga. Murder Black said, as he quickly picked up his cell phone and started dialing Mike's number.

CHAPTER 36

A lot of tension in the air

Leaving out the kitchen, Lartesha made her way towards where Marie was at, wanting to let her know that she was leaving soon, but in the process of her approaching Marie. She took a quick look over in the direction she last left Vince and saw that him and Rell were in a conversation. What bother Lartesha and made her stop so suddenly in her tracks was the strange looks Veronica was making behind Vince's back. Lartesha stood staring in disbelief saying to herself, what is wrong with this bitch? Lartesha was beyond annoyed with Veronica for the way she has been acting and seeing all the crazy facial expressions Veronica was making towards Vince had Lartesha furious. Instead of her going to say goodbye's to Marie; she stormed over toward Vince and Rell, and as she approached them, they both could see that something was bothering her by the look on her face. Rell quickly caught the crazy glare that she gave Veronica.

Lartesha! What's up baby girl? You all right? Rell asked as he stood in front of her and put his hands on her shoulders.

No, the question is if she all right? Come on, Vince; let us go before somebody makes me hurt them up in here. Excuse me Rell for interrupting you but we must leave because some people need to grow up but call me okay. Lartesha said as she kept rolling her eyes at Veronica.

Huh… Veronica said, with a smirk on her face.

Lartesha wanted to walk up to Veronica and slap the smirk off her face, but she did not want to disrespect Jay's Mothers' house. She turned and walked off. Veronica knew she was getting under Lartesha's' skin. She also knew that Rell would not let Lartesha make any crazy moves on her in Jay's mother' house. As Lartesha headed towards the door Marie cut her off by stepping in front of her.

Going somewhere, Miss. Thing? Marie asked, putting both her hands on her hips.

Oh, I'm so sorry Marie, but I was on my way to let you know a minute ago, but I got thrown off by that bitch over there. I don't know what's her problem, but somebody better talk to her because I ain't the one. Lartesha said, pointing toward Veronica.

I hope you not still carrying on from what you were arguing about on the ride over here because you are too old for that; you hear me. Marie said.

Excuse me ladies, Lartesha, I will be out in my car all right. Vince said as he approached them.

Okay Vince. I'll be right out in a minute.

Girl! He's cute, how long have you known him? Marie asked after Vince walked off.

Oh, a few months. Yes, he is cute, Marie; I have to go, so I'll call you okay. Lartesha said, leaving out the door.

All right girl, be safe and don't do nothing I wouldn't do. Marie said, with the wink of her eye and a smile.

Carlos was walking out the kitchen when Lartesha was making her way towards the door.

Aye yo Lartesha! Remember to have your phone on because this is important. I'm leaving in a few. Carlos yelled out across the room.

Okay, Carlos… Lartesha yelled back before closing the door.

Carlos walked up to Marie and leaned over and kissed her on the cheek. When she looked in his face, she could sense that something was bothering him, but she did not pursue it. She let him spark the conversation up if he wanted her to know what was bothering him. Marie stood there in quiet mode, letting Carlos capture the beauty that he loved so dearly because he was just staring at her, until Rell came up from behind him and tapped him on the shoulder.

Aye yo Carlos! I'm about to be out. Is Ms. Williams' still in the kitchen? Rell asked.

Yeah, she's in there and I'm about to leave. I will hit you on your cell after I make that move, all right? Carlos said.

Yeah… Yeah…. all right, playboy. Rell replied.

Aye yo Rock… Black! Carlos yelled.

Carlos… I will go tell Ms. Williams we are leaving okay. Marie said.

All right, Marie. Carlos said.

What up Carlos? Rock said as he and Black walked up.

Aye yo you remember I told you it's going down tonight so be ready because I will hit you on the cell when everything is everything nah mean? Carlos said.

All right, then. Black said.

After they spoke about the moves, they were planning to make, they all headed towards the kitchen to see Jay's Mother before they left. They want to make sure she would be all right when they left. When they enter the kitchen, Marie was in the middle of hugging and kissing

Ms. Williams on the cheek, then after Marie turned walked out. As she walked by Carlos, he could see the tears coming down her cheeks and the same expressions on her face when she thought about her family's death.

I'll be waiting in the car for you, Carlos. Ms. William, please call us if you need anything. Marie said as she was walking out.

All right, Mami. I'll be out in just a minute. Carlos spat back.

Jay's mother looked back and forth at them both strangely because of the names they were using for each other. She didn't understand it, and Rock caught the frown; she was making, but he just shook his head and smiled because he knew she didn't quite understand what the hell they were saying.

Carlos, what did you say… Mami… what is that your name in Spanish or something? Ms. William asked out loud while Marie was walking out of the kitchen.

No… that's not our names in Spanish, it's just some nicknames we call each other, that's all. Carlos said.

Okay baby, or should I say Carlos also? Ms. William said.

No, it's fine, Ms. William. Carlos said with a smile.

Ms. William, I'm so glad to see that you're staying strong. Black said as he walked up and hugged her.

Carlos was watching Ms. William closely. He knew how badly she was hurting in the inside; he knew she was trying to hide it. Carlos stood there waiting for his turn to hug her and let her know he was there for her no matter what it was. As he was standing around watching Rock talk, he started thinking about Tricks' condition, which made him walk up and interrupt the conversation Rock was holding with Ms. Williams. He knew he had so much to do in so little time and wanted to make it to the hospital, to see Trick, to see how his mother was holding up because that was something eating at his conscience badly.

Ms. William I am so sorry, but I have to go Marie is outside waiting for me. I have so much to do but here is my number call me anytime okay. I'll be stopping back by soon, so I want you to take good care of yourself okay, and excuse me Rock for interrupting you, but I really have to run. Carlos said, as he stepped in front of Rock to hug Jay's mother.

Oh, baby, I will be fine. Thanks to you all, you all were an enormous help and I really appreciate everything you have done for me and my baby. Carlos go handle whatever it is you have to do because there's nothing else to do here and I will stay strong and I'll call you if something comes up; but I'm sure I'll be just fine, okay. Ms. Williams said.

All right, Ms. Williams take care. Black said, as he was walking out.

Wait… hold up one-minute Black. I will need you to bring her the money tomorrow, okay. Carlos said as he walked up to Black.

All right, no problem, I'll handle that. Black spat back, then he walked out.

When Carlos was walking towards his car, he hoped that Ms. Williams was not lying about being able to handle the loss of her only son. Then he started thinking about Trick. It was just so many things that were running through his mind. He did not know if he was coming or going. Marie had to lean over the armrest and tap on the window he was standing there not moving he was deep in thought. After she tapped on the window, he hopped in the car and pulled off. Still deep in his thoughts, Marie kept looking over at him.

Carlos, are you all right? Marie asked.

Well, no, and yeah. Carlos said, as he kept his eyes on the road.

What's bothering you then? Marie asked.

Everything from the move. I'm supposed to be making with your uncle, too. My man Trick is still in a damn coma. Carlos said, gripping the steering wheel tight.

Carlos, why are you having all these negative thoughts? Marie asked.

Marie, I'm not having negative thoughts about anything but while we're on this subject. Does your uncle have a key to your apartment building? Carlos asked, as he was slowing down for a red light.

Carlos, he owns the building. I'm sure he would, I thought I told you Carlos. Marie said.

Marie, you never told me that your uncle owned this building. Carlos spat, looking back and forth at Marie and the red light.

I mean Carlos, what does it matter? Did something happen that I should know about? Marie asked with a frown.

Okay, now that I know, it matters, and I mean it matters a lot! I do not want somebody I am doing business with and I state illegal business; to have a key to the building I live in Marie and yes, I understand this is your uncle. But nothing is fair in this game so hear me out, I need you to be by my side 100% and trust me on whatever decision I make. It is all for the best.

Carlos, what are you talking about? I do not understand where you're going with this. Marie said.

Marie, what I'm saying is after I make this move with your uncle tonight, we're not staying there anymore. Carlos said, as he was pulling off from the light.

What? Why not Carlos? Marie asked.

Come on, Marie! Didn't I ask you to trust me? Carlos said shaking his head with both hands gripping the steering wheel thigh as he plead.

I do… it is just… come on Carlos; I know you do not think my uncle would try something funny; Carlos he is serious about his business. He would never put me in harm's way, I'm his only niece and he knows you stay with me. Marie said.

Marie, I come home from the mall today and as soon as I walk in the door, it's a damn envelope with a note in it on the floor, like somebody slid it under the door. Who? I do not fucking know, but I know that your uncle has been following me because in the note he states what I am driving. Unless you told him that, and from the way he is doing his move, I can sense he does not trust me. The feeling is mutual, so that's where I stand on that. Carlos said.

Carlos, please listen to me…. My uncle did business with you because I asked him to, now whichever way he went, I told you how he was, but I know he wouldn't do you or do me any harm Carlos. Marie said.

Like I said, Marie, I know that is your uncle and you probably love him dearly; I made my mind up. I really don't want to talk about it anymore. Carlos said, as he was pulling up in front of the apartment building.

Carlos, what do you mean you don't want to talk about it anymore? I have a life also and I'm a lady not a child so I think I can make my own decisions, because I totally disagree with you this time! Marie said, as she jumped out the car and slammed the door behind her.

Carlos had so much running through his mind he figured by Marie not following along with his plan, it was not making the situation any better. He loved Marie and if he knew that dealing with her uncle would cause this effect on their relationship, he would not have asked for the deal. Now that it was in position, he was not having doubts about turning his back on the move. Carlos sat in the car for about five minutes before pulling off, and as he was coasting slowly through the city streets, he said; to himself, Nigga, this game is way too serious to be letting emotions sink in now! This is the life you chose, so live and abide by what you feel is right nigga. Talking to himself, which Carlos did often, he felt that he could somehow get a better understanding out of the things he did and the positions he put himself in all the time, if he spoke it out to himself. This time he knew his relationship was on the line, so before picking up his cell phone to call Lartesha, he was slowing down at a stop sign. He said to himself, What's next... my damn relationship? I already lost my damn homie to this game, and another one is in a damn coma. What is fucking next? Carlos said, as he stopped at the stop sign and slammed his fists on the steering wheel. Then he grabbed the cell phone and started dialing Lartesha's' number.

Hello?... Lartesha said as she answered on the first ring.

I'm on my way, be ready. Carlos said, and then he hung up.

Damn Carlos ain't no...... Lartesha said before she heard the tone.

CHAPTER 37

No stopping just yet

While Murder Black was sitting in the hotel parking lot talking with his cousin Mike on the phone. Justin was relaxing, reclined in his seat, attempting to pay close attention to the conversation Murder Black was having, seeing Murder Black shaking his head with a frown on his face. Justin quickly assumed something went wrong. When Murder Black got off the phone, Justin did not waste time asking what happened.

Why were you shaking your head like that? What she got back on the bus or something? What did he say? Justin asked, sitting up in his seat.

Now! That nigga Jordan is mad Mike said, he was saying shit like he does not want to do business with me anymore, that's why I'm shaking my head. I can't afford that loss, nah mean. Murder Black said, as he was looking back and forth out of his window and back at Justin.

Why did something happen to that chick? Justin asked.

Damn! Here we go with the question again. Nah, nothing happened to the chick. She's right here at this hotel. We got the right place. She called Jordan and let him know where she was at. Murder Black said.

Then what the fuck is he tripping over if nothing happened to her? Justin asked.

Man, I don't even know but let me go get her real quick so we could be out. Murder Black said, as he jumped out the car.

Murder Black entered the hotel through the back door, then he quickly took the flight of stairs to the room Mike had told him she would be in. When he knocked on the door the first time, he did not receive no answer, so he took a step backwards to look up at the room number and make sure he had the right room. He knocked again, but before he could, the door flew open with a young Spanish girl in the doorway who could not look any older than 19 years of age. By the expression she gave Murder Black, he knew she was mad at him. Instead of explaining, he told her to follow him as he spun around and headed towards the stairs. Justin was in the car with the music turned up loud to where he was not paying attention to his surroundings. He never even noticed the hotel police patrol pull up behind him and get out. When the officer walked up and tapped on the window with his flashlight Justin quickly looked up and turned the music down. He then rolled his window down a little with butterflies in the middle of his stomach.

This is a no-parking zone. The police officer said, with the flashlight shining in Justin's face.

He's coming right out, officer. Justin said, with his hands trying to block the bright light.

When Murder Black walked out the back door of the hotel and turned the corner he immediately stopped in his tracks, at the sight of the police officer standing by his car talking to Justin with his flashlight shining throughout the car. Murder Black waited for a few more minutes, so he turned around and waved for the young Spanish girl to wait. Murder Black wanted to absorb the officer's movement from a distance because he did not know what was going on, he said; to himself. That damn stupid bitch Peaches, I know it; I know it! As Murder Black said that to himself, the officer was putting his flashlight away and pulling out a small notepad while he was walking around to the driver side of the car. Murder Black saw that he was just writing a ticket, so he eased up and walked out towards his car with the young girl on his heels.

What's going on? Isn't that the police? The young Spanish girl asked in her broken English accent.

Yeah don't worry, just let me handle this, you get right in the car. Murder Black said, looking back over his shoulder as they were walking towards the car.

As Murder Black approached the officer on the driver's side of his car, he made sure he stayed calm because he knew the officer was absorbing everything and he did not want to show no sign of guilt or suspicion. He knew by being in the area that they were in; the police did not play fair, and he didn't want to take a loss with his two bricks of cocaine.

How may I help you, officer? Murder Black asked politely as he looked at the officer in the face.

Are you the driver of this vehicle? The officer asked with a firm tone in his voice, as if he was trying to intimidate Murder Black.

Yes officer, is there a problem? Murder Black asked as he kept his cool.

Yes, there is a problem. Can you read that sign over there? It says clear as day, no parking. The officer said, rudely.

Damn! That is my fault. I was so much in a hurry I missed that sign officer; I was not long. I came right back out. Murder Black said, trying to talk his way out of a ticket or anything else.

Yea, you are right, your fault. Now I will need to see some license and registration. I don't have all night either. The officer said rudely while looking at Murder Black directly in the eyes.

No problem… no problem. Murder Black said as he opened his driver side door and reached over in his glove compartment to retrieve his registration.

This is a mighty nice car, so you're the owner? The officer asked as he was looking over the car some more while waiting for Murder Black to give the information he asked for.

No, this car belongs to a family member and they let me drive it officer. Murder Black spat back as he handed the officer his license and registration because he knew where the officer was going with his question.

Okay, a family member, huh? Just wait right here, I'll be right back. The officer said sarcastically. Then he walked off towards his car.

CHAPTER 38

I will hold us down

Pulling up in front of Lartesha's apartment building, Carlos quickly blew the horn and stayed in the car because he did not feel like talking. He knew Lartesha would ask a million questions. So that was something Carlos refused to go through right now. He figured maybe Lartesha would get the point that he was in a rush and did not feel like being bothered. Unfortunately, when she walked up to the car with the bag in hand, she tried to open the passenger side door but Carlos quickly rolled the window down because he was trying to avoid the conversation, Lartesha was not trying to hear that at all.

Carlos, if you don't roll this damn window back up and open this damn door! Lartesha said.

Lartesha. Not right now. I have so much to do in so little of time. You are holding me up, just throw the bag in please. Carlos said.

Don't fucking please me! Open this damn door! I am coming with you. Marie called me Carlos; she was crying so when you said that you were on your way; I made my company leave so open the damn door! Lartesha yelled.

I don't want to talk about it. Carlos said, as he pushed the unlock button to let Lartesha in the car.

Oh well, whippy do! You do not want to talk about it, but guess what? I don't care, we will talk, Carlos! Lartesha spat back as she got in the car, slamming the door behind her.

Look Lartesha I've been through too much over the last couple of weeks and if she can't just trust me, I will not force her. I love her, but this is something I have to do. And I made my decision. Carlos said, as he was riding in and out of the city back streets.

But Carlos have you ever stopped to think about her feelings Carlos, that girl loves you and you have been together too long, you shouldn't act this way. Lartesha said.

Lartesha listen to you. Let me tell you something and I want you to listen. As soon as I get all emotional in this game that's when it gets the best of me! And believe me, I ain't come this far to let that happen. So, I will move with what's best for me and not get lazy; and know better. So that's the end of this conversation. Carlos said.

But Carlos... Lartesha said.

That's it, Lartesha. I do not want to hear no more about it!

When Carlos cut the conversation off Lartesha left it alone she knew Carlos had so much running through his mind. They rode in silence until they pulled up in front of Marie's apartment building, right behind his truck. When he threw the car in park Lartesha looked at him strange.

Come on, we're about to ride in your truck, I need to go to the hospital to see what Trick's condition is. Carlos said, as he was pushing the bag of money under the passenger seat like the note said.

What are you doing with that? Why are you putting it under there? I know you're not going to just leave all that money in this car, Carlos! Lartesha asked.

Lartesha you're starting to work my nerves you know, now come on and stop asking so many questions. Carlos said, as he dropped the key in the ashtray, then opened the door to get out.

Well, at least you could lock the doors. Lartesha said as she was getting out.

NO! Now come on! Carlos yelled.

Getting out the car Carlos looked up and down the street, but he saw no one, not even Vince who was sitting low in his car with his binoculars to his eyes watching Carlos and Lartesha's every move. They never even saw him following them because he stayed so far behind, but as Vince sat and watched, he said; to his self. Why are they changing cars? They then pulled off. He waited a few seconds, then he pulled off right behind, keeping his distance. Vince then turned off after seeing the direction they were going in. He had other plans.

Carlos we cannot see Trick, it is late, and they won't let us in the room, only visiting hours. Lartesha said.

I know all that Lartesha, but I still can see how his mother is doing and ask her about his condition. Carlos said, as he was unfastening his tie while he was driving.

Murder Black was trying to keep the young Spanish girl calm. She was acting very paranoid. He knew he didn't have any warrants, so he had nothing to worry about. Justin was paranoid, but he didn't show it because he kept all the way quiet, keeping his thoughts to himself. When the officer walked back up to the driver side window with the ticket in his hand, they felt at ease.

Next time I will have this car towed. Am I making myself clear? The officer said, as he was handing Murder Black his ticket with his license and registration.

Yes, understood officer. Murder Black spat back quickly, making the officer feel like he did something.

After receiving his ticket, Murder Black quickly threw his seatbelt on right in the office's presence just to play it safe. Justin didn't think to hesitate, he was putting his on right along with his cousin. The Officer gave Murder Black an evil grin, then walked off. When Murder Black pulled off, he knew he had to get to one destination and one destination only because running into the law again was out of the plan.

Aye yo baby girl, first thing tomorrow you'll be back on the bus unless you want to catch the taxi back to the bus station. This ride here is one way, and that goes for you also Justin in the morning. Murder Black said.

That's cool with me. I'm not trying to go home tonight, anyway. Justin spat back.

No....! Hey, I have to get back on the bus now! the young Spanish girl shouted.

Calm the fuck down! You'll get back on the damn bus but not right now because first thing is dropping my drugs off, everything else can wait. Murder Black said, as he was driving.

Walking into the hospital Carlos had chills running down his spine from just thinking about how he lost Jay in the same place not even a month ago and he was hoping Trick's condition changed for the better. As Carlos approached the nurses' desk with Lartesha by his side, he got the attention of the closet nurse available as possible because they all looked busy.

Excuse me, Ma'am. I'm looking for a patient by the last name Walker. Could you help me? Carlos asked.

Walker...... Walker.... mmm.... here we go. He's in room 205. His condition hasn't changed yet. Are you his immediate family because if not visiting hours are tomorrow in the morning? The Nurse asked, after looking up Trick's name for Carlos.

Okay, Ma'am but if it's possible I would like to speak with his mother if you could page her for me? Carlos said.

Yes, I'll do that, if you could just go in the waiting room and have a seat for me and give me a minute. The Nurse said as she picked the phone receiver up.

I told you we wouldn't be able to see him. Lartesha said while walking towards the waiting room.

Yeah, I knew they would not let us in, but I needed to see his mother to make sure she's doing okay. Carlos said.

While they were waiting for Tricks mother to come, Lartesha tried to spark a conversation up about Marie, but the way Carlos looked at her, she knew he didn't want to talk about that. Now and with the look, he also asked her a question that put her in a state of shock.

Why the hell do you keep insisting on questioning me about my damn relationship with Marie? You are not a damn marriage counselor, or are you? Carlos asked.

Lartesha was so shocked Carlos spoke to her like that. She was just sitting there with a stupefied look on her face. Wondering why he would say such a thing to me like that. But Lartesha quickly did what she welled and didn't hold back on her word.

Carlos! Wait one minute, I will not make no scene in this hospital, but don't you aggressively talk to me like that ever again. You aren't the only one that's going through something! Lartesha spat back.

I'm not trying to hear that shit! Stay out of my relationship then! Carlos spat back aggressively.

Before Carlos could say his last words, Ms. Walker appeared in the doorway looking like she was up for nights and like she hasn't been getting the proper rest. After Carlos saw her enter the room, he immediately got to his feet, and he was feeling every bit of the pain and grief that she was going through. Because he has been going through the same thing. What stopped Carlos in his tracks as he was approaching her was the smile that appeared on her face. It confused Carlos. He didn't know if she was hiding the pain and sorrow behind that smile; so, he stood patiently preparing himself for whatever.

Carlos… Carlos, he will make it. Ms. Walker said, as she was walking towards him with a smile on her face and tears coming down her cheeks.

Ms. Walker, I don't understand what do you mean by that? Did he wake up from out of the coma? Carlos asked with a hesitant look on his face.

Yes, baby! He opened his eyes. And he will be all right. The doctor said it before I came down here because there up in the room right now. Ms. Walker said, with a sign of relief in her voice.

CHAPTER 39

Time to recruit

Vince got his night started off in front of a group of seven detectives in a small room in the downtown police station, with pictures of Carlos and his friends on a bored, as Vince filled the detectives in on his investigation he's been running for these last past year's, he spoke with pride being that he was on the inside of the case and had some real good information on a dangerous crew to send them away for a long time, while Vince filled his team of detectives in he gave a brief description of each member of the crew, until he came to Lartesha picture and that's when he put the twist in the story do to the feeling he held for her.

Do you see this young lady here! I want to make myself clear; you are not to do any surveillance on her, and she meets with me and me, only this is my C.I. okay! Vince shouted this with an emphasis on his words, as he pointed to the picture.

Vince continue to speak on about Carlos and his crew, to his team of detectives as they listen carefully and analyzed the pictures in front of them making their own examination in their minds, it was this one detective who had only been on the team for only one year and a half as he looked at the pictures the faces became more and more familiar to him from his days in the blue and white, when he was on the beat in the streets chasing young hoodlums, he said to himself I ran up on that guy on many of occasion while he was staring at the pictures he saw underneath that it said deceased that just made him raise his hand.

Excuse me, sir! Detective Vince, I just had to ask, but are these guys part of that car crash from the police chase a while back? Detective David asked with a curious look on his face.

Yes, detective these are the guys who put our officer life in jeopardy on that car chase, I was the one who called it in and witness the shooting, so we have them on a few charges as of now but not enough yet. Detective Vince replied.

I'm sorry detective Vince, But I must ask, what more could we have on them? You've been on this investigation for a few years' now! Detective David said with a frown on his face.

Detective David just opened the door for the rest of the detectives in the room to ask a question. And detective Vince answered them as they came but didn't want to talk anymore about his confidential informant, which didn't last long because detective Natalie insisted on knowing more about Lartesha.

Excuse me, detective Vince, but I have to ask how old is this young lady among the group? Detective Natalie asked as she stared at Lartesha picture.

To answer your question detective she's 24years old, I am wrapping it up with questions for now; I have a package for each of you to take as you leave out and it show what partner you would be with and the suspect you would do surveillance on and the days we meet, now let's get back to work and get these criminals off the streets.

Detective Natalie felt that Vince was brushing her off, so as everyone was leaving the room she waited and approached Vince to ask him some more about the young lady in the group.

If there's anything you need to know about this, it's right there in that pack detective, I am press for time; I have another meeting to attend, and we will talk another day about this. Vince said with a firm voice and grabbed his belongings, then walked off.

Detective Natalie was in disbelief the way Vince spoke to her and walk off she stood there for a minute infuriated and as she stormed through the pages of the package of information on the crew, there was more information on the guys and hardly anything on the young lady of the group which didn't sit right with detective Natalie.

CHAPTER 40

Guilt and relief

The weather was cool; the sky was dark, and the moon was bright. As he was leaving the hospital Carlos had so much on his mind. While driving home, he was hoping Marie was asleep, because their last encounter wasn't the best and he didn't want to argue. After hearing that, Trick came out of his coma; he felt guilt and relief, because he got them in this situation, so he had to be the one to get them out. While he drove through the city streets, Carlos had a lot weighing on his mind. He pulled up in front of his apartment building and parked. Carlos sat in the car for a few minutes, trying to let go of the frustration he felt towards Marie for not listing to him. After he felt calm enough, he got out the car and went into the building, opened the apartment door and found Marie sound asleep. She wore white sheer boy shorts with her half-cut t-shirt, that read (MY HEART IS YOURS), showing her beautiful skin tone that Carlos loved to touch. Carlos took in his woman's beauty as he took off his clothes and lay next to her. He put one arm around her, and he fell asleep. While asleep throughout the night, nightmares dreams would come to Carlos, in a horrifying way.

No…. No…. No… were the sounds coming from Carlos as he laid next to Marie.

Marie woke up startled, as she turned over to see if Carlos was all right. The sight of Carlos in so much sweat made Marie shake him, waking him up out of the bad dream he was having.

Carlos…. Carlos…. Marie yelled as she was shaking him.

What…. What…. Carlos screamed as he woke up. You were having a bad dream, and you are sweating, are you all right? Marie asked as she was sitting up, looking down on Carlos as he laid there.

Yes, Marie, I'm good, it's just so much has happened, and I go to sleep with a lot on my mind. Carlos said as he laid there.

Carlos, I know we went through something last night, but I love you and no matter what we go through, I'm here for you. Marie said as she laid her head on his chest.

Marie, I love you too, very much it's just I really need you to trust in me, please. Carlos said with a sleepy voice.

Carlos, I trust you, let's just say I'm a woman and I have a voice in this relationship. Marie spat back as she looked him in the face.

Yes, that is true Mami you have a voice, I'm not trying to take that from you, when it comes down to me taking care of you that's what I will do, because I love you and I know how dangerous things could get, when you're in the streets. Carlos said as he looked Marie back in the eyes.

But Carlos! This is my uncle we are talking about, and he cares too much about me. Marie spat back in her pledging tone of voice.

Marie let's get this straight, what makes you or me safe in this life of ours or should I say mine, because I brought you into this life of no way out or should I say dead end cause this is what it is. Carlos spat back as he laid there holding the pain in.

Seeing the pain in Carlos eyes Marie moved closer to him, because dealing with the loss of his friend she knew that it was very hard for him, and she felt every bit of that pain because, it's something she went through with her brother, when he passed, so as Marie moved closer to Carlos she pressed her body up against his and looked him in the eyes just to let him know and see that she was feeling every bit of his pain and she was with him 100%.

Marie…. Through all this I have to remain strong, it's just that I brought them in this and I have to wear that on my shoulder now, when I look in Jay's Mother eyes it hurts cause all I can think is only if I just let that nigga have it right where I seen, him then this would have never happened. Carlos said.

Carlos I know if you knew what the outcome would have been, you wouldn't have done it that way, but you did it Carlos and you cannot take that back, that's what's bothering you, that same thought hit me every time I think about my brother… and… and… I just wish. Marie said as the tears fell from her eyes and she stutter with the words she spoke.

As Marie spoke her last words Carlos put one finger to her mouth to quiet her, he then held her in silence because he knew how emotional his women could get when thinking about her brother, so as Carlos laid there looking at his queen, he knew he had to remain focus because he knew that emotion could rock a man to sleep, and cause him to lose everything including his life and the people around him so that was something he refuse to let happen because the pain that he felt he knew he couldn't see himself going through it again for him not doing it himself like Marie said, so as the pain set in and the mission became clear he assured his queen that everything was under control with a firm grip and a straight stare in the eyes.

Marie there isn't a day that will go by, that I will not mourn and hurt for what has happen to my friends, I know you feel the same way about your brother, when he passed away and that wound gets reopened every time a death is in the air. Carlos said to Marie in a soft tone of voice as he stared her in the face.

Carlos, it's just…. When you hurt, I hurt…. I just want you to be smarter about your decisions, think things out first Carlos. Marie said as she took breaths in between her words.

Your right, Marie…. You're right! Carlos said as he was looking Marie in her face.

As the conversation went, the sleep came, and the sun rose, but the dreams never stop for Carlos as he tossed and turned, faces came in a clear vision like something of a reality check, as Carlos dream went on he saw himself being chased by guys with hoodie on, as he ran for his life in his dream he became exhausted from running and stopped to make out the faces, but as he looked he couldn't make out the weapons, they had in hand until they got closer… closer and closer that's when the dude put the gun to Carlos; he woke up screaming.

NO… NO…! Carlos yelled as he jumped up.

Jumping out of his dream in a screaming state caused Marie to stop doing what she was doing in her kitchen and quickly walk in the bedroom, to where Carlos was at just sitting up shaking his head in disbelief of how he was taking everything and not being able to sleep.

Carlos is everything all right? Marie asked as she hurried in the room.

As Marie sat next to Carlos and looked him in the face with so much concern, she could only imagine the pain he was going through, she sat there on the edge of the bed rubbing his back in silence.

Marie, I just must do this one run, I'm done with this because it's too much that comes with this street shit and it's affecting me. Carlos said as his head rested in his hands while he spoke.

Yes… yes Carlos, I agree with you. Marie spat back as she continues to rub his back.

CHAPTER 41

Making critical decisions

As Murder Black laid on his stern foster mattress, with his polo pajamas on that made him feel relaxed, he couldn't help but think about the PCP he brought and who it was for, He held it in the air with his right hand only imagining the fun that awaited, but he also knew that real business had to be taking care of and with that thought so many other things crossed his mind like, Mike with the connect, Justin and his situation which he knew would not be good if anyone got wind of him making moves with him, Murder black laid in the bed just weighting his option, while Justin laid on his couch with his phone off in a deep sleep away from worry until he woke up to reality which was awaiting him, Murder Black rolled out the bed and headed toward his dresser to get his phone now that he had his package, he knew he had to make his customers aware, being that he didn't have any drugs for some weeks. His phone had messages backed up; Murder Black turned it back on to scroll through it as he headed towards his living room where Justin laid sound asleep.

YO… JUSTIN… YO… Murder Black yelled as he continues to scroll through his phone.

Huh…. huh… huh…. Justin said as he woke up wiping the sleep out of his eyes.

Yo fam… it's time to make it home, don't you think? Murder Black asked as he was looking at his phone and back at Justin.

Well, damn fam, I got to knock this package off first and I can't take it home. Justin said as he was getting up from where he laid.

Hold on now! Let me run something by you. When you got in these streets, living with me was not in your plans or hiding out either. Also, I hope you're not trying to play this game full time because I can't hold your hand. Murder Black said with a firm look and his hands waving with the phone.

Fam… fam… Calm down… I just wanted to flip this and then I would chill and then go home, I just thought maybe you could help me knock some of this shit off. Justin said as he held his hands in his defense.

Listen, Justin… You need to go home and check in with your mother before she has Carlos out here looking for you, you will not be with me. Murder Black spat with his voice getting a little louder and firmer.

All right… You right, I'll do that and then I'll come back out tonight and call you, but can I leave my package here? Justin asked, referring to his drugs as he agreed with Murder Black.

While Murder Black stood in front of Justin, scrolling and texting on his phone, Justin sat back on the couch thinking with his head back staring at the ceiling which made Murder Black walk off towards his room.

Yo I'll be ready in a minute, I'm about to jump in this shower and make a few calls after so make sure you're ready. Murder Black spat as he walked away from Justin.

Justin didn't respond because he was mad and he knew Murder Black was right he just didn't want to admit it, so while sitting and thinking he said to himself shit I can't fuck with J-Love anymore being that he don't like my cousin and no telling what he did to get out of jail then he thought well maybe my mother won't take it so hard and just punish me for a few weeks until I get my grades up in school, she not home half the time anyway, but what if she already spoke with Carlos he said to himself?

Oh, yeah... You might as well cut that phone back on. Murder Black yelled from the bathroom with a smile.

Man, mind your business! Justin spat back as he sat on the couch with his phone in hand.

CHAPTER 42

Still not feeling the vibes

Starting her morning off was not like any other morning. Veronica couldn't let go of the way Lartesha felt about Vince, her gut feeling about Vince didn't sit right, as she got herself together this morning, there was nobody other than her friend on her mind, the thought of her hitting the ground that night at the bar made a tear come down her cheek as she thought about it while looking in the mirror, brushing her teeth Veronica said to herself why... why, would you do this why... why? she then stopped brushing and started staring in the mirror for a moment, then her phone rang, bringing her back to reality as she went to wash her mouth out. Her phone continues ringing. She stopped what she was doing to hurry to the phone.

Ring... Ring... Ring.

Rushing out her bathroom into her bedroom, towards her dresser where her phone laid ringing and vibrating with her favorite ring tone song by Keyshia Cole every time this song played during her hard times it would bring back memories of her past with Tyron her ex-boyfriend, who she never stopped loving, but his street ways had a bad effected on her, she felt that she had to have his back during him doing wrong which on two occasion almost cost her life, as she missed the call she held the phone, while standing there looking in her dresser mirror, reflecting on the past, she thought of that moment when he sent her to answer the door, because he was too busy counting his money in the other room, as she screamed out who is it while approaching the door it flew open with a powerful force sending her to the ground screaming, as she looked up it was four men in mask one with his gun in her face telling her to get up, thinking about how foolish she was for Tyron she still had feeling for him, Veronica knew he would not change and after her second encounter was with the police she had, enough so she left Tyron, which he ended up going to jail for 5 to10 in state prison, but thinking about that raid and her whole life experience had her on point this time around, cause so much chaos that has happen in her life, now she feel bad that her friend has choosing to live that same dangerous life and bring her back into it, which the person who Lartesha was seeing didn't sit right, with Veronica at all, Veronica walked away from her dresser towards her closet to find something to put on when her phone went off again.

Ring… Ring… Ring

Hello…… Veronica answered.

Hey girl! How are you doing on this beautiful morning? Kim asked, sounding excited.

I'm okay just a little down over here, thinking about my life and all that I've been through, even with Tyron and trying to get dressed at the same time. Veronica said as she was pulling her polo shirt out with a pair of Levi's jeans.

Girl… I know you aren't thinking about his no-good ass, shit you left him for about two year's now girl… You need to get a grip and put that loser behind you. Kim spat back as she frowned her face with every word.

It doesn't just stop at Tyron, Kim, It's more to it that's just a wound that has opened back up from something else girl, what are you doing later on today maybe we could get up and talk cause I haven't seen you in a month or two? Veronica asked as she walked back into her bathroom to run her shower water.

That sound great call me girl; I'm here for you any time. Kim spat back as she was hanging the phone up.

Okay will do… love you Kim. Veronica said hanging the phone up.

Love you too. Kim spat back quick.

Veronica got in the shower and let the water run over her body until she felt relaxed, she enjoyed the conversation she had with her friend Kim, when they had the chance to speak, Veronica and Kim has been friends ever since high school coming up they both lived on the east side of town, only around the corner from each other, growing older and going in different direction was the hand that life dealt so Veronica sat under the water and collected her thoughts on how her life would have been, if she took the same path as Kim going to college and achieving a career in the business field, she thought would I have met Tyron which she didn't have any regrets behind her past, Veronica always have considered herself as a strong woman and was happy to hear from Kim she couldn't wait to meet with her because Kim was a stress reliever, also she was a very exciting person, out spoking and fun to be around during hard times, Veronica never held back when it came time to talk face to face with her, Kim was the person who would help Veronica when she was going through it with Tyron, getting out the shower Veronica had a great idea come to mind she wrapped the towel around her and said I could meet Kim at the library she wanted to look Tyron jail address up to send him a card. Also, Vince came to mind as she smirked to herself, then she headed out the bathroom with that thought in mind as she got dressed.

CHAPTER 43

The drop off

Thinking about his dreams and seeing what comes from this street life, Carlos knew that he didn't want to make this a lifetime thing, as he ponders on the thought he couldn't understand how his uncle could keep going back and forth to jail for this life, so as Carlos was getting out the shower to start his day, he started thinking about how Victor would handle the move; he hoped that he didn't tear the car up being that it was a rental, and it was in Marie's name. While he was thinking this, he could hear the phone ringing and Marie answering it.

CARLOS! THE PHONE! Marie yelled out.

WHO IS IT! I'M GETTING OUT THE SHOWER! Carlos yelled back.

ITS BOBBY... HE SAID CALL HIM!!!! WHEN YOU GET OUT ITS IMPORTANT! Marie yelled back as she was hanging the receiver up.

OKAY MARIE THANK YOU! Carlos yelled back

As Carlos walked out the bathroom he thought to himself, damn another one of these young boys from off the east side did something to one of my cars again, then he picked the phone up off the bed were his outfit laid, dialing Bobby number expecting to hear the worst.

Ring.... Ring.... Ring.... Carlos held the phone as it was ringing.

Hello! Hello! Bobby answered with a stutter.

Bobby, it's me! Carlos, what's going on? Carlos asked as he sat on the edge of his bed.

Carlos! Carlos! These Spanish guys came by here with a tow truck and drop that rental car off you was driving, I tried to get his name, but he told me no... Speak no English! I just took the key. Bobby said as he walked back and forth in the shop office.

Okay, Bobby.... Okay.... Just pull it in and I'll be there in a minute, listen, do not touch it. Carlos said as he shook his head in disbelief.

Carlos sat on the edge of the bed as he hung the phone up with Bobby, just trying to figure Victor out he said to himself how did he know about the shop then he called Marie in the room, but he held back with everything he had in him, he knew that he has taking Marie through enough and he asked her for this, Carlos felt that any problem was his from here on and it was time to man up and stop pointing the finger at the people who he had on his side, he got dressed and called Rell, Rock, Black and Lartesha to ask them to meet him at the shop later on today he knew the move was ready. He wanted to let everyone know how things would get moved.

Ring.... Ring.... Ring. Carlos held the phone receiver as it rung.

Hello! Rell answered with a loud enraged tone of voice.

Yo! You all right, damn you mad loud my dude, what's good with you? Carlos asked with concern look on his face.

Man! I know you hear this bitch in the background. Rell said, referring to his girlfriend.

Ha... ha... ha... When isn't, she not tripping? But anyway, yo meet me at the shop in a few hours okay; I need to fill you in on something. Carlos said as he laughed a little, then shook his head.

I got you… shut up bitch can't you see I'm on the phone, yo Los I will be there if I don't go to jail for fucking this chick up. Rell said as he yelled at Kelly while talking to Carlos.

After hanging the phone up with Rell, Carlos shook his head because he couldn't see what Rell saw in Kelly, and that he couldn't stand her ass, for his own reason which Rell had already known and as Carlos got dress and thought about the time when Jay had told him about what he said to Rell, while they was riding Carlos couldn't hold back the smile, with that thought in mind he finished up what he was doing and headed into the living room, where Marie sat on the couch eating her meal she had prepared for him and her.

Hey Carlos… I was thinking maybe I could go register for school just for something to do, because I'm bored. Marie said as she was looking over her shoulder because she heard him coming towards her from out of the room.

Marie, you want to go to school, that's great, so what are you going to major in? Carlos asked as he leaned over her shoulder and kissed her on the cheek.

I plan to major in law Carlos, but enough about me. How are you feeling this morning, being that last night was awfully hard for you? Marie asked out of concern for her man.

Marie, I'm okay… but not to change the subject, but that's a great major, now for what I'm dealing with I'm okay, I will stay strong you know. Carlos spat back as he sat down in his recliner chair.

As Carlos said that he laid his head back and closed his eyes, because he knew and Marie knew that he had a lot on his shoulder, so while he sat there collecting his thoughts, Marie looked at him and back at the T.V. until she said to herself let me make my baby his plate, as she got up to go in the kitchen she leaned over him and kissed him on the forehead.

Carlos everything will be okay, I love you. Marie said as she walked in the kitchen.

Carlos took those words in without responding. As he focused on his day to come, his phone started to vibrant.

Hello! Hello! Carlos answered.

Morning! Carlos! Lartesha said in a low tone of voice.

Oh, hey Lartesha morning to you also, I was about to call you anyway, how are you doing? Carlos asked as he talked with his eyes close, laid back still.

I'm hanging in there Carlos, I was calling you cause, I'm about to head up to the hospital to see Trick, being that he is out the coma and no telling when the police will pull that same shit, they did with Young Chris. Lartesha said as you could hear the grief in her voice.

You right...... Yup you sure is right, okay I will meet you up there, I will be on my way, see you there and then I will tell you, what I had to tell you at the hospital, I'm about to be on my way. Carlos said as he was getting up.

Okay, Carlos, see you there. Lartesha said as she was about to hang the phone up.

Hey! Hey! Lartesha, can you call Rell back? I just spoke with him and I told him something different. Carlos said before hanging up.

Okay, Carlos, I got you. Lartesha spat back.

After hanging the phone up with Lartesha, Carlos quickly called Black and gave him the rundown, as he was hanging up, Marie was coming in with his plate, but as Carlos was thinking about Trick, Carlos wasn't in the mood for any food but not to make Marie mad he took the plate and got up from his seat ate it as he walked back in the kitchen.

CHAPTER 44

When it hurts

As Young Chris sat in the jail cell staring at the stained and smelly walls, while laying on a plastic mattress that didn't make his pain feel any better as the medication slowly became weaker reality quickly set in, as he thought about the small amount of food left in his house, he couldn't help but feel bad about his action and think about his little sister who was only 7 yrs. Old with no one to care for her, with those thoughts in Young Chris mind he couldn't wait to use the phone to call his aunt, he knew his mother and father followed each other everywhere whether it was to find something to steal or find someone to get them that next crack rock not caring about their baby who sat at home hungry and tired, crying herself to sleep wondering when and where was her brother her pride and joy going to walk through the door with their meal for the night, as she waited for him, Young Chris waited for the phone continually repeating the words he never thought he would ever speak, he spoke.

Please, Lord…. Please, Lord…… Please Lord let my baby sister be safe. Young Chris said to himself as he waited in his jail cell.

As Young Chris was laying there patiently, the flashbacks of the accident came to, which put him in the position he was in. It came clearer and clearer as he thought about it; the thoughts brought his boy Jay to mind which made him more infuriated, Jay was somebody who Young Chris looked up to and trusted in the neighborhood, being that he didn't even trust his own parents, and knowing that Jay didn't survive the car crash and not being able to attend the funeral really had him mad, but with them thoughts in mind Young Chris slowly got up and walked to the door of his jail cell, while doing that he saw lights coming on one by one.

Click... Click.... Click.

When the doors opened Young Chris stood there not knowing what the noise was, while standing at his door he could see a few guys rushing out their doors to get to the phone, when he gave his door a slight push to see, the door went open Young Chris walked out his cell slowly, under his condition he didn't want to run into someone he didn't like from the streets, he knew he wasn't in any shape to be fighting making his way towards the phones; he heard someone shouting his name.

YO! CHRIS! YO! CHRIS.... Oh, shit damn man what the hell your wild ass done got into? Damn, son! You real banged up. Rick said as he was walking over to Young Chris.

Yeah, Rick I'm a little fucked up word son, I was in a car chase, but we crashed. Young Chris said as he was looking back and forth at the phone line and Rick.

As Young Chris was talking and watching his surrounding, he heard someone else yell out his last name from a far, turning his head towards the voice he could see it was the correctional officer at the desk.

Mr. Robinson! Mr. Robinson! Mr. Robinson! The correctional officer shouted as he sat behind his desk.

Yo Chris that C.O. is calling you, shit you probably made bail, yo go see what he wants I'll hold your spot for the phone. Rick said as he looked at the people waiting for the phone too.

Yo, good looking, Rick. Young Chris spat back as he walked off.

Walking toward the desk Young Chris had so many thoughts going through his head, but the most important thought was for him to get in contact with his aunt, so she could go get his little sister, Young Chris also knew that they weren't giving him any bail because the lawyer Carlos set him up with already told him, but he also told him he would do everything he could to get him another bail hearing, so as Young Chris slowly made his way towards the desk as nervousness set in.

Mr. Robinson, I have a package that came for you, if you would please sign right here. The Officer asks as he handed Young Chris his bag and a pen and paper to sign.

While Young Chris was signing the paper the C.O. was Yelling chew time, so Young Chris grabbed his package and headed towards his room, to put his package up because he wanted to make his phone call with a few funny stares he kept it moving, the only thing was on his mind was the phone, he didn't have a taste for any food.

YO... CHRIS HURRY YOUR ASS UP! I'm trying to eat. Rick yelled out as he was holding the phone receiver.

Coming out the cell making his way towards the phone that Rick was holding Young Chris was feeling the pain with every step he took and he knew the medication was wearing off, but the thought of his little sister helped him bear everything and getting in contact with his aunt was his every hope.

Good looking, Rick. Young Chris said as he walked up and grabbed the phone receiver as he held the pain.

Yo, no problem.... Yo, you not going to eat? Rick asked as he was walking away to go get his tray of food.

Nah! I'm good for right now. Young Chris spat back as he was dialing numbers on the phone.

Yo yell out to this C.O. that I could have your tray homie word. Rick said as he was back peddling toward where the food was being server.

HEY C.O.! HE COULD HAVE MY TRAY. Young Chris yelled out.

GOOD LOOKING CHRIS!!!! Rick yelled back with a smile on his face as he took the tray of extra of food.

Letting the phone ring Young Chris was getting restless because he knew his aunt was home and he also knew that it was a little early in the morning so after a few more rings the answer machine picked up, but do to Young Chris tenacious personality he tried to call once again.

Ring…. Ring…. Ring.

Hello! Hello! Mary answered.

You have a collect call… from Chris; the operator said.

Answering the phone, Mary had a bewildered expression on her face from hearing her nephew's name as the operator spoke.

If you accept press five, if you wish to block this caller from calling press…

The operator didn't get the chance to finish speaking because Mary was pressing five unpleasantly.

Hello! Hello! Auntie! Auntie! I'm so sorry for calling you like this, but Destiny is home alone, and you already know how your sister is. Young Chris said as he held the phone tight to his ear.

Yes… I hear you, and I feel sorry for the both of you, now you're in jail and your sister need you the most, Chris, I have read the newspaper boy and I am not proud of your action. Mary said as she was shaking her head with every word she spoke.

TWO MINUTES TO LOCK IN! The correctional Officer shouted.

After hearing the disappointment in his aunt voice, Young Chris stood there holding the phone lost for words, because he felt every bit of the pain from his action, also he knew that he was facing a lot of time, when the correctional officer yelled locked down in two minutes that brought Young Chris back to his surroundings.

Auntie! Auntie! I know you are extremely disappointed in me and I'm very sorry; I have to go lock in, if you don't mine, I will call back? Young Chris asked as he was looking around and watching other inmates walk to their cells.

Yes, I want you to call me back, but you will not run my bill up, do you hear me, you will not run my damn phone bill up, damn it. Mary spat back as she put emphasis on her words.

Yes! Yes! Young Chris said he was hanging up the phone.

CHAPTER 45

When a mother hurt

Ms. Johnson stared out her kitchen window, as the water ran in the bucket in her sink, the fresh smell of pine sol filled the room along with her music by Luther Vandross, with her day off from work she felt that a clean house would relax her, but with so many other things on her mind she wanted to stay busy, breaking her stare and making her way towards the sink, she said to herself why in the hell isn't Justin answering his phone, as Ms. Johnson stood at the sink she thought about her past up bringing, just being in the house with her brother and sisters had her thinking as she walked away from the sink with the words in her head that her mother use to always say never live to get old, live your life put a smile on her face, the signs Justin was showing made Ms. Johnson reflected as she continued picking up her house she said to herself first the damn skipping school, then the coming home late then she shook her head and headed towards the phone with them thoughts on her mind then she started thinking about Carlos and the things he's going through in the streets with his friends dying and the money he's been giving her, she didn't want to tell him no because she knew she needed it but now with the thought of him being in the streets made her nervous and Ms. Johnson knew money couldn't bring her son back, she held the phone receiver as she thought about her brother who stayed in and out of jail for drug-related charges which brought a tear to her eye because she didn't want that for her kids, so as she sat there with the receiver in hand her phone beginning ring.

Ring…. Ring… Ring.

Ms. Johnson looked at the phone very puzzled before answering it, because there was no number on her caller I.D. it had said unknown, so when she picked up, she did it real slow.

Hello! Ms. Johnson answered with low and hesitant tone of voice.

This is the operator with a collected call from Larry at a state correctional facility press five if you accept...

After hearing her brother's name, Ms. Johnson never gave the operator a chance to finish another word. She presses five quickly.

Larry! Larry! Oh, my lord Larry. Ms. Johnson shouted through the receiver in excitement.

Hey sis! Yes, it's me how have you and the boys been, I know it's been too long. Larry said as he held the phone while feeling the emotions from his sister's voice.

Larry, you just don't know how happy I am to hear your voice; I've written you never wrote back. Ms. Johnson said.

As Ms. Johnson was speaking her brother quickly cut her off.

Hold on! Hold on! Sis I understand but I don't have long, I don't really write letter's please understand me my time is short on this phone I love you very much Sis did Carlos tell you I called? Larry asked as he looked around while he held the phone to make sure no one was close to him.

After Larry mentioned the phone call, he made when he first went to jail Ms. Johnson stood up with a puzzled look on her face as she was holding the receiver to her ear, not wanting her brother worrying she quickly answered him.

Yes!… Yes! Larry, he told me you called. Ms. Johnson replied with a perplexed look on her face.

Okay that's great, so are the boys doing the right thing out there I was reading the newspaper and I see a lot of things are happening in the streets. Larry said.

They are driving me crazy right now Justin is skipping school and lord knowns what Carlos is into he moved out, his friend passed away the other one badly injured all in some damn car chase with the police these streets are taking my baby's. Ms. Johnson said as she was shaking her head with every word.

As Larry held the receiver, he was feeling every bit of the pain in his sister's voice; he didn't intend on calling and receiving bad news, but he knew what a mother could go through with two boys who didn't listen.

So, sis, I didn't mean to cut you off again. Damn, I didn't know that was his friends. Okay, now I see what's going on out there. Larry spat back with sympathy in his voice.

Yes, Larry! Yes! But I need you to stay positive and don't worry about this out here you come too far, remain strong I got this out here this is your sister. Ms. Johnson spat back as she felt confident for her brother.

I know your strong sis! I know! I have my release coming soon, so you remain strong and tell my nephews I love them, sis, I have to get off this phone, but I will call again, I love you sis. Larry said as he kept the strength in his voice.

I love you to Larry! I love you too. Ms. Johnson said as she was hanging the phone up.

Getting off the phone with her brother had Ms. Johnson inferior do to her brother situation and because her own son didn't tell her he was in jail, her neighbor Brenda down the street had to tell her Ms. Johnson felt she had a very close relationship with Carlos, as she sat in her living room with so many thoughts in her mind Ms. Johnson was, disappointed in herself as the self-pity set in her mind she being questioning her motherhood saying to herself I do everything that a mother does... I do everything... I bust my ass as Ms. Johnson was saying this to herself, then a curious thought came to mind that made her get up and walk over to the spot she knew her brother would hide thing only to find it empty which was strange to her. Ms. Johnson shut the closet door, went back into her living room and sat down with a puzzling look on her face. She reached over and picked the phone up to call Justin again as Ms. Johnson dialed Justin's number again; the worry set in as she asks God to keep her boys safe where ever they were; she wanted to hear his voice, but as Ms. Johnson held the receiver to her ear, all she continued got was a ring than Justin's voice mail came on, and the sound of his voice touched her heart.

Ring! ... Ring! ... Ring.

Hello! Hello! Well, if you will not talk, I'm hanging up just playing leave your name at the beep. Justin's voice mail picked up.

Holding the receiver and hearing Justin voice had Ms. Johnson nervous and tormented with a tremble in her hand as she was about to hang the receiver back up then she called Carlos instead because she needed him to go find Justin and she also wanted to know why he never told her that her brother called when he first went to jail.

Ring! Ring.

Hello! Carlos answered.

Hello! Carlos this is your mother I'm losing my mind over here because your brother is not answering his phone, I've been sitting here worried bad about the both of you. Ms. Johnson screamed as she walked back and forth.

Mom! Mom! Calm down please I will find him and don't worry about me, I'm doing fine. Carlos spat back as he was getting in his car.

Oh, and we need to talk, I spoke with your uncle this morning he called me for the first time in three and a half years and I've always told you to hold nothing back from me. Ms. Johnson said with so much stress in her voice.

Holding the phone to his ear and putting the key in the ignition with his right hand as he heard his mother last words he quickly stopped what he was doing and looked out his car window with a frown on his face as if a sharp pain was in his stomach.

So, what did Uncle Larry say? Carlos asked as he sat staring out the car window.

Just come by and we will sit down and talk about that but until then baby please find your brother for me! Please! Carlos. Ms. Johnson spat back as the tears fell with the breaking of her voice.

Okay!!!! Okay!!!! Mom stop crying please I will get on that right now. Carlos spat back as he gripped the steering wheel as his angry boiled.

CHAPTER 46

Who is being watch

Getting off the phone with his mother had Carlos caught up in a daze. Trying to imagine the conversation his mother and uncle had. Not to mention, he was also angry with his little brother. So, as he sat reclined back in his seat deep in thought, he spoke the words of his uncle to himself look at your little brother. He will follow your lead. This street shit is a never-ending cycle as Carlos spoke and imitated the words of his uncle. He shook his head at those thoughts as he started the car up. His uncle was right, and he knew it, but he was hardheaded to the facts. Not looking in his rearview mirror or staying focus on what lied ahead of him, Carlos pulled off. Not noticing the two cars that pulled off along with him, as he drove, he said to himself when I find Justin little ass, he will get it. Then his phone rung.

Ring… Ring… Ring.

Hello! Hello! Carlos answered as he kept his eyes on the road.

Carlos! Carlos! They said, Trick can't have visitor's, I've been up here going off on the receptionist, this is crazy. Lartesha said, as she paced back and forth outside of the hospital.

What? Calm down! Calm down! What the hell is going on? Carlos asked as he slowed down for a red light.

Well; I just got here, and she will not let me in, nor will she tell me why. Lartesha spat back as she titled her head back and the sighed her last words.

SSSSSSSSSccccccuuuuuuuurrrrrtttttttt... Boom! Boom!

Oh shit; Tesha let me call you right back! Carlos shouted as he looked in his rearview mirror.

Quickly hanging up the phone, Carlos got out the car to witness a three-car accident. The first vehicle was just inches away from his bumper. As he stood there looking, he could see the second car had two angry men jumping out of their car waving their badges and screaming. That made Carlos walk back to his car. Unaware of who was in the third car; that caused the accident. Carlos quickly turned around and got in his car. He didn't want no dealing with the law. The light turned green, and he pulled off, looking in his rearview mirror. While looking in the rearview mirror Carlos noticed the police pulling a Spanish-looking gentleman out of the third car, Carlos picked his phone back up to call Lartesha.

YO! Oh, shit, you wouldn't believe what just happens! Carlos shouted through the phone hyped like he had an adrenaline rush for the sight of the police as he drove.

What Carlos? What? Lartesha spat back as she was walking back to her truck.

Tesha YO! This damn car was just inches from hitting me. It was a three-car pile-up; the one behind me just missed me and the second one had two police in the car word! As I pulled off, I saw the police pulling a Spanish-looking dude out of the third car word!! Do you hear me? Carlos spat back as he was still hyped about what just happen.

Damn that shit sound crazy!!! Lartesha said sounding depressed as she got in her truck.

Yo Tesha, I'm headed to the shop and I want everyone to meet me there. We will find out what's going on at the hospital later. So, hit them dudes up for me and let them know. Oh, tell them I have a A.P.B. out on my little brother so if you know or hear anything let me know. Carlos spat back as he drove.

Carlos drove with so many thoughts in his mind, keeping his eyes on the road and not the people he passed. He was so overwhelmed with everything; this was something he vowed to not let happen. Losing focus because of the adversity and pain that he knew came with this lifestyle. So, while in his thoughts and emotions, Carlos looked in his rearview mirror. He wanted to step on the brakes and make a u turn in the middle of the street. Instead, he said to himself in due time, in due time as he shook his head with every word watching the BMW vanish in his rearview mirror, Carlos would continue to look in his rearview mirror from time to time. As he pulled up in the shop's parking lot, Bobby was outside.

Bobby, what's up, man? Carlos shouted as he got out the car.

Hey Los, you already know! Same shit different day, just trying to get these cars cleaned up. Bobby said as he stood up with a towel in his hand, he was using to wipe the car with.

The passion Bobby had for the shop and working on cars come from years of experience. Whatever it was, in dealing with a car Carlos knew Bobby had the touch for it. Being at the shop alone was more the better for him because he felt that he got a lot done with no one in his way. Bobby was also a person who Carlos would get a lot of advice from. So, as they walked making their way into the shop, they never noticed the black tinted out Lincoln MKS pulled over watching them from down the street.

So damn Bobby, the dude didn't give you no note or nothing, Carlos asked as they stood looking at the car

Carlos I'm telling you! He told me no English and gave me the key. Bobby said imitating the Spanish guy as he was going in his pocket to remove the key.

Ha... ha... ha... ha! Damn, that's crazy word; I see you changed this place up a little to Bobby. Carlos said as he was making his way around the shop.

Yeah, I had to! Oh, and you see that sign right there that goes for those damn cell phones. Bobby spat back as he was pointing to his sign. He put up that read NO CELL PHONES ALLOWED IN THIS SHOP THANK YOU!

Bobby didn't like cell phones, he became annoyed when he was talking to customers and they were on the phone; he preferred them off before entering.

Ha... ha... ha... ha! Yeah, that's what's up Bobby I like that. Carlos said as he laughed while turning his phone off.

Carlos also knew Bobby was schooling him on the low, and that was just the way he put you on to things you either picked up on them or you just missed the message, so as Carlos made his way towards the car Bobby handed him the key. Carlos opened the trunk only to see that it was empty, but had a piece of paper with writing on it, as Carlos picked the paper up with a puzzled look on his face, Lartesha, Black, Rell and Rock made their way through the door, causing Carlos to look up from the paper he had in hand.

Yo if any of you have your cell phone on cut that shit off... no better yet put them in your cars, yo Bobby when everybody come back in lock the doors shop is closed for now.

Carlos, what's wrong? Lartesha asked with a concern look on her face.

Lartesha please no time for question. Carlos spat with a serious look.

As everyone went to their cars, Carlos then focus back on reading the note.

Welcome to the family Carlos, all we ask of you is trust and loyalty don't be like my nephew. He couldn't. I will not make this note long, but I hope we have a good understanding, now you will find everything in the doors, the extras are a gift, burn this note!

Carlos! Carlos! Bobby yelled.

Everybody was just staring at Carlos as he stood there with the paper in hand like he just got the worst news ever and what they didn't know was to Carlos it was tragic to know that Marie the love his life was being deceived by her own uncle someone who she trusted, Carlos knew the hurt it would cause Marie if she knew the truth of her brother's death, as Carlos looked up everyone was staring him in the face with Bobby calling his name repeatedly, Carlos shut the trunk and walked around to open the door placing the note in his back pocket.

Yo Bobby gets the tools, I want these doors took apart. But I want nothing broke or missing when it's time to put it back together because this is a rental car okay. Carlos said as he opens the passenger side door, looking around at everyone as he spoke.

CHAPTER 47

Other plans

While sitting in the library parking lot waiting for her friend Kim to show up, Veronica was so deep in thought and overwhelmed behind the way her and Lartesha has been arguing; she said to herself I have always been a good friend to Lartesha Veronica sat with a puzzled look on her face as she just stared straight until Kim tapped on her window and shook her up a little causing her to jump out her seat, Veronica body jerked before she turned and saw it was Kim and laughed it off, but was very nerves in the inside.

Hey girl, do not scare me like that. Veronica said as she was opening the car door, laughing in between words.

Girl, please! You not scared... Now come give your girl a hug; I missed you. Kim spat back, laughing as she walked around the car door with her arms out.

Aw... I miss you to girl! Veronica said, hugging Kim back.

Girl... Let me get a good look at you. Veronica said as she stepped back to look Kim up and down as she walked around her, taking in the purity of her skin tone. Which made her body transformation stand out and as Veronica took in her friend's appearance and attitude, she was excited to see that veronica had become an ambition independent, headstrong woman who didn't let her journey beat her down.

Girl... What.... Are you smiling at? Kim asked as she put her hands on her hips with a confident look, giving Veronica a smile back as she was spinning with a shake in her hip showing off her body.

Girl... You killing that Michael Kors one-piece suit... oh, and I love the matching bag girl! Veronica said overly excited with her friend.

Aw.... Thank you, Vee Vee. Kim said as she was walking up to Veronica with her arms extended.

Kim and Veronica were so excited with each other's presents, nothing else existed around them, as they took in one another's beauty and shared words that uplift them both. The day has come just like they could only imagine, but what Veronica had in mind it deeply disturbed Kim behind the information Veronica's provided of her past events with Lartesha. She couldn't believe what her friend was telling her. She stood there with her eyes wide, just listing to the horrifying danger she was in. While Kim's expression was of distaste, she never discourages Veronica from proceeding with her plan. She was right along with her friend with a few plans of her own. Veronica could see and feel the change in Kim's demeanor as she spoke of her life-threatening encounters.

I have always told you Vee Vee... That's not your friend... she does not care about you... I can't... I can't. Kim spat back as the tears filled her eyes with anguish in her voice.

But Kim, I feel that they pressured her... I... I... just don't have Lartesha doing this herself and they killed him.... Do you hear me, Kim...? shaking Head... they killed him right in front of me. Veronica said as she strutted with a shaky voice.

Okay, Veronica, so why do you still want to follow through with what you have in mind.... Because you could see that these people are not playing. I want you to know that I am down with you no matter what; please don't get me killed okay. Kim spat back with anger in her voice as sympathy fill her facial expression.

Girl… I am not trying to put you in harm's way; therefore, I told you the whole situation. I am not holding anything back from you… like Lartesha did me… shaking her head…. No; we are friends now, let's handle this business. Veronica spat back as she extended her arm out, grabbing Kim's wrist and moving it with every word.

Making their way into the library, Veronica's stomach filled with butterflies and her mind raced with intrusive thoughts, not wanting to get her friend hurt. But the emotion overpowered her decision making, and during these times she always had Kim to call on. But at this moment Kim was getting irritated at everything she heard, the indignation feeling Kim was having because she wanted justice for her friend, but not in the literal way of justice. Approaching the young lady at the desk, they quickly changed their facial expresses, giving the women a warm smile.

Hello Ma'am… we would like to occupy one of your computers please? Veronica asked as they had approached the desk.

Sure… No problem, I'm just going to need either photo I. D. or something with a valid address. Kate replied, giving Veronica a friendly smile.

Hey Vee Vee, we will find nothing in here, I might have another way, do you remember Natalie, she joined the police force? Kim whispered in Veronica's ear.

Oh, I know you didn't Kim… you know we did not get along over Tyron girl…. I'll join the police force to if my man put his hands on me the way Mel used to beat on her, I will pass on her Kim, I don't need the police help. Veronica spat back titling her head down with her first words then continued giving the lady her photo I.D.

Veronica, that shit is so damn old, people are changing every day for the better, you better get with the program, get out the pass. I don't know why in the hell are you holding on to them feelings for Tyron, you will never know how bad you had it with him until you let that special someone in, that will love watching the moon go down in the presents of you, and cherishing every morning you share watching the sunrise. Kim spat back, sharing with Veronica her prospect of a good man.

Okay... okay.... shaking head.... Kim, we have this damn conversation every time we bring Tyron's name up. Veronica replied looking at Kim as she was turning around to walk towards a computer.

CHAPTER 48

Being blind

The full moon filled the sky, as it glowed on the wet pavement, the air had that steady muggy feel as mist from the fog-covered parts of the streets. They broke the streetlights for the hoodlums that wanted to stay in the dark. Tonight, was not a normal night, there was no one in sight, police cars were strolling the streets. Justin did not have a clue what he was in for, although he's determined to sell the cocaine he had purchased, even after his cousin warned him to go home and check in with his mother. Picking up a few tricks that he learned from his cousin, Justin thought moving through the streets would be a piece of cake. He felt confident tonight as he rode his bike through the back streets. As Justin turned another corner, he ran into Dollar and Felicia who were just flagging cars over and yelling at each other as they rushed to the cars. They never notice Justin as he rode up on his bike. He pulled up on the sidewalk close to the wall in the dark with one foot down and one foot on his bike pedal just in case he saw police pull up. Justin recognized Dollar from the night J-Love hit him with his car. He also remembered Dollar getting J-Love sent to jail for that sell. Justin did not really want to take any chances with Dollar tonight, but he was watching Felicia jump in a car and pull over down the street for 5 minutes and jump in another car right after. Justin stared with a puzzled look because he thought Dollar was getting her sales, but then Justin said to his self she look too dirty to be hustling as he continue to watch with the same puzzled stare, leaned over his bike handlebars wondering what the hell she was doing in them cars. Only this time Dollar spotted him, but he never noticed that someone had spotted him until Dollar ran up on him.

Hey, little boy! Dollar shouted as he grabbed Justin's bike handlebars and jerked his bike with his last word.

Don't be running up on me like that, dude! Justin yelled as he yanked his bike away.

Wait... I know you from somewhere... yes, I do.... yes, I do... yup you are Carlos little brother the one Toya was talking about that night that fucker hit me with his car... wow that fucker got everything he deserved that night. Dollar said with a slight laugh as he was pacing back and forth all hype.

Yeah, okay now that you know who I am, and I know who you are... don't be running your mouth telling people you saw me. Justin said.

It's late... what are you doing out here away? Dollar asked.

I'm trying to get this money like that girl right there. Justin said, pointing at Felicia as she jumped in another car.

Dollar busted out laughing and started running in circles from what Justin had just said because Felicia was a prostitute hooked on heroin who did whatever it took to get her next hit and she paid Dollar well to protect her that's why she had the guys that pulled up; pull over down the street. Felicia made her way towards Justin and now he could see why Dollar was laughing and carrying on like he was. Felicia white face had scares; her arms all bruised up from the needles she used.

Okay, Dollar, I need a fucking break... I want a fucking hit, Felicia said as she walked up to Dollar and handed him some money.

All right, bitch! You can get your fucking fix, but after that it's back to making money! Yo nigga you got some work on you. Dollar yelled at Felicia, then turned to ask Justin for some crack.

Yea what you working with? Justin asked.

I got one hundred… and I need a good deal because I don't just smoke; I sell to… so hook me up with two grams. Dollar said with his eyes wide as he spoke.

Nah nigga… Nah nigga… Nah nigga! Toya yelled as she was skipping down the sidewalk all fast.

Justin saw Toya coming towards them as he was getting off his bike and walking towards the side of a building to take a gram of crack out for Dollar because that's what his cousin Murder Black taught him and he also schooled him on what crack heads would say just to get more, acting like they was hustlers and knowing they would smoke every rock. So Justin did what Murder Black taught.

Huh… Dollar, here's two grams for your hundred and I want you to run me some sales, I just hooked you up. Justin said as he gave Dollar the gram of crack.

I will… I will… I will!!! Toya yelled as she was all hype in Justin's face.

Okay… Okay… but you make the sell and after you bring me the money, I will be right here on the side of this building waiting. Justin said to Toya as he was getting back on his bike.

Okay… Okay… but I need something to get me started. Toya spat back all hype.

Huh Toya now get out my face. Justin said as he gave Toya a piece of crack to smoke.

The night was going just as Justin was hoping it would and he was glad in a way that he ran into Dollar even though he didn't know him like that, but what Justin didn't know was that Felicia had to contact her supplier for her heroin fix and Justin was in for a big surprise. With Toya running sales she was out doing everybody that filled the street, Justin was so occupied with what Dollar and Toya brought that he never notices Felicia slide in the old black STS Cadillac that pulled over down the street.

Okay… Okay… give me mines with this sale, I got right here. Toya yelled as she was speed walking up on Justin.

Hell, No! I will pay you for every five sells you bring, not every damn sell Toya. Justin spat back as he stood up and poked his chest out with his words.

While Justin and Toya were busy talking, they never paid attention to the old black STS Cadillac pull up on them with the widow halfway rod down.

Hey, young blood! What you doing out here? Old Timer Luke asked as he pulled up on Justin in his car.

Why… who wants to know? Justin asked with a glare.

How's your brother doing? Tell your mother Luke said hello, you be safe out here young blood. Old Timer, Luke said as he pulled off.

Old Timer Luke always had a thing for Justin's mother growing up, she never took Luke serious because of his slick ways and all the women he attracted from his street credit and flamboyant lifestyle. But Luke still made it his business to stop by her place from time to time; because he enjoys flirting with her and would offer a helping hand, which she never took.

CHAPTER 49

Reminisce

As the loud bass rumbled through the apartment walls, you could hear the music echoing through the hallway, you even felt the vibration from the walls. Outside the snow covered the ground and the cold air hit the building; while Lartesha moved through her apartment lip singing Evelyn Champagne King (love comes down) a song she grew up on. As the song screamed through the speaker Lartesha was shaking and dancing like she did when her mother would play it. She was in a zone like a kid all over again, so captivated by the words and the melody. Being that winter was here, Lartesha didn't mind the weather because she had the chance to wear all her fur coats, sweaters and timberland boots. So as the sun was shining through her window she continues to dance and sing as she straightened up her apartment; before she headed out for the day. Lartesha saw that her cell phone was vibrating, so she rushed over to see who it was, when she seen who it was she started dancing to the song even more throwing her hands in the air screaming I JUST CAN'T STOP THE WAY THAT I FEEL…. I JUST CAN'T STOP THE WAY THAT I FEEL… with a smile and the shaking of her hips. But before Lartesha could walk away from her cell phone, it started vibrating again.

Hey Carlos… what's going on? Lartesha asked.

Well, don't you sound like you're in a good mood. Carlos spat back.

I am, let's just say that, so what's on your mine? Lartesha asked as she continue picking up her apartment.

Damn, I'm sorry to be the one to be giving bad news and putting a damper on your day. But I just got the news on Trick status. Carlos said.

Oh, no... what happened? Lartesha asked with her shocked voice.

So, the reason you could not get in there the other day is because the police have stopped all visits and only his mother can be in the room. But the police must be in there to with her. Carlos said.

Oh, no.... Oh, no... Lartesha yelled as tears started coming down her cheeks.

But that's not the half Lartesha... they are taking him to jail today. I have never heard of something happening like this Lartesha. Carlos said.

What can we do, Carlos...? What can we do? Lartesha asked as she cried out.

This shit isn't right Lartesha he's not recovered yet; I am about to get on top of this right now with a lawyer, I will hit you back. Carlos spat back.

Okay, Carlos, please call me back. Lartesha said in a pleading tone.

I will Lartesha... I'm sorry to get you all down like this. Carlos said as he was hanging up the phone.

No, don't worry Carlos, just call me back and let me know something, please. Lartesha spat back.

As Lartesha sat on the couch thinking about Trick, she could not stop crying. Meanwhile, Vice was sitting in his car listing and watching her building from down the street. Lartesha sat on her couch so overwhelmed with so many thoughts, especially after all the things that have happened over these last few years, the tears were flowing down her cheeks as she sat there still holding the cell phone in her hand; Lartesha went back to the text message she received before Carlos called giving her that bad news. Lartesha stared at the message Jordan sent, something she didn't get from him often; Jordan would usually send post cards or gifts. Today Jordan texted her to let her know he was stopping by to visit. Lartesha closed her eyes to imagine Jordan holding her in his arms, telling her that everything would be all right. What Lartesha never knew is that each man was closer in present than she could imagine. Vice was doing his police surveillance and Jordan who was following the orders of his boss Victor, which he gave him some months ago. Victor knew of the relationship Jordan had with Lartesha and from monitoring Carlos' entire crew he saw that she was big access to all of them. He also found out that Lartesha has been sleeping with the police. Victor had Jordan use the top of the line listen devices and cameras you could think of. Jordan even got an apartment in the same building as Lartesha having the maintenance man install mini cameras in her hallway pointing directly at her door, which she never noticed. Gathering the strength to move and go about her day was hard for Lartesha as she sat on her couch emotionally depressed, but she picked herself up to go about her day. Hoping for the better. Then she heard a knock at her door. Lartesha headed towards the door with so many thoughts on her mine, she thought to herself who could be on the other side of this door. Which made her stop before answering the door; she rushed to her room to grab her gun. Lartesha said to herself everyone had to be let in the door so who could this be.

Knock… Knock…

Lartesha never said a word as she started tiptoeing towards the door to look through her peek hole.

Knock… Knock… Knock.

Looking through her peek whole seeing who it was knocking, Lartesha rushed to her draw, pulled her gun out, then she rushed back to open the door.

Well, hi their stranger. Lartesha said as she opened the door with a smile.

CHAPTER 50

When it is so close

Marie was in the bedroom separating clothes, getting ready to do some laundry. She did not like winter and would much rather stay inside to get a few things done. Some months back Marie signed up for an online college course, hoping to occupy her mind and time with something of value. She figured if she sat around the house all day doing nothing, it would only lead her to thinking about Carlos every minute on the hour. While separating clothes Marie thought about how far behind, she has gotten in her schoolwork and had plans on catching up with everything today. Marie was deep in thought as she was going through Carlos' pants, making sure he had nothing in his pockets. Marie felt a piece of paper and pulled it out, she unfolded it then her phone started ringing. Marie dropped the pants and the letter on the bed and rushed over to her phone, thinking it would be Carlos.

Hello… Hello… Marie shouted as she answered the phone

MARIE… LISTEN… YOU FUCKING TELL CARLOS TO STOP DOING WHAT HE'S DOING THE POLICE IS WATCHING HIM AND HIS FUCKING CREW! Victor yelled through the phone.

Before Marie could even respond, Victor hung up the phone. Marie stood staring at the phone, puzzled and speechless in total disbelief. Marie never saw her uncle mad; she could feel the anger in his voice as it rumbled through the phone receiver. Marie immediately started dialing Carlos' number.

Hey Marie… What's up with you? Carlos asked.

CARLOS! YOU NEED TO COME HOME NOW!! Marie shouted through the phone.

I'M ON MY WAY!!! Carlos spat

Before Marie could ever respond to Carlos, she dropped the phone to the floor. She rushed to the bathroom where she felled to her knees in front of the toilet. Marie was vomiting as she held the white porcelain toilet with a tight grip. Carlos was on the phone yelling Marie's name after hearing the phone hit the ground with a loud thump. Which made him drive franticly. Carlos kept yelling through the phone at the same time he blows the horn at cars who he felt were driving to slow for him. Marie had found the strength in her little body to make it back over to the phone.

CARLOS!!! CARLOS!!! Marie shouted through the phone.

MARIE!!! MARIE!!! I AM NOT FAR… DO YOU HEAR ME… I AM NOT FAR… I'M COMING MARIE… Carlos yelled as he drove faster.

Marie had to use the strength she had left to walk back into her bedroom. She sat on the edge of the bed next to where she placed the letter; she pulled from Carlos' pants pocket. Marie still felt very nauseous and drained from the vomiting. She knew the symptoms all too well from seeing her friends go through it, Marie knew for a fact that she was pregnant. When Marie look to the side of her, she reached over to pick the note up recognizing the handwriting she being reading it while Carlos was still on the phone. It was like someone took the soul from her body the way the phone dropped out her hand as she sat motionless. Marie was numb from what she had just read, she was furious with the hurt and revenge boiling in her gut. All the strength left Marie's body as she lay across the bed.

Carlos was still yelling through the phone as he pulled up in front of his building. Marie laid across the bed; she was in a daze, feeling like she couldn't trust anyone. Carlos stormed through the door yelling Marie's name.

Marie... Marie... Marie! Carlos yelled as he hurried through the apartment door, heading towards the bedroom.

Marie heard Carlos yelling her name, but never answered. Hearing Carlos get closer to the room made Marie's blood boil from the betrayal she felt behind Carlos not telling her about the letter. So, the closer he got to Marie, she began regaining some of her strength back as she got up from the bed right before Carlos walked in the room.

Marie! Carlos yelled as he was rushing through the door.

Marie was standing up as Carlos rushed through the door, meeting him with a stare that stopped him right in his steps towards her.

What's wrong Marie, why are crying and what's that stare for? Carlos asked, standing in front of Marie.

What's wrong... what's wrong...? I can't believe you would stand in my face and ask that... Carlos, what's this! Marie yelled in Carlos' face as she waved the piece of paper aggressively with her right hand close to the side of his face.

LOOK MARIE... I TOOK MY PANTS OFF AND FORGOT TO TALK TO YOU ABOUT IT!!! But I have so many other things going through my mind, we'll handle that. Carlos yelled as he became frustrated with Marie's accusing him, he walked closer to Marie as he lowered his voice.

Carlos, that's not it... I think I'm pregnant, I've been vomiting consistently and I'm weak, I think I need to go to the hospital now. Marie said with a weak and faint look as Carlos walked up to her and put his arms around her.

CHAPTER 51

Vengeance set in

The squeaky noise that came from the room filled the air like the sounds and the aroma of passionate sex, as she moaned with every stroke; she also contested every stroke, feeling in control of the moment. But Murder Black had other feelings and thoughts going through his head as he gripped Carmen T-shirt in a ball with his right hand pulling hard at it with every stroke, caught in the moment of anger and betrayal Murder Black thought he was rough housing Carmen, but she loved every bit of this side he was displaying, so in fact she lowered her abdomen closer to the bed laying her head to the side on the sheets and spreading her legs open wider as she being climaxing all over his dick Murder Black continued stroking Carmen from the back with her juices flowing all over him and on the sheets.

Uh daddy, you are killing this pussy, was I... I... a bad girl... uh... uh... uh... don't stop daddy. Carmen shouted as she stuttered while pushing back with every stroke.

That made Murder Black blood boil when Carmen said don't stop because he wasn't trying to please her, he was trying to hurt her, so he released Carmen T-shirt from his hand and moved both of his hands towards her neck, making his hands in the form of Carmen's skinny neck. Murder Black slightly leaned forward and grabbed the back of Carmen's neck, forcing her face into the mattress as he continued to stroke her, Carmen became so frantic from the pressure Murder Black applied to her neck. Carmen was not in the mood to continue having sex; she was swinging her hands at Murder Black as if she were fighting for her life. This made him let go of her with a slight laugh.

Get the fuck off me… what the fuck has gotten into your ass nigga? Carmen yelled as she was swinging frantically at Murder Black.

Quickly jumping off the bed and out of the way of Carmen swinging, Murder Black rushed over to his underwear to put on, still laughing and looking at Carmen as she got up from the bed, feeling infuriated as she walked towards the bathroom. Murder Black grabbed his pants and pulled out half the Dutch he was smoking on, while making his way back over to the edge of the bed he lit the cigar up and inhaled a gigantic cloud of marijuana smoke, making him cough.

You better save me some of that motherfucker! Carmen yelled from the shower.

DON'T WORRY… I GOT YOU… Murder Black yelled in between puffs of his cigar.

Murder Black had a devilish grin on his face, as if the moment was too good to be true, as he moved through the room quietly, putting on his pants, taking the cigar out of his pocket that he dipped in PCP. Murder Black held his laugh in; while placing the PCP cigar on the nightstand then he grabbed the remote and turned the T.V. on and continued smoking the rest of his Dutch. Carmen came walking out the bathroom wrapped up in her towel headed straight towards her fate in which karma held for this day and Murder Black sat waiting acting as if he was all into the T.V. while finishing his cigar.

Give me your lighter. Carmen spat as she waved her hand with the Dutch in between her two fingers.

PLEASE… IS HOW YOU ASK BITCH! Murder Black yelled as he turns and threw the lighter at her.

I GOT YOUR BITCH NIGGA... I'm still waiting for you to tell me what's the problem, oh you still mad about your cousin... ha... ha... shit rent had to get paid, sorry for him. Carmen spat as she was shaking her head with every word, then she lit the cigar, giving it a powerful pull.

Oh, yeah... sorry for him, huh? Murder Black asked sarcastically and aggressively as he stood up looking her straight in her eyes repeating her last word.

Carmen stood by her nightstand slowly exhaling the smoke, quickly she became lightheaded she placed the Dutch back down on the nightstand looking away from Murder Black with a look of discomfort on her face as if she was in pain, the PCP had started instantaneously working Carmen felt herself drifting, Murder Black stood watching his plan take its effect, seeing Carmen's body language change he began grinning at her, her vision of him had got faint Carmen only heard Murder Black last words YOU STUPID BITCH, I HOPE YOU DIE! echoing in her ear as she started stumbling off balance rocking back and forth she began reaching for her nightstand causing her to fall face first hitting her head on the corner of the nightstand sending her to the floor motionless.

Murder Black was wide eyed, and mouth open as Carmen head hit the edge of the nightstand, he walked over towards where she laid only to see blood coming from her forehead. Murder Black grabbed the PCP Dutch off the nightstand and walked towards the bathroom not feeling any sympathy for Carmen as she laid on the floor in her own blood, he tossed the Dutch into the toilet pulled his hoodie over his head while watching it disappear. He turned around to make his way towards the front door walking past Carmen's body looking at her and saying his last words before walking out the door.

KARMA IS A BITCH... HA... HA? Murder Black yelled through the house as he opens the door to walk out.

CHAPTER 52

When the time is right

Carlos sat holding Marie as she rests her head on his chest. They both sat patiently waiting for the doctor to come back with her results. Marie was feeling weak and nauseous as she kept her eyes closed. Carlos held Marie in his arms while he rested his face on her long jet-black hair to inhale the sweet chemicals of coconut milk shampoo that Marie used often.

Damn Baby, your hair always smells like some fruits and berries. Carlos said as he kept inhaling with a burst of sight laughter.

You better stop doing that before I vomit all over you. Marie spat back in a weak tone of voice.

After Marie got her last words out the doctor appeared in the doorway with a smile on her face when she began reading Marie's result.

Congratulations Marie your test was positive, we recommend you staying overnight and getting some rest and IV Fluids in your body because you have become very dehydrated. The Doctor said as she stood in front of Marie and Carlos.

Meanwhile, as the doctor was talking Carlos's phone being to vibrate, causing him to nudge Marie so he could get up to step out of the room and answer his phone. Carlos stepped out of the room and looked at the screen, causing him to smile as he answered.

Hey mom... you called at the right time I'm at the doctor's with Marie... she's pregnant... mom! Carlos said with excitement in his voice but very composed with his body Language as he stood in the hospital corridor.

Oh, my lord, Carlos...! I'm about to be a Grandma, okay well tell Marie I said congratulations... how far along is she? I really hate to call you right now during this time and spoil this beautiful moment baby. Mr. Johnson said as she held the phone receiver to her ear with an annoyed facial expression.

Carlos sense a little worry in his mother's voice, which made his posture change as he stood straight and more attentive to the conversation with a bothering expression on his face as he was holding the phone receiver to his ear.

I will let her know what you said mom, but what's on your mind? Carlos asked as he rested his body up against the wall.

Carlos... an old friend of mine just called me... he saw your fucking brother on Elk street selling drugs... I am about to KILL HIM! Mr. Johnson yelled as she was angry and hurt.

Carlos heard the hurt and pain in his mother's voice as she yelled through the phone.

Carlos... I bust my fucking ass to make sure the bills paid... I fucking bust my ass to make sure the both of you have... but what I get; sneaky lying ass kids!! Mr. Johnson spat as she started walking around in her house.

Carlos didn't say a word he was so confused, angry, with a perplexed look thinking to his self who and where his little brother got the drugs from. While Carlos stood in the bright corridor of the hospital with doctors, nurses, and patients walking pass, his mind started racing from knowing the dangers of the streets, and not wanting to lose Justin to the street or jail. While in his thoughts, the doctor steps out of the room and waved, hoping she caught Carlos' attention. His mind was elsewhere. Mr. Johnson was still yelling through the phone receiver, which made Carlos snap out of the daydream he was having. Immediately turned to walk back in the room with Marie while his mother continued to yell through the phone. Mr. Johnson was mad with Justin and Carlos, Marie heard Mr. Johnson voice coming through the phone and could hear some bad words being used causing Carlos to take the phone from his ear to shake his head as his silent response causing Marie to give him a bewildering stare. Carlos press the phone back to his ear only to hear his mother last words.

I CAN'T EVEN TRUST YOU ANYMORE!!! Mr. Johnson yelled through the phone as she stood staring at Carlos and Justin's picture sitting on her fireplace.

Click.... Was the last sound Carlos heard coming through the phone receiver after Mr. Johnson hung up in his ear, Carlos stood baffled at how his mother was handling things. Marie was still laying on the hospital bed just staring up at Carlos as he stood over her with an empty and emotional look that made her sit up.

Carlos... what's wrong? Marie asked as she sat up.

That fucking... Justin will make me kill him... my mother just got a call from a friend that told her Justin is on Elk street right now selling drugs. Carlos spat back, putting emphasis on his words as he walked up closer to Marie.

Carlos, you go get his ass right now... I mean right fucking now! Marie shouted as her anger showed through the words and her facial expression as she spoke.

Marie, calm down... I... got this. Carlos said as he wrapped his arms around Marie.

While Carlos and Marie were holding each other, a nurse appears in the doorway calling for Marie to come with her.

Carlos go handle your FUCKING Business... I will be here when you get back... oh and I will text you the room I'm going too. Marie spat back, filled with anger.

Okay, Marie... I will call you. Carlos said as he was backing out the way of the nurse and Marie.

Carlos saw the anger and disappointment in Marie's eyes as she spoke, causing the guilt to set in his mind along with other thoughts that only angered him more. Carlos pick his jacket up and made his way out the door, shouting his last words to Marie.

I love you, Marie! Carlos shouted as he walked out the door.

Made in the USA
Middletown, DE
06 May 2022

65177325R00170